My Brother Peter

to Donna —
with warmest wishes and thanks —
fondly,
Kerri

Canadian Cataloguing in Publication Data

Berger, Nomi

My brother Peter: was it murder or suicide? 30 years later, a sister's quest for peace, and the truth.

ISBN 1-55207-010-7

1. Berger, Peter.   2. Brother and sisters - Canada.   3. Suicide victims - Canada - Biography.   4. Murder victims - Canada - Biography.   5. Narcotic addicts - Canada - Biography.   I. Title

HV6548.C3B47 1998   362.28'092   C98-940260-6

Nomi Berger

My Brother Peter

ROBERT DAVIES PUBLISHING
MONTREAL—TORONTO—PARIS

Robert Davies Multimedia Publishing Inc.
330-4999 Saint-Catherine Street West,
Westmount, Quebec, Canada H3Z 1T3

This book may be ordered in Canada from
General Distribution Services:

☎ 1-800-387-0141 / ☎ 1-800-387-0172
🖷 1-416-445-5967;

in the U.S.A.
from General Distribution Services,
Suite 202, 85 River Rock Drive, Buffalo, N.Y. 14287
☎ 1-800-805-1082

or from the publisher, toll-free throughout North America:
☎ 1-800-481-2440 🖷 1-888-RDAVIES

e-mail: rdppub@vir.com

The publisher wishes to take this opportunity
to thank the Canada Council for the Arts,
the BPIDP program at Canadian Heritage
and the Ministère de la culture du Québec (SODEC)
for their generous support for its publishing programs.

To my beloved brother, Peter.
For all you were, and all you might have been.

Acknowledgments

Although my brother led the way, this was not a journey I made alone. And so, to my many, loyal travelling companions, I offer my love and my gratitude.

To L-J, for being there from the very beginning, for believing in the rightness of what I was doing, for bolstering me when I faltered, and for acting as my fellow Holmes.

To my mother, for enduring the ordeal of a reawakened agony, for worrying about me, and for supporting me in more ways than simply the ways of the heart.

To Paul, for his wisdom and advice, patience and guidance, as, together, we unlocked the door to the past.

To my brother's friends, for their empathic kindness, and for helping me, through their memories and insights, discover my brother and the times that shaped him.

To those officials, who, in their humanity, bent the rules for me.

To those few, very special friends, whose ears were always open and whose shoulders were always solid.

And finally, to Robert, for taking this chance with me.

Some names have been altered
to protect the privacy of certain individuals.

if only we could start again,
equal partners in a second genesis;
baptized in kinder waters,
and blessed by hindsight's generosity,
what might have been
might have the chance
this second time to be;
cursed with the naiveté
of the child I still am,
I want to believe
that *if* I believed,
even the impossible
would be possible;
for then I'd fill the cracks
of your fragmented heart,
replate the tarnished surface
of your brave, flawed dream,
and set you firmly
on a clear and compassed course;
forewarned, we'd guard with vigilance
the fragile sanctity
of this, your second birth,
as proof that even destiny
can indeed be vanquished;
but wishful thinking
is, at best, a minor force,
too weak to spin a ballad
from a requiem,
or raise you up,
my soul's failed Lazarus,
from the dead;
the most, then, I can do
is dip my pen
in absolution's sweetness,
and inscribe upon
your stonebound epitaph
an earthly smile,
endless as eternity;
there, in the cradle of its curve,
may you find the peace
so long denied you,
safe within the constancy
of a sister's love.

Foreword

"*H*elp me."

Those were the last words my nineteen-year-old brother, Peter, ever said to me.

We were huddled in the den of my parents' Montreal apartment. His long, thin arms were clamped around my waist, and I was crying. My husband had to drag me forcibly from the room.

I never saw my brother again.

Three weeks later, he was dead.

The date was September 26, 1968.

And since that date, I've remained haunted.

Haunted by that final image of the two of us together, and by his final words to me. He'd asked me to help him. But help him, how? What, exactly, had he meant?

Haunted, too, by my own, unremitting guilt. A sister's guilt. I *should* have saved him. I *could* have saved him. Why *didn't* I save him?

No one has ever been able to relieve me of that guilt. No argument, no matter how well-intentioned or how logical, has ever succeeded in lessening its weight. I still wear my guilt like a mental hair shirt, close to my skin. Perhaps in justifiable penance for what I've always perceived as my life's greatest failure.

And I still have not found closure.

It's been kept from me by a combination of many things: denial and grief, anger and sadness. An ongoing sense of loss, of being cheated. Of never having learned the full truth of what happened. And pain. At times barely noticeable, at others so excruciating, it can stop my breath.

Whenever I've looked for answers to the question as to why my brother died, I've been told, "Hey, it was the sixties."

What a catch-all phrase that is. Facile and dismissive. It's like a lazy yawn, a shrug of the shoulders, a simplistic, "ah well, that's the way it was." It's the rug, under which the nastier bits and pieces of an entire decade have conveniently been swept.

As if that explains it. As if that justifies it. As if that settles it.

To blame the times for his destruction seems logical enough. For if ever someone defined and epitomized the sixties, it was my brother. Brilliant. Inquisitive. Adventurous. Impulsive. Fearless.

A marginal student, he dropped out of Bishop's University in Lennoxville, Quebec, at the end of his sophomore year. For the next fifteen months, he lived with an expanding and fluid circle of friends as a member of Montreal's hippie counter-culture. And it was there, in that dusky netherworld of drugs, mysticism, and pseudo-Eastern philosophies, that he rose, quickly and briefly, to become one of its darkest stars.

When all else failed, my parents, in a last, desperate bid to save him, signed papers committing him to the Douglas Hospital in Verdun for observation and treatment. Two days before his scheduled commitment, he was arrested for drug possession by the RCMP and jailed. He was released on bail to enter hospital, only to be discharged — without my parents' consent — after a mere, twelve-day stay.

Six days later, on the morning that he was scheduled to appear in court for a hearing, he was found dead in the bedroom of a friend's house.

We were told that he'd committed suicide.

But I never quite believed it. To me, it wasn't only unthinkable, it was impossible. I was certain that he'd been murdered. To silence him. Whether denial or wishful thinking on my part,

I didn't know. All I did know was that my brother's grisly death had upended my safe and ordered world, and changed my life forever.

When he died, I stopped using his name. To me, it was tantamount to sacrilege. Like taking the name of the Lord in vain.

And I never talked about him. Not to my parents, not to my husband, not to my friends. I simply couldn't. The shock was too great, the pain too intense, the loss too acute, the guilt too profound.

Locked inside my solitary grief, I was unreachable and, as such, inconsolable. Time did little to improve the situation, and I was eventually confronted with two choices: live with it and go mad, or bury it and go on.

I chose to bury it.

But my unconscious demanded — and found — an outlet for the myriad, tangled and conflicted feelings I'd managed to suppress: my writing. Through my various poems, short stories, and novels, I was able to achieve some small, though temporary, measure of relief and comfort. Through those same writings, in one incarnation or another, my brother, my beloved brother, was able to live again.

What a relief it was to move from Montreal to Toronto in 1983. It meant a new start, new people. How comforting to be able to omit from my biography one whole segment of my past life. Now, whenever newly-met strangers asked, "Do you have any brothers or sisters?," I could say no.

To have said yes would have been to elaborate. And I couldn't. I *still* couldn't. It was less a negation of him than a preservation of me.

Then, in the spring of 1995, as I was beginning work on a new novel — my first attempt at a murder mystery — something strange occurred.

I found myself overwhelmed by an eerie and curious sensation. A kind of restlessness, a whirling and spinning inside me. It was as if I'd been taken over by some otherworldly power, held in thrall to some mysterious force I could neither comprehend nor explain.

Until I heard a single question form in my head: "Why write fiction when you can write a true-life story?"

His story.

I was stunned.

Why now? I asked myself.

And the answer came back, "Because it's time."

The words, like a body blow, took my breath away and doubled me over in pain. It was a familiar pain. Sharp and bittersweet. As strong now as when it first began: on the day he died.

Within moments, there was chaos. Everything I'd considered safely buried for so many years, suddenly and inexplicably, was refusing to *remain* buried. It was like being subjected to a ferocious, internal mutiny. I could almost hear the ripping of the entrenched, but fragile, scar tissue that had allowed me to survive for so long.

And I knew. It *was* time.

As the days passed, I found myself consumed. By a startling rush of energy. Of purpose. Of anticipation. And the greedy, desperate need to know.

To know, once and for all, how my brother *had* died.

Had he been murdered as I'd believed, or had he committed suicide as we'd been told? And if he had, in fact, taken his own life, I needed to know why.

But I also needed more. I needed to know how he'd lived. I needed to know everything about him — from those who'd known him as I, perhaps, never had.

I would, I decided then, embark on a quest. Set out on a journey of discovery and, at the same time, self-discovery.

I'd return to the past. Begin at the beginning. Ask all the questions I'd never dared ask before.

Then, hopefully, by journey's end, I'd have the answers I needed. Enough to enable me, finally, to set down my lifetime burden of guilt. And take those first, long-delayed steps toward healing.

One

"*N*orah, would you do me a favour?"

Norah was one of my oldest friends. She'd once worked as my father's legal secretary, and still lived in Montreal.

"Would you try to find out if the RCMP still has a file on my brother?"

"You're kidding."

"No. I'm not."

"After all these years?"

"It's a long shot, I know, but it seems like the most logical place to start."

"Start? Start what, may I ask?"

Australian by birth, Norah's clipped tones lent a formality to her speech, which, as always, made me smile. But that didn't keep my voice from quavering as I answered, simply, "My search for closure."

For a moment, there was silence, then the sound of Norah's whispered, "Oh, No-mi."

After that, there was nothing more for either of us to say.

The journey had begun.

Little did I know what I'd set in motion that early evening in mid-June. Little did I know how many lives I'd touch or how many lives would touch mine. Little did I know that the straight and simple path I'd envisioned for myself would prove as convoluted as a maze and as dizzying as a rollercoaster ride.

To prepare for the project, I bought a three-ring binder, a packet of lined, looseleaf paper, a clipboard, and a spiral notebook. Then I sat down at the computer in my study and drafted two separate lists of questions: one for the friends who'd known my brother during his brief life, and one for the officials who'd figured in it only at the end.

Think of it as an adventure, I told myself as I typed. Think of the different hats you'll be wearing, the various roles you'll be playing: lawyer, sleuth, investigative reporter, judge, author, sister ...

Sister. Suddenly, I wavered. No one, except Norah, knew of my plan. I could stop right now. Tell her to forget it. Erase the questions from the computer screen. And retreat. To the safety of not knowing.

Of never knowing. Of never healing. Of never finding peace.

And then another thought struck me. What would I do if I found my brother *had* been murdered? Set out, on my own, to track his killer down? Have him arrested? Have *him* killed?

Would he still be alive? I wondered. Would he even be living in Canada?

What if he discovered what I was doing and came after *me*? Was I, by initiating this inquiry, placing my*self* in jeopardy?

Was I mad?

Before I could lose my nerve completely, I shut off the computer and snatched the notebook and a pen from my desk. Then, after stopping just long enough to pick up my keys, I left my apartment and hurried toward the elevators. While I waited anxiously for one to arrive, I tried on my lawyer's hat for the first time and steeled myself for the questioning of my first witness: my own mother.

Yet as I rode down to her apartment (we live in the same building, twenty floors apart), I felt sick with guilt for daring to dredge up from the darkness of her *own* past, its most horrific memory. But I knew of no other way to begin.

I found her, as I usually did, nestled in the large, leather lounge chair in her bedroom. Perching myself on the edge of her bed, I drew a deep breath, and turned nervously to face her.

Then, in a low, hesitant voice, I told her of my plan.

To my amazement, she didn't seem the least surprised.

"It's about time," she said.

I stared at her open-mouthed.

"I only wished you'd done this sooner, it would have spared you years of needless heartache."

"I couldn't. I wasn't ready."

"And you are now?"

"Yes."

"For what?"

"The truth."

When I explained the two main thrusts of my search, she said, "As to the first, we already know how Peter died."

"No, we don't. We were *told* how he died, but I didn't fully accept it then, and I still don't accept it. Face it, mom, even *you* had doubts. Weren't you the one who said he wasn't the suicidal type? Weren't you the one who first suggested it might have been murder? Or at the very least, a post-hypnotic suggestion?"

When she didn't respond, I pressed on. "Weren't you also the one who said he'd boasted that he was going to 'spill the beans' in court that morning?"

My mother frowned. "I don't recall saying that."

"Well, you did."

"Whatever suspicions I may have had at the time, I put them aside long ago. For me, that entire episode is no more than a distant memory. Again, I only wish you could have — "

"So do I. God knows I've tried."

"Peter is dead. To me, *how* he died is irrelevant. All those years ago, I had a choice of turning it into an obsession — "

"Which you think I have — "

"Or putting it behind me and getting on with my life."

"Which you're saying I haven't."

Over the years, I'd really, only missed my brother in spurts. Most of the time, the memory of him lay dormant inside me. Most of the time, the unhealed wound of his death bled on in darkness and in silence.

Except for those instances when I caught myself looking at his brass-framed photograph on the table beside my bed ...

Except for his birthday ... and the anniversary of his death ...
Except for holidays ... and Sundays ...

Then I'd feel those familiar pangs of loneliness, emptiness, and regret.

At other times, though, all I'd feel was anger. And I'd curse him, over and over again, for having left me.

I was so engrossed in my thoughts that I missed what my mother was saying.

"What exactly," she repeated, "do you intend to do?"

"Go back," I told her, "to the beginning and ask questions."

"Of whom?"

"Of anyone who knew him."

"Who do you expect to still be around? And how accurate do you think their memories will be? This all happened a long time ago."

I looked at her quizzically. Was she merely playing devil's advocate or was there something else involved? Was she trying to protect me? Her? Both of us?

Clearing my throat, I tried a different tack. "Mom," I began, "when he — "

"Peter."

" — he died," I continued as if I hadn't heard her, "part of me froze, literally and figuratively. And that part of me's still frozen. But I realize now it was more than that. I froze *him* in time as well. My memory of him stopped during that last, terrible year.

"All I have left of him are fragments. Incidents taken out of context and out of sequence. Most of them are frightening, some of them are shocking. And because they *are* so shocking, I've never been able to look at them closely enough to deal with them.

"What I need is something to act as a counterbalance to that final year. Other aspects of him, of his life; good and bad, happy and sad. Because I'm convinced that, unless I can see my brother as a whole person, I'll never come to terms with what happened to him, and I'll never be able to let him go."

"Do you think you're well and truly prepared for what you might hear?" she asked. "For what you might find out?"

"I think I am. But I'll only know once I've started."

Opening up my notebook, I drew a long, unsteady breath. How could I do this? I demanded of myself. I may have been the sister, but *she* had been the mother. What right had I to meddle with someone else's healing just because mine was incomplete?

"Mom," I began, then just as quickly stopped. Pausing to wet my lips, I tried again. "Mom, forgive me, but I have to start with you."

"It's all right," she assured me. "As I've told you again and again — and I know you still find it hard to believe — I dealt with this a long time ago. I'm long past the pain. My fear is for you. Whether or not *you* can handle it."

"If I can't, I can always stop." With a click of my ballpoint pen, I signalled that I was ready. "What are your memories of him through the early years?"

I heard her sigh, and the sound tore at my heart.

"Mom, I'm sorry," I whispered, "I'm so — "

"Shh, I'm fine, really." Another sigh and then, "To put it simply, Peter was an easy child to love."

As I recorded that first sentence, I felt a prickle of childish jealousy. By her own admission, I'd been difficult.

"He could charm people. He had quite a mouth on him, and people would fall for him. He was so small, with this winning grin, big round, dark eyes, and long, long eyelashes."

As she continued speaking, my mind, as it so often does, divided itself in two. One part focused on my moving hand, the other on my brother.

How I'd adored him when he was little, especially his head. I couldn't get enough of squeezing his head. Could that have been the start of his problems: my passion for squeezing his head?

"He was left-handed, small and short, with rather large ears that stood out. We even took him to a plastic surgeon once, because of the teasing he got about his ears. But he refused to feel self-conscious about them, saying it was the other guys' problem, not his. I recall the doctor's being impressed with his attitude. And his brightness."

I was smiling now as I wrote, thinking of those Sunday mornings when I'd tuck him, a snuggly bundle, into bed with me, and regale him with made-up stories about the mud pies. I'd long forgotten what they were about, but they'd lived on in my brain, simply as "the stories about the mud pies."

"I wanted to keep him in nursery school an extra year, but public school insisted he be registered for kindergarten, because there was room for those born after the start date of September. His November birthday made him nearly a full year younger than the other children, and I felt that he just wasn't ready. It was the beginning of the system's failing us, and it followed us throughout his life.

"At Christmas, I begged his teacher to keep him back, again because he was still so small and so young. But I was told that it was impossible because he was too bright. In grade one, it was a repetition of the same thing."

"Tell me more about his personality," I urged.

"Among other things, he was unrelentingly inquisitive. He used to follow me around and pepper me with questions. If he had any favourite word, it was 'why?' He also, much to my dismay, showed little sense of fear. He was impulsive, with an enormous zest for life. He was always ready for new adventures. He never thought that he *couldn't* do something.

"He did, however, have a quick and searing temper."

Ah yes. His temper. As children, we played a lot of board games: Monopoly, Clue, Chinese Checkers, Sorry, Snakes 'n Ladders. Whenever he lost, my brother would throw the board into the air, scattering everything all over the living-room floor. That would lead, inevitably, to one of our famous wrestling matches.

Being four years older and much taller, I knew — thanks to my mother's constant warnings — not to hurt him. And I never did. I never could. I loved him too much.

And so, while I held back, he'd either get me in a head-lock or give me one of those awful Chinese burns. My howls of laughter only made him angrier, until it finally hurt so much, I had to yell, "Mommy, help!"

And mommy would hurry to my rescue and pull him off me.

"As Peter grew older, his capacity for developing hobbies, interests, and skills was impressive. He played both the guitar and the piano. He painted, sculpted, and did ceramics. He was an excellent skier. We were told he was Olympic material, he was that good.

"He could build anything, from model airplanes to crystal radios, and he could repair anything as well. He had a hard time focusing, though; he liked to try everything."

How different we were. Where he thrived on risk, I opted for safety. Where he was scattered, I was focused. Where he was good at everything, I did only those things I knew I could do well.

"Surprisingly, though, he never achieved academically." My mother's voice, as she continued, had taken on a sombre note. "I started worrying about him in high school. I'd lie awake at night, wondering where he was, and if he was coming home. Then I found a joint in the pocket of his jeans and knew he was in trouble.

"Although his SAT scores were near perfect, his grades weren't high enough to get into McGill. We thought a small, more personal school like Bishop's would be perfect for him. And he seemed very enthusiastic about going there."

She paused then, and I could almost feel her gathering herself up before she said, "He was so exceptional. That's why what happened to him was that much more puzzling, and that much more heartbreaking."

"What a waste." I didn't realize that I'd spoken aloud, until I heard myself repeating those same three words, over and over again. There was a dull pain in my right temple, and I pressed my fingertips against the spot to ease the throbbing.

"Are you all right?" my mother asked.

I shook my head.

"Do you want to stop?"

I nodded, gulping back a sob. "Sorry," I said.

"Is this going to be too much for you?"

I shrugged and made myself look at her. "I don't know. I hope not."

I thought of the boy I'd revered, the teenager I'd loved with helpless trepidation, the young man I'd buried in grief and anger and despair. Then I thought of the questions that still needed answering, the closure I so desperately wanted. And I vowed that no, it *wouldn't* be too much for me.

"Do you not think you're asking too much of yourself?" my mother said.

"No, I don't. This is something I *have* to do, for him, as much as for me. You weren't there in those last months, mom, you didn't see what I saw. It was like being caught in a doorway between two worlds. On my side of the threshold, it was all brightness and normalcy; on the other, blackness and mystery.

"You didn't feel the contradictory feelings I felt. Fascination and revulsion. Curiosity and dread. Love and hate. But most of all, terror. Part of me wanted to give in, to cross the threshold, to see what it was really like on the other side. But I was too frightened, so I never did." My voice began to break up then. "Oh, mom," I whispered, "I know I could have done more."

"No, you couldn't," she argued. "You couldn't have done a thing."

"I could have saved him."

"Once again, you're wrong. You *couldn't* have saved him, no one could. Only Peter could have done that, and he chose not to. When are you going to accept that and stop blaming yourself, stop crippling yourself with senseless guilt?"

I appreciated her concern. But that didn't keep my brother's final words to me from starting up their familiar chant inside my head. And I knew that, whatever the cost, this quest was my own, last hope.

Two

*W*ithin the hour, my mother and I were scouring our memories for the names of my brother's friends. My intention was to begin with those from his childhood and end with those who'd known him during the final phase of his life. When I saw how short our list was, I was disappointed. There were only five names on it.

Four were, indeed, childhood friends; the fifth, Phil Gaucher, once dubbed "the evil genius" by my mother, had been the most destructive of my brother's later friends. I decided to save Phil for last, and start with the other four.

But back in my own apartment, I suddenly became concerned.

How would these now, middle-aged men respond to my barging into their lives so unexpectedly, and asking them to cast their minds back to when they were kids? Would they consider it an invasion of their privacy and resent me, or would they be sympathetic and try to help me? Would they even remember my brother? If they did, just *what* would they remember? And would *I* be prepared to *hear* it, whatever it was?

Forcing aside my doubts, I settled myself on the slipper chair in my bedroom and placed the clipboard, with its single page of printed questions and several sheets of looseleaf paper behind it, on my lap. Then I reached for the telephone on the small, console table beside me. Praying the four men still lived in Montreal, I dialed Information there, and crossed my fingers.

Within minutes, I'd gotten all four numbers.

The adrenalin surged and my body trembled as I lifted the receiver again. Nervously rehearsing the speech I planned to make, I punched out the first of the numbers.

I hung up before the phone could even ring once.

Obviously, I wasn't as ready as I'd thought.

One week later, I tried again.

This time, I stayed on the line until I heard a voice I hadn't heard in nearly forty years. After giving Howard Decker my name, I began what quickly became my standard opening.

"I know this is going to sound strange, and I don't know how you'll react," I said, "but after twenty-seven years, I'm finally trying to come to terms with my brother's death. What I'm attempting to do is put together as complete a picture of him as I can with the help of those who knew him at different stages of his life. And I was hoping you might be able to fill in some of the missing pieces for me."

His response was immediate and brought a rush of grateful tears to my eyes.

"Wow," he said, "what a brave thing for you to do." Then, after a brief pause, he continued, "I wish I could *really* help you, but we were just childhood friends, you know, kids. We'd do things like fly kites or look for ants at Ponsard Park. We were in the Cub Scouts together.

"He was a very interesting kid, your brother, he had a real scientific mind. He was always reading, *Scientific American*, things like that. He was always in some science group. I must say he had a calming influence on me."

"Did you see him at all, once you'd reached your teens?"

"A few times. We'd go listen to the music on Crescent Street."

"Did you see him in the last year of his life?"

"No."

"Did you hear anything about his death?"

"Only that he'd killed himself."

There it was. Voiced aloud by one of his friends for the first time. I picked up a separate sheet of paper, one I'd divided into two columns and headed with the words: MURDER and SUICIDE.

I shuddered as I wrote Howard's name in the column under
SUICIDE.

"But then," he added, "how can you have fear, when you're
told it's better on the other side, and you'll find a father who'll
never say no to you?"

I was so taken aback by what he'd said that, for a moment,
I couldn't speak.

"You know," he concluded in a wistful voice, "lots of my
friends died then and since then; they could never change their
innermost self."

Within the hour, I was repeating my opening for the second
time.

I tried to match the deep voice of Jack Sternthal to the voice
of the boy I once knew as Jackie, and failed. Like Howard,
Jack's recollections of my brother were few.

"I remember Peter as a brilliant, brilliant kid and a great
guy," he said. "He was the brain, the real genius in school. He
helped me with school work. In university, though, he seemed
to take a whole right turn. I was surprised that someone who'd
lived within the system, could have been so influenced by the
sixties' thing, that he went out of the system completely."

Then came that same, unhappy indictment.

"Over the years, I've known dozens who've died as a result
of drugs and so on. The sixties affected a lot of people."

The following day, I called the third person on my list:
Robin Billick. I was fortunate in my timing. Robin and his wife
were about to leave for Europe to celebrate their twenty-fifth
wedding anniversary.

Robin married twenty-five years? I couldn't believe it. I
didn't *want* to believe it. It was further proof of just how much
time had gone by.

"I was shocked and crushed by Peter's death," he said. "It
had a poignant impact on me."

He then provided me with snippets of his own, distant
memories.

"We were friends until after high school. For the most part,

Peter was a normal, playful kid. Tough, resilient. He was talented, sharp, creative. We'd do scientific experiments together, ski, play indoor hockey, those kinds of things."

"When do you think he started to change?"

"At Bishop's."

Several years after my brother's death, his former adviser had stunned my parents by informing them that the students at Bishop's had been making LSD in chemistry lab. And no one, it seemed, had been told. According to him, "The smart kids were into drugs, the dumb ones were into beer."

"When was the last time you saw my brother?" I asked Robin now.

"Just after he'd come back from his first trip to Jamaica."

My stomach muscles clenched and I promptly stopped writing.

Jamaica.

If my brother had carried within him the seeds of his own destruction, they were subsequently nourished and nurtured by what he'd found in Jamaica.

For it was there, that one of his friends had come upon a farmer. Not just any farmer. But one who called himself king of the Rastafarians. Who held out the promise of power in one hand and marijuana, as the basis of that power, in the other. Who, like the serpent in Eden, slithered into my brother's world, and took it over.

As if confirming my own thoughts, Robin said, "Peter was different, distant. He'd started to get into drugs and spiritualism, and had been transported. I later heard he'd become involved with a guru type of person. There were rumours that he'd become involved with a group that espoused self-sacrifice as the epiphany. And ... and that he'd killed himself."

Grimly, I entered Robin's name under Howard's. Then he surprised me by saying, "I suggest you call Andrew Cowan. He'd know more."

Andy, of course. I quickly jotted down the number Robin gave me. Then, in words eerily reminiscent of both Howard's and Jack's, he said, "You know, there were lots of casualties of young men in that era."

*   *   *   *

That evening, Norah called. She'd contacted not only the RCMP, but the Montreal police as well, and neither of them had a file — at least not anymore — on my brother.

"There is one bit of good news, though," she said. "I visited the Archives on Bleury, where old court files are stored, and I found the file of his arrest on drug charges."

I was so stunned, I actually gasped.

"Among the papers," she continued, "was a copy of the coroner's report, together with the file number. My next stop will be the *Centre d'archives de Montréal* to see if I can locate the actual coroner's report."

"Oh, Norah, I don't know what to say." I was shivering now, jubilant and frightened and anxious all at once.

"There's nothing *to* say," she told me softly. "Except," and she paused a moment before continuing, "except to say you've got my full support on this. I've thought for years it was something you should have done."

While the sleuth in me revelled in Norah's discovery, the rest of me waited with nail-biting nervousness for her next call.

She didn't disappoint.

"I went to the *Centre d'archives*," she said, "gave the clerk the number of your brother's file, and asked if I could see it. He disappeared for a good half-hour, and returned with a copy of the coroner's report which, he said, was the only paper in the file. I mailed it off to you immediately."

"Was the report the same as the one in the court file?" I asked.

"It appeared to be."

"Then you read it."

"Yes." There was a pause, a long, long pause, and then, "God, I didn't realize he'd died in such a ghastly way. I'd always assumed ... I mean ... I didn't know he'd — "

"Don't say it. Please."

"I'm sorry, it was just such a shock."

I was struck then, by what I'd subjected Norah to when I'd

first asked for her help, and I was deeply shaken.

"I'm the one who's sorry," I told her, "truly, truly sorry. I never stopped to think about what we might be getting ourselves into."

She assured me — twice — that she was all right. Yet her parting words to me were, "Brace yourself."

In the morning, I got the phone numbers for the MUC (Montreal Urban Community) police headquarters in Montreal, as well as for the RCMP, in both Montreal and Ottawa. Knowing I wouldn't be satisfied until I'd spoken to them myself, I called each office in turn.

And with the first of those calls, a pattern was established. I'd explain, gently and apologetically, that my French wasn't good enough for conversation, then ask if there was someone around who spoke English.

Usually there was, occasionally there wasn't. But what astounded — even humbled — me, was everyone's courtesy, interest, and kindness. We'd invariably end up laughing together, and poking fun at our deficiencies — mine in French, theirs in English — while we struggled to make ourselves understood.

If I'd hoped for a different response, I didn't get one. There simply *were* no files on my brother. Anywhere.

But I still wasn't ready to drop the matter.

I called Montreal again, and spoke this time with the Honourable Fred Kaufman. My father had asked Fred to represent my brother at the time of his arrest, but my brother had refused the offer and had chosen his own lawyer.

"Did you ever meet my brother?" I asked Fred.

"Once," he replied. "I went to the Douglas Hospital in a quasi-legal capacity to see him, and had a long talk with him."

"Do you remember anything about your talk?"

"Only that it was a pretty rational conversation."

He then said he'd have someone from his office check into my brother's missing files, and call me back.

When he did, it was merely to confirm what I'd already been told. Several times.

"If a death's been ruled a suicide," he explained, "any existing file can legally be destroyed after five years. If it's a solved murder, the file can be destroyed after twenty-five."

"But what about microfilm?" I asked. "Surely, they don't just physically tear up files and throw them in a waste basket."

"Apparently, with files dating back to the sixties, that's precisely what they did."

"How very professional of them," I muttered.

"I also checked to see if *I* still had a file on Peter, but I don't. It was too long ago."

As I hung up, I could hear my mother's words echoing in my ears. *"I only wish you'd done this sooner."* Dammit, I thought, so do I.

Swallowing my frustration, I channelled my energies into contacting Andrew. And after three failed attempts, I finally got him.

"Peter was an intense guy," he told me. "We were close friends as teenagers. Every kid feels like a bit of a misfit in his own way, and we were misfits together for a time. Every teenager feels the world is screwed up, but they grow up, get older; he didn't. He hated hypocrisy like all teenagers, only more so.

"He was a person of extremes; it was always 'more' with him. He had lots of frustrations. Being short was one of them, it was part of who he was. He could be a pain in the ass, could enjoy annoying people on purpose. But he could also be extremely nice.

"I used to play the banjo. We lived in an apartment, and my playing really got on my father's nerves. One day he snapped the neck of my banjo in half. Needless to say, I was wrecked. Peter said, 'Let's fix it,' and he did.

"In the basement workroom of your house, he glued it together, put in screws, sanded, and refinished it. And you know what, it wasn't perfect, but it played. That was a great thing for him to do; it helped a lot."

"Are you still playing the banjo?" I asked.

"No, the guitar. As a matter of fact, it was watching your brother play that got me interested in the guitar. We played music together, we'd even go to folk festivals together. We were going in the same direction as friends then, but toward the end, we weren't any more. We'd gone off on different paths."

Suddenly, his focus shifted.

"Everyone was doing drugs then; it was a way of life. But they were different, a real trip, almost innocent. Now, it's big business. It was a whole culture back then. There was supposed to have been a revolution, but it didn't get quite big enough. One percent wanted to change the world. Ultimately, convention won out.

"Drugs," he said, "strip away whatever stands between you and whatever's out there. They're relaxing; they enable you to lose things that skew perception in that way you've built up. They allow a kind of openness, and that's a nice thing. They relax you, help you focus, help you understand where people are coming from. When they wear off, so does the mindset, and that's disappointing."

I waited a moment, absorbing what he'd said, then I asked, "Did you see my brother in the last year of his life?"

"Only once. It was in the spring of '68. My girlfriend and I had had a child together. I hadn't seen Peter in three years. We met, he came over to our place for an hour, and it was a disagreeable meeting.

"He thought I was hopelessly square, not hip to myself, burying myself in the conventional world, hiding from myself. He was hip, he was onto something, and he was almost aggressive about it."

As to the matter of my brother's death being a suicide or murder?

"Suicide was possible, because Peter was extreme in that way. He died facing something he couldn't face. But then, someone could have helped him die."

I put down the phone with Andrew's name virtually straddling both columns.

Three

*W*hen the envelope from Norah arrived, I opened it with panicked dread. I scanned the brief note she'd enclosed, then took my time unfolding the long, thin sheet of paper accompanying it.

The coroner's report.

The breath lodged in my throat when I saw my brother's full name, Peter David Berger, written in bold, black script across the top of the page.

It was the first time I'd seen his name written that way for years — except for his tombstone. The shock of recognition was more pronounced, I knew, because it was *his* name, and no one else's.

As irrational as it may have been, I felt a surge of sisterly protectiveness. It isn't possible, I thought. They can't be referring to my brother. Not *my* brother. How dare some stranger study him, poke and probe him, then write about him? How could his privacy be so invaded, the sanctity of his person be so defiled?

My stomach was churning, as though I'd eaten something that hadn't agreed with me, yet my gaze remained fixed on the flow of black ink spelling out my brother's name.

Its damning position at the top of the report contradicted what I suppose I'd always wanted to believe. That he wasn't really dead, but was simply out there someplace, hiding.

My eyes moved slowly to the right. To the small box in which his age was written: nineteen.

I swallowed hard. Nineteen. So young. He'd been so young.

My eyes dropped lower. And there in French, were the words that had so shocked Norah. The ones she'd warned me about. The ones I hadn't let her say out loud.

"Stabbing."

"Knife forced through the left breast into the heart."

Nausea burned the back of my throat and I squeezed my eyes shut against the pain. Who, I asked myself, who in God's name, chooses to die in such a gruesome way? It had to be murder, it had to be. *He* couldn't have done this to himself. *How* could he have done this to himself, how?

And yet, despite my incredulousness, there at the bottom of the report, was the official conclusion of the coroner: "suicide in a moment of mental alienation."

Mental alienation?

What did that mean? And how could a coroner, in looking at a *body*, describe that body's state of mind?

With the report clutched in my left hand, I punched out Fred's phone number with my right, and asked him to explain the term "mental alienation" to me.

"Historically," he said, "Catholics who'd committed suicide, were forbidden burial in consecrated ground. But if they were deemed mentally incompetent, they *could* be buried there. So coroners simply started applying the term to everyone, regardless of their faith."

Although I accepted the basic premise of his explanation, I still wasn't satisfied, and returned — once again — to the missing files.

"How," I asked, "can I pursue this matter further? I mean, how do I know it's not a question of some bureaucrat somewhere being too lazy to even try and find them for me?"

His suggestion: look into the new Access to Information Act.

Lying in bed that night, attempting to fall asleep, I couldn't close my eyes without seeing my brother. Dead, with a knife in his heart. No matter how many times I blinked, no matter how often I shifted postions, no matter how many other subjects I focused on, that ghoulish image of him remained.

As I lay there in my agony, I imagined him lying there in *his* agony. Whether by his own hand or by someone else's, one fact was now, at last, irrefutable. My brother had died with a knife in his heart.

I remained awake for most of the night, but near dawn, I must have drifted off, because I woke up, dreaming.

In my dream, I was with my brother. He was a child, perhaps six or seven years old. We were in a clothing store and he was trying on various kinds of clothes. Everything was too big for him — the clothes of a man trying to fit onto the body of a young boy. I had to keep rolling up the cuffs on his pants and turning back the sleeves on his shirts.

A woman asked which of us was older. When I said I was, she said that *he* looked older. Ignoring her, I gave my brother a hug, while he simply stood and looked up at me with his huge, black eyes.

I told him that I loved him and pleaded with him not to do anything rash. Hugging him even tighter, I told him that I'd die if anything happened to him.

I kept repeating, "Promise me that you won't do anything bad," until he finally said, "I promise."

And that's when I woke up.

The dream had been so real that I could still see his eyes, so large and so warm, gazing up at me. I could still feel my arms clasped tightly around his narrow back. I could still feel the closeness of him, the dear and precious closeness of him.

And I missed him. God, how I missed him.

I decided to pursue a different aspect of what seemed, for the moment at least, to be a stunted paper trail. All it required was another long distance call to Montreal. To my old friend, Charles, who worked as a psychologist at none other than the Douglas Hospital. Perhaps *they* still had a file on my brother. And if they did, I wanted it.

When I reached Charles, I put the question to him and asked him to let me know as soon as possible.

He called that evening with the answer.

Yes.

There *was* still a file on my brother. He even gave me the file number.

I broke into a grin. "Only joking now, Charles," I said, "but do you think you could get hold of the file, make a copy of it, and send it to me?"

Unfortunately, he didn't see the humour in my suggestion. And I knew, even as we said goodbye, that I hadn't been joking at all.

The following morning, I called the Douglas Hospital and spoke with France Lemieux in the Medical Records Department. After explaining who I was, what I was doing, and why, I gave her the number of my brother's file and asked if I could see it.

At first, she sounded sympathetic. Then I made the mistake of telling her that I was a writer. Alarm bells must have sounded in her head, because her tone changed immediately, and she refused my request outright, saying there was no access whatsoever to those files.

When I persisted, she told me that I could put my request in writing, according to the "Act respecting access to documents held by public bodies and the protection of personal information," and send it to Richard LaBranche, associate director of Professional Services.

"You must," she added, "include proof of your identity, as well as proof of your brother's death, and the reasons you want access to his file."

When I put down the phone, I was fuming. What had begun as a matter of curiosity had become, in an instant, a matter of utmost necessity. The very fact that I'd been denied access to my brother's file made me want it all the more. And the more I wanted it, the more determined I was to get it.

Within minutes, I was dialing the hospital again. This time with the intention of locating and speaking to Dr. Heinz Lehmann, the psychiatrist who'd been the hospital's clinical director in 1968.

I hadn't even rehearsed what I'd say if I reached him, and when I was put through to his office, I was almost relieved to learn that he'd retired. But, I was told, he still came in several times a week. Brazenly, I asked for his home phone number, and, astonishingly enough, I was given it.

I called him early that evening. He didn't say hello; he answered by announcing his name. I gave him *my* name and told him about my search, then filled him in briefly on my brother's stay at the Douglas in September of '68. To my utter amazement, the man actually remembered him.

He even recalled my brother as being "articulate," and stated, most emphatically, when I inquired, that "he wasn't psychotic." Then, after I'd described how he'd died, Lehmann said, "Psychologically, it doesn't make sense."

My feelings exactly.

I explained that the hospital had refused me access to my brother's file, and appealed to him, on humanitarian grounds, for his help. He admitted to being intrigued and agreed to speak with France Lemieux. Then he told me to call him back the next night at the same time.

In the morning, I turned, finally, to the fourth name on my list: Michael Cukier. But I found myself speaking instead with his ex-wife, Jennifer. When I explained who I was and the reason for my call, she told me, "I remember Michael saying over and over, 'My best friend died.'"

And, in what was becoming a familiar lament, she added, "There were many suicides from your brother's class, yet no one's ever forgotten *him*."

She gave me Michael's number then, and wished me luck.

Hearing his voice, the most familiar of them all, was an emotional jolt. It flung me back in time and pinned me up against the wall of the past. For Michael had been a constant fixture in our house when we three were growing up. To me, he sounded the same as he had thirty years ago.

"Peter wanted to know it all and to be a leader," he said. "He had to direct the show. I couldn't teach him anything; it was my responsibility to learn from him. But he was also insecure.

"He was ultrasensitive about his height, and had to compensate for his shortness. He wanted to be tall and strong; he never felt strong. Even when he'd grown tall — inside the tall guy, he was still a shrimp."

There it was again, that same observation about my brother's height. The classic Napoleonic complex. Could that have been a factor in the choices he ultimately made?

"He became a heavy Bob Dylan fan, and took lots of his information from song lyrics. He was also influenced by Kahlil Gibran's *The Prophet* and by the *Siddhartha*. He saw himself as the Walrus from the Beatles' song.

"He tried to get me to smoke pot, but I wouldn't, because I didn't want to get into trouble. It was illegal, and I didn't want to break the law. The more he smoked, the less I saw of him. Often when we'd be together, he'd say 'Gotta go now.' I did go with him once to Night Magic in Old Montreal, but I felt uncomfortable, with all the drugs around the place and the new music.

"During our college days, we drifted apart, not because of anything in particular, but because our lives had already begun taking separate paths. We saw each other very little in the last years. The best and closest friends historically go their separate ways."

"Did you know they were making LSD in chemistry lab at Bishop's?" I asked.

"It wouldn't have surprised me."

"Why not?"

"Because Peter was always inventive. This simply became more extreme. Manufacturing LSD was no different than his building a model plane or a rocket. I see that as a continuum, an exaggeration of the essence that was there, more than a change. What he did, he always was. But like a girl getting pregnant at that time, a nice, Jewish boy doing and dealing drugs wasn't socially acceptable.

"Do you know I felt more connected to him *after* he died? I had nightmares. I kept thinking, 'How could he do this to me? I was his friend.' If he'd met a woman and fallen in love, everything might have been different."

How simplistic, I smiled, how sweetly naive. But, as I looked down at what I'd written, I shuddered. My brother did have a girlfriend of sorts toward the end. Someone named Kathy. She'd died in a plane crash not long after my brother's death.

According to my mother, Kathy's brother had paid them a surprise visit one night and had given them back a ring he'd found among Kathy's effects. It was the ring I'd bought my brother for his Bar Mitzvah.

Michael tore me from my thoughts with an apology. He was on his way to a meeting, and would have to call me back.

After I'd hung up, I sat in my chair awhile, simply staring at the phone. I felt as if I were nibbling on canapés at a buffet. Yet, the more I ate, the hungrier I became. And now I was ravenous.

To my growing list of "wants," I added a new one: the switch.

The switch that someone or something had thrown to divert my brother from the path he'd been on at the start of his life, to the one he'd followed at the end of it. I was looking for the incident, the moment, the epiphany, whatever, that had changed him from what he was into what he became.

I glanced at the clipboard on my lap, examining more closely what Michael had said. Two sentences, in particular, stood out.

"I see that as a continuum, an exaggeration of the essence that was there, more than a change. What he did, he always was."

Could it have been as simple as that? Not a change at all, just more extreme?

At seven that evening, I was back on the phone with Heinz Lehmann.

"The woman's on a power trip," he said, referring to France Lemieux. "She remembers speaking with you. She knows you're a writer, and she's afraid you might be getting ready to write something about this. She did, however, tell me something *I* didn't know, and that is, after a person's death, their file is sealed."

Was that true, I wondered, or was it merely a delaying tactic on Lemieux's part?

"I told her that I wanted to see the file," Lehmann continued, "that I may, in fact, have been the doctor of record in the matter. She said, 'Only if you give me your guarantee that you won't tell her what's in it.'

"I said I would guarantee her nothing, and that I wanted to see the file. She told me to come back in a week, because those files are stored elsewhere. I suggest you call me again next week at the same time, after I've had a chance to look at it."

"I truly appreciate what you're doing," I told him. "I know this is highly unusual, and goes beyond the call of duty."

"You've aroused my curiosity."

"Of course, if you feel like taking some notes and sneaking them out with you, I wouldn't mind," I joked — again not joking at all.

Unlike Charles, Lehmann, at least, rewarded me with a laugh.

Four

On Monday, at precisely 7 p.m., with my clipboard poised and ready, I placed my third call in a week to Dr. Lehmann. I could barely contain my excitement when he confirmed that he'd seen and gone through my brother's file. But it was his subsequent remark that set the tone for the rest of the conversation.

With a wry chuckle he said, "Did you know that your father was the first person who ever wanted to sue me?"

"No." I feigned surprise, knowing full well that my father had indeed considered such a suit.

"I even had to hire a lawyer to protect our interests, but it wasn't necessary, as he never proceeded with the action."

That was because Victor Goldbloom, then Member of the Quebec National Assembly, and a friend of my parents, had discouraged just such an action, citing, among other reasons, my father's precarious health, the emotional costs, and the gruelling nature of such a case should it go to court. He had also, I was told, promised them that "something like this will never happen again."

Something like what? I'd always wondered.

"Why do you think my father wanted to sue you?" I asked, feeling the anger begin.

"Oh, he mentioned in his letter something about homicide or suicide, and that he was holding the hospital responsible for what happened to your brother."

Stung by the offhandedness of this statement, I found it

difficult to keep my temper in check. I only managed by quickly directing the man's attention back to the file itself.

"According to the records," he said, "your brother was seen as a nice, witty, polite, young man. He was articulate and highly intelligent, if somewhat impulsive and immature. He was neither depressed, nor psychotic. His responses were perfectly normal. He did well on all his tests.

"He apparently said something to the effect that 'life is beautiful, although it can sometimes be very difficult.' It appears he did his best not to show any morbid features. There was not much wrong except the drugs."

"Not much wrong except the drugs!" I cried. "Wasn't that wrong enough?"

"I could understand the concern of your parents to keep your brother out of prison," Lehmann replied, "but this wasn't the purpose of the hospital. Besides, a drug detoxification program takes months, and doesn't work without the consent of the person in question. And, as I said before, since his tests were normal, and since he was neither depressed nor psychotic, we saw no reason to keep him."

"But you released him without first consulting my parents. According to my father, he received a letter asking for permission to discharge my brother *after* the fact."

"I have no recollection of that."

"What about the staff's being so impressed with my brother's knowledge of LSD, that he was asked to come back and lecture them on it?"

"I have no recollection of that either."

Whether true or not, my brother had boasted it was Lehmann himself who'd issued that infamous invitation.

I could sense a growing tension on the wire, and at this point, the conversation lagged. Moments later, Lehmann ended it with the suggestion that I contact Khalil Geagea, a psychiatrist at the Jewish General Hospital. As I repeated the name, it sounded vaguely familiar. Then I realized why.

Geagea was the name of the resident who'd been in charge of my brother's case.

Restless and agitated now, I prowled my apartment in search of diversion. Within minutes, I found myself sitting crosslegged on the floor in the study, my oldest photo album in my lap. Turning to the first page, I began a slow, all-too-brief walk through my childhood, with my brother by my side.

Each small, black and white snapshot of him had a different pet name printed in tiny, block letters at the bottom: Petie Boy. Peter Pumpkin. Pete-Boy. Petie. Petie Poo. There were no more than a dozen photos in my paltry collection. He was no more than six in the last of them.

How small he was. How cuddly. With his wide grin, large, round eyes, and straight, dark hair. And what I'd come to think of as his Clark Gable ears. I stiffened suddenly, thinking back. As he lay in his casket, I, in my desperate, aching need to make a connection with him one, final time, had reached out to touch him. And what had I touched? His right ear.

I slammed the album shut and took out a second, smaller one. I knew just the photo I needed to see. It was taken the evening of my high school graduation dance. There I stood, posed, beside a neighbour's magnolia tree, elegantly serene in a short, full-skirted dress of white lace over pale blue satin. I was smiling down at my brother, my adorable brother, whose head barely reached my chest, and who, with a twinkle in his eyes and that special grin of his, was gallantly kissing my left hand.

I closed that album, too, then opened my wedding album.

I'd gotten married in May of '68. Four months later, my brother was dead. And my marriage died with him.

These were my last photographs of him, and the changes in him were shocking and profound. In each of them, his head was down. Now slightly taller than I, his once-straight hair had grown into a kinky, semi-Afro, his face was pale and gaunt, and a thin, straggly mustache stretched across his upper lip. Gone was the elfin grin, the twinkling eyes, the glint of humour. Gone were all vestiges of the boy under the magnolia tree. In his place stood a spectre. Removed, by the blankness of his expression, from all that was going on around him.

Hastily, I put all three albums away. But I still couldn't let go. By opening up those albums, I'd opened up the past. Now, it was inviting me to stay awhile.

I went to my closet and knelt in front of the bookcase that held my records: worn and warped LP's in shredded jackets, scratched and scratchy, vintage 45's. Scanning them hungrily, I looked for anything I could find from the sixties. Then I tugged them, one by one, from the shelves, and placed them in a stack on the floor.

First Edition ... Beatles ... Rolling Stones ... Bob Marley ... Paul Butterfield Blues Band ... Bob Dylan ... Jimi Hendrix ... Janis Joplin ... Otis Redding ... Doors ... Jefferson Airplane ...

I recalled going with my brother to see the Jefferson Airplane when the group played Montreal in '67. The two of us had stood, along with thousands of others, on the vast, outdoor square fronting Place Ville Marie, holding flowers, passing around flowers, and moving to the music.

I dropped *Like a Rolling Stone* onto the turntable of my stereo, and turned up the volume. As Bob Dylan's wailing voice and hypnotic, repetitive rhythms filled the room, I closed my eyes and allowed myself to drift. When the record ended, I put on Janis Joplin's *Summertime*. I followed that with the First Edition's *Just Dropped In*, then Otis Redding's *Dock of the Bay*.

When Otis Redding was killed in a plane crash, my brother had told me, eerily, unnervingly, "It was his time. His work here on earth was done."

I shivered as the fingers of the past slid up and down my back. And soon, all that existed for me was the music.

In the morning, I called the Jewish General Hospital and left a message for Dr. Geagea. Even as I did, I wondered if I'd ever hear from him.

Later that day, I had my answer.

The anger returned the moment he identified himself. Only this time, it was directed at *him*. I described my conversation with Heinz Lehmann, refreshed his memory about my brother, and asked if he had any recollection of the case.

He did.

And I was astounded.

Again.

Astounded by my brother's obvious impact on people. Astounded that, after twenty-seven years, he was someone they hadn't been able to forget.

"I recall we interviewed him," Geagea said, "and found him to be bright and articulate. He had tremendous personality power. I presented him in rounds to Dr. Lehmann. Away from the drugs, he was coherent and made a good case for himself."

"But if you knew he was using drugs," I asked, "why did you let him go?"

"The issue was commitment and his having the right to leave. We felt his condition didn't warrant our keeping him there. We didn't feel he had to be forced to stay."

"What, Dr. Geagea, was the age of majority in 1968?"

"I believe it was eighteen."

"Then why did the hospital send my parents a letter asking for their permission to release my brother because he was a minor? He was nineteen at the time, and, therefore, according to you, *not* a minor."

"The hospital would never have sent your parents a letter asking for their permission to release him."

"According to my mother, they did."

"Did she see the letter?"

"I don't know. All I do know is that my father told her about it."

"Then she must be mistaken."

I bit down hard on my bottom lip to keep my anger under control.

"You know," he told me then, "your brother fit that era; he was a part of that whole era."

What a rationalization. As if that excused *them* for what they'd done or, rather, for what they hadn't done.

I took a deep breath and played my final card.

"Do you recall putting your arm around my brother and taking him out one evening for a barbeque chicken dinner, Dr. Geagea?"

"Whoever told you that was mistaken. I never did such a thing."

"Then I guess my mother was wrong again. You did it right

in front of her. Thank you, Dr. Geagea, for all your help."

And with that, I hung up.

Two days later, my mother unearthed another name for me.

Howard Berson still lived in Montreal, and when I called him, he, like the others, couldn't have been kinder.

"Peter and I were friends in high school," he told me. "We shared the same enthusiasm for woodworking and building things. His work habits could be quite careful, and he could make nice things, but he'd become impatient, frustrated, angry, with anything that took a long time.

"By the end of high school, no one was yet into drugs. The interest was there, but no one had a clue as to where to find any. People were different then. One of my friends drifted into some light dealing, with a tentative movement toward going into it big time. Peter was enthusiastic about going into it big time."

Of everything I'd learned about his final year, this had been the hardest to accept. That my brother, *my* brother, had dealt in drugs.

And about that final year?

"He was into different things," Howard said. "We didn't spend much time together. I didn't find his scene particularly attractive. I did, however, score some great acid from him at a Be-In at Fletcher's Field. You know, it wasn't a crime to have LSD then."

For the first time, it was appropriate for me to ask my next question.

"Did you ever meet Bas?"

The name was like bile on my tongue.

Bas.

Basil Harcourt Hawthorne. The serpent of pure evil in my brother's world.

"I met him a few times."

"And?" I prompted.

"There was great reverance toward him. I remember being told that anyone could speak with Bas, but that they had to remove their shoes before going into his room. I said 'No thanks' and this irked Bas. So I'd just sit in the sun porch while he held court."

"What was it that so attracted my brother to someone like Bas?"

To me, this remained one of the great mysteries surrounding my brother's final year. That he, with his background, his brilliance, and his abilities, could have been so taken in and so taken over by an ignorant, uneducated farmer from the hills of Jamaica.

"Peter thought Bas had some important, philosophical viewpoints to which he himself aspired. He believed Bas had the knowledge and he, Peter, had the keys to that knowledge. It all revolved around the jargon of the time, terms like 'psychic power' and 'other planes.' It sounded too much like mysticism to me, and I was resistant to it."

"Why?"

Why could Howard resist what my brother, apparently, could not?

"I didn't buy it. Bas was just a guy. I found him distasteful. I don't know what makes some people seek simple paths."

Was that what my brother had been doing: seeking simple paths?

"Did you ever hear anything about how my brother died?" I asked.

"I heard that a few nights before it happened, he stabbed himself with a can opener, and exorted the others to do the same."

I recoiled in disbelief and nearly dropped my pen.

And, as to my brother's actual death, Howard said, "Apparently, he'd been absolutely certain he wasn't going to die. He was simply going to a different place. The place Bas had talked about going to."

I was so chilled by his words, so sickened by the horrible image they conjured up, that I could barely breathe, let alone write.

Little did I know the horrors had only just begun.

Five

*T*he following day, I did two things. I opened a file on my computer, headed SCHEDULE, to serve as my daily diary. And I booked a flight to Montreal.

I plotted my four-day trip with precision care, listing the people I planned to interview, the places I intended to visit, and the time I'd allot to each of them.

My mother suggested I stay with one of her friends to cut down on expenses, but I refused. For what I was about to do, I needed privacy. I needed space. I needed to be alone.

But from a more practical point of view, without a car, I needed to be centrally located. And that meant a downtown hotel. Where a cab was only a doorman's whistle away, and where I could entertain guests simply by summoning a waiter or dialing room service.

My flight left Toronto early on a sweltering July morning and arrived an hour later in the equally blistering heat of Montreal.

But as I disembarked from the plane, all I felt was cold.

My first, scheduled interview was with Michael. And as he came through the front door of my hotel, I felt the years dissolve, sweeping me away on a bittersweet wave.

We sat at a window table in the lobby dining-room, two grown strangers who'd once been childhood friends, while my brother's presence hovered in the air between us, like the phantom pain from a missing limb. After several minutes of playing catch-up, I opened my notebook and turned to the real reason for our meeting.

"Did you ever meet Bas?" I asked without preamble.

"No, I only heard about him."

"What did you hear?"

Michael sighed. "For the first time in his life, Peter deferred to Bas. Bas was his oracle. To him, the man was the truth, the man was god. Peter had a sense of omnipotence. He'd found the answers, he'd found the way.

"He was recruiting, but not in a formalized way. He saw himself as enlightened and wanted to enlighten those still left in the darkness. He spoke in parables. But as much as he tried to bring me into the fold, I never really tried to bring him back out.

"His attitude was: 'I'd tell you about my god, I'd tell you more, but you wouldn't understand. Since you don't know what life is, it'd be too hard to explain it to you.' In short," Michael added grimly, "he had a new god, a new family."

A new family. The very idea set my teeth on edge, made me bristle with anger and resentment. And something else: jealousy.

"My feeling," he continued, "is that after his arrest, Peter was caught between his old family and his new one, and he didn't want to betray either. Although he'd turned against the establishment, he respected your father tremendously. His new life was undermining everything your father had built. It was at war with everything he believed in. By his actions, Peter was shaming him; he was a blot on your father's good name.

"If he testified, he'd be betraying his new family; if he went to jail, he'd be betraying his old family. All the forces combined. He had nowhere to go. The arrest killed him as much as Bas, although the physical act was by his own hand."

"Then you don't think he might have been murdered?" I asked.

"Not in the traditional sense. He was murdered by convention and society. He died of shame and embarrassment for what he was doing to your father. To me, it was a phase in the extreme;

he flew too close to the sun and burned. If he'd gone in a different direction, I could see myself being interviewed about him when he won the Nobel Prize."

I smiled sadly at that, and added Michael's name to my growing list.

"You know," he said, as he stood to leave, "you should call Tom Gottlieb when you get back to Toronto. He lived in the house off and on. If anyone knew what went on there, Tommy would."

In the taxi en route to my next appointment, I thought of the door Howard Berson had opened, and which Michael had opened farther still. But the wider it opened, the darker, not lighter, it became. For beyond it, lay the void. The yawning hole of blackness that had enveloped, and ultimately, consumed my brother. And into which, by my actions, I myself was stepping.

Dave Schatia had been my father's law partner at the time of my brother's death. He was the one who'd accompanied my father to the house on Coloniale Street, where my brother's body was found, and later, to the morgue. He was the one who'd acted as liaison between my parents and the police investigating my brother's death. He was the one who'd confirmed to my parents that the police had ruled it a suicide.

He was also the one who'd told the funeral home to shave my brother's face and remove his mustache. Perhaps he saw it as a way of returning to us the boy we'd once known.

But, for me, his good intentions had backfired. It may even have been one of reasons I never fully came to terms with my brother's death. For the clean, sweet face of the young man in that coffin was not my brother's face. It belonged to a stranger.

Despite having seen Dave on several occasions over the years, I felt uneasy about seeing him now. But his greeting was affectionate and warm, and when I asked him what he remembered about my brother, he responded without hesitation.

"He was very quick-witted, skilled at repartee, and very philosophical. But his behaviour, over time, became increasingly bizarre. He seemed to be a very troubled young man. I remember one of the last conversations we had.

"He told me, 'Everything is a matter of perception. You see life one way, I see it another.' He pointed to a doorknob and said, 'To you, it's a doorknob; I don't necessarily see it as one.'

"He was so different from your father. Your father never shared, he was a very secretive, private man. It was as if he knew, but didn't know."

"Forgive me if I sound a bit ghoulish," I said, bracing myself, "but could you tell me exactly what you saw when you got to the house on Coloniale?"

"It's a sight I've never forgotten," he said, gazing off into space. "The room was dark and dismal. He was lying, fully dressed, on an unmade, messy bed."

"Was there any sign of a struggle?"

"No. There was a sense of calm to the room."

"Was there a blood trail leading to the bed?"

He shook his head. "I don't recall even seeing blood."

"Can you describe him ... you know ... "

"He was lying face up on the bed, eyes looking up, the handle of a long butcher knife protruding from his chest."

I fought the urge to retch, and continued. "Was he holding the knife?"

"Perhaps one hand or both, I can't recall precisely."

"Anything else?"

"There were a few scared-rat kids in another room. None took any interest in what had occurred, and that made your father furious. You know, it was all so long ago ... " and his voice trailed off.

Try as he might, he couldn't dredge up anything else which may have been of use to me. We rose at the same time.

"I believe your father never got over it," he said as he walked me to the door. "He never spoke of it again."

I felt numb as I went out into the summer heat. What Dave had described didn't sound, to me, like a murder scene. No struggle ... no blood trail ... a sense of calm ...

And yet ...

*   *   *   *

In the morning, I walked to the nondescript, brick building on Bleury Street that housed the Archives.

Following Norah's instructions, I rang the bell outside the locked, inner door several times, then waited. When I was finally admitted, I found myself in a large room with a low, wooden counter to my left and several tables to my right. Shelves of file folders lined the walls behind the counter, and, opening off the main room, was a series of similar, shelf-lined rooms.

I filled out a request form and handed it to the clerk on duty. He gave it a cursory glance, then sauntered off.

A few minutes later, he was back, carrying a bulky, manilla folder, which he transferred to me with the merest of nods.

My legs were shaking as I made my way to one of the empty tables, and sat down. I placed the file, together with my notebook, pen, and reading glasses in front of me, then waited. Until I could find the courage to begin.

What little I did muster, faltered instantly at the sight of my brother's name on that ominous-looking folder.

Suddenly, I wanted to run. Before I was confronted with something I might not want to face. Before I saw something I might not be *prepared* to face.

But I didn't run. I forced myself to sit there and take a chance. On myself. On my being able to handle it, whatever *it* was. Very quickly then, I opened the file.

Staring up at me was a document headed, in French, by the words "Court of the Sessions of the Peace." It was a "Bill of Indictment," charging my brother with "committing an indictable offence under section 3 (2) of the Narcotics Control Act" for the possession of approximately three ounces of marijuana and six pieces of hashish.

My heartbeat quickened at the sight of his name, Peter David Berger, typed in upper case letters. Next to it, was the name of his co-defendant: Basil Harcourt Hawthorne. Bas's name, however, had been Xed out. Leaving my brother's name to stand alone. Leaving my brother himself to stand alone.

A second document headed "Recognizance," noted that my father had pledged the sum of nine hundred and fifty dollars to have my brother released on bail. I peered dismally at the two signatures near the bottom of the page. The first was my father's.

My father. Upstanding and honourable, principled, and proud. A lawyer whose hallmark was integrity. How his heart must have broken. How torn he must have been, how shamed. To have had to put his name on so degrading a document.

The second was my brother's. I studied it, long and hard. Written in a cramped, upright scrawl, only the three capital letters, P, D, and B, were clearly distinguishable. But what struck me most was the line he'd drawn through his entire name, starting with the last letter in his last name, and curving back to slice through the first letter in his first name.

What did it mean? I wondered. A negation of that name? A negation of himself? A slash through the heart of his name, like the one through his own heart three weeks later? I shuddered and moved on.

Among other things, the file contained the testimony of the two RCMP officers, Joseph St. Denis and Richard Rougeau, who, on September 7, 1968, conducted the drug raid on my brother's place; a letter, dated September 13, 1968, from Helga Ast, chief of services at the Douglas Hospital confirming my brother's admission to the hospital on September 9th; a copy of the coroner's report; the transcript of Bas's court hearing; and the judgment of the court dismissing all charges against him.

For the next few hours, I was spellbound. Using the various documents as a guide, I managed to reconstruct the events surrounding the RCMP drug raid that fateful September night so long ago.

There was a knock at the door. Phil Gaucher answered it. One of the RCMP officers entered.

Phil said, "What do you want? Who are you?"

"I'm a policeman," he replied.

The second RCMP officer entered and walked to the other end of the house.

Phil asked if they had a warrant, and he said, "I don't want to be a dictator, but if you don't sit down and shut up, I'll call the Montreal police, who'll not only search these premises, but also rough you up a little."

Not long after, they left with my brother, saying, "We have what we want."

A half-hour later, both men returned, accompanied by twelve or thirteen other men, including Montreal police, more RCMP officers, and plainclothesmen. They arrested Bas, Phil, and two juveniles, and took them down to RCMP headquarters for questioning.

Among the exhibits listed in the indictment were various boxes, bowls, and Indian pipes, some blue capsules, and several envelopes and plastic bags containing marijuana and hashish.

In an interrogation room at RCMP headquarters, my brother was questioned and advised of his rights. He reflected for nearly a half-hour, then at 11:55 p.m., signed a declaration, stating that all of the drugs seized belonged to him and no one else.

After he'd signed the declaration, which, needless to say, wasn't in the file, he was left alone for three hours, while the officers questioned the others they'd taken in. Then they returned and led my brother off to a cell.

I let out a groan. I couldn't bear it. I couldn't bear the thought of him, sleepy, disoriented, and probably terrified, being locked inside a jail cell. And I still couldn't bear the thought of him — he, who could have been anyone and done anything — as a drug dealer.

My next stop was MUC police headquarters on Bonsecours Street. There, two uncooperative security guards stood between me and the elevator that would have taken me to the third floor where the records were kept. I had no file number, they said, no papers. They couldn't let me pass without them.

Despite my protests, pleadings, and explanations, they remained firm. The answer was "no."

Finally, in a voice as cold and menacing as I could manage, I said, "Listen to me. You're only security guards. You know nothing about police procedure and nothing at all about this particular matter. Now, if you won't let me speak to someone on the third floor, I want you to bring someone down here to speak to *me*."

It worked. The younger of the two men agreed to do it, and got into the elevator. A few minutes later, he returned, alone, and beckoned me inside. We rode up to the third floor in silence, and when the door slid open, I smiled a thank-you and got off.

Facing me was a long counter topped by a pane of glass that reached to the ceiling. Behind the glass was a large room filled with desks, computers, files, and people.

I promptly explained to a young man who spoke English, and a woman who didn't, that I was trying to locate the file on the police investigation into my brother's death. Then I showed them my copy of the coroner's report and the photocopy I'd made of the "Bill of Indictment."

Both were kind, but pessimistic. The file, they said, repeating what I'd already been told, would probably have been destroyed long ago. They did, however, ask me for my brother's date of birth, then fed it, along with the other information I'd given them, into their computer.

Nothing.

They advised me to put my request in writing and send it to the Police Archives. If the file still existed, which was doubtful, they'd be the ones to locate it. What I needed, though, was a letter from someone in authority to vouch for the fact that I was who I said I was.

Disappointed, but hardly surprised, I thanked them and left. In the lobby, I located a pay phone and called Fred Kaufman. He agreed to write the letter I needed, and I told him simply to mail it to my Toronto address.

I then contemplated what to do next. Should I go on to RCMP headquarters or just forget about it? While I debated the matter, I decided to begin my search for Phil.

According to the court documents, he'd given Baie

Comeau, Quebec, as his place of residence. I promptly dialed Baie Comeau Information and asked if they had a listing for him. They didn't. I checked the Montreal directory, then called the only two P. Gauchers it listed. The first number was no longer in service; the second wasn't registered to a Phil.

So much for him, I thought, and left the building to hail a cab. In a split-second decision, I gave the driver the Dorchester Street address of RCMP headquarters.

Once again, I found myself confronting a door that wouldn't open to me. I spoke over the intercom to an officer at the front desk and told him what I wanted. He gave me a number to call, and I did. But after being shunted, with utmost courtesy, from one department to another, I finally asked, "Is it possible for me to speak with someone face to face?"

"Sure," came the reply. "I'll get a room and meet you in the lobby."

As quickly as that, I was allowed past security and into the building. I signed in at the front desk, then settled down on a couch to wait.

Ten minutes later, a young man came walking toward me, an amiable expression on his face. After introducing himself as Constable Richard Huard, he picked up a key from the desk, and led me down the hall to an interrogation room.

It was like walking onto a movie set. There were no windows in the room. In the middle stood a long, wooden table with several chairs grouped around it. On one wall hung a framed notice, in both English and French, stating the rights of the person being interrogated. I gulped, and Huard must have noticed.

"Yeah," he said, motioning me to a chair. "The two-way mirror, the whole thing."

He seated himself across from me and opened his notepad. I automatically began to talk. But while I talked, I could feel my mind again dividing itself in two. Soon, it was no longer me sitting there, but my brother.

What had he been feeling? I wondered. What had he been thinking? A nineteen-year-old kid, late at night, half-stoned, being questioned by two, perhaps more, RCMP officers. Faced, for the first time, with his own vulnerability. Faced, too, with the realization of his own, worst fears.

"I'm sorry?" I blinked and tried to focus.

"Do you have the names of the arresting officers?" Huard repeated.

I gave them to him, along with the name of the liaison officer, Y. Fortin, and he dutifully wrote them down.

"Maybe some of the oldtimers will remember these guys," he said as he stood up. "I doubt if we still have a file on your brother, but let's see what I can come up with. I'll leave the door open, so you won't feel so ... you know ... "

As soon as he'd gone, I slumped forward with my head in my hands, suddenly drained. And I stayed that way until he came back.

"Sorry," he said.

"Nothing?"

"Nothing. But you could write the Archives in Ottawa. If for any reason, the file wasn't closed, they may still have it."

I sighed and pushed back my chair. We exchanged cards, then, as we shook hands, he smiled and wished me luck.

Six

"*I* hope you don't mind, but I'm going to need you for a couple of hours."

The taxi driver looked at me and grinned. "It's Saturday morning, I'm all yours."

I returned his smile and slid into the backseat. Then I had him drive to the nearest grocery store, where I bought some red carnations and white chrysanthemums.

"I'm going on what you might call a nostalgic journey," I explained. "I've come back home to lay some ghosts to rest."

"Don't feel you need to apologize," he said, his eyes warm and kind in the rearview mirror. "You don't know how many people get into my cab to do the same thing."

Our first, official stop was the Royal Victoria Hospital, where both my brother and I were born.

I placed a red carnation beside the imposing entrance to the Women's Pavilion and stepped back to take a picture.

In my mind's eye, I was a child again, nearly four, clutching my father's hand as we approached the great stone portico outside the building. It had rained that bleak November day, leaving the pavement slick and flecked with puddles. I was immaculately dressed in a matching coat and hat. When I saw my mother seated in a wheelchair, holding the bundle that was my baby brother, I gave a shriek of joy, dropped my father's hand, and started running.

Seconds later, I tripped and fell headlong into a giant puddle.

"Mo-mm-ee!" I wailed. "I'm wet."

My mother immediately handed the bundle to the nurse, leapt from the wheelchair, and hurried to comfort me in my humiliation.

Such was my introduction to Peter David Berger.

Our second stop was the large, semi-detached house in Outremont, where we'd lived with my mother's parents until I was six and my brother two.

I placed a red carnation at the bottom of the front steps and took a picture. Then I sought out the second-storey window that had once been his.

I saw myself standing in his room one day, while the pediatrician examined him. I remember hovering, close to his bassinette, holding a glass of milk. No sooner had the doctor removed my brother's diaper, than an arc of pale yellow urine cut through the air and landed in my milk.

I was laughing as I turned to leave, but beneath the laughter, a quiet ache had begun.

Our third stop was the compact, white stucco house in Snowdon. The house of our childhood, our youth, our early adulthood. The repository for most of my memories of us, both the sad and the sweet.

I placed a red carnation next to the long, stone walk and snapped a picture. Then I simply stood there, remembering ...

Those Saturday mornings, when my brother and I rode the bus downtown to Montreal High to attend the Children's Concerts conducted by Wilfrid Pelletier of the Montreal Symphony Orchestra. And how we'd always stop first at Laura Secord to buy ourselves candy before the performance.

Those Saturday afternoons, when my brother and I filled the saddlebags on our bikes with cookies and fruit and peddled off, with the intention of getting lost. But we never did. Instead we'd find a park, lay our bikes down, and settle ourselves under a tree. Then we'd while away the time, eating our food, and counting the number of Chevrolets like ours driving by.

Those Sundays when, good sport that he was, my brother agreed to play dress-up with me. I always chose a different theme: pirates, gypsies, storybook characters, historical figures, cowboys, Hawaiians. Then we'd prepare an appropriate theme supper for our parents, and, on occasion, their friends as well.

Those weekday afternoons, when I dragged my brother to the jewellery counter at Woolworth's, and pointed out the rings I liked. Once, he even bought me one. It was wonderfully garish, with a large, red, cut glass centre stone flanked by a pair of rhinestone-encrusted crescents.

That spring, when I inadvertently hit him in the head with a baseball bat. It was a sound, a hideous, cracking sound I never forgot. A little nearer the temple, we were told, and he would have died.

Could that have been the cause? I'd always wondered. Could that blow have scrambled some vital circuit in his brain, changing him from what he was into what he became?

That summer, when we got our first pet: a tiny chameleon I named Frisky. It was with the greatest pride that we strolled the neighbourhood together, walking Frisky on the long string attached to the short, fine chain around his neck. When Frisky died, my mother unceremoniously flushed him down the toilet.

That autumn, when my brother received a hamster for his birthday. I dubbed him Tricky Pinky Paws, because of all the tricks we taught him, poor thing. How we adored that hamster. But after my mother developed asthma, we had to give Tricky away. When he died a short time later — of, my brother and I were convinced, a broken heart — my grieving brother went up to my mother, pointed a shaking finger at her, and sobbed, "Murderer."

That winter, when he strapped on skis for the first time and rode the rope tow to the top of the hill at Beaver Lake. I stood, a cheering section of one, at the bottom, and watched, enviously and admiringly, as that small, dear figure cut a swath through the snow with confidence, ease and grace.

Memories, so many memories. Days of them. Seasons of them. Years of them. Too many to recount at one time. And the metre was running.

*   *   *   *

We stopped next at Ponsard Park, two blocks away. I placed a red carnation next to a bank of swings, and took a picture.

Those swings ...

I couldn't have been more than seven the day my friend Frances ran back from the park, shouting, "Peter's eye fell out! Peter's eye fell out!"

Panic-stricken, I climbed onto my bicycle and, making a noise like a siren, took off for the park. When I arrived, I found my brother cradled in the arms of our maid, blood streaming down his face from the long, deep gash in his forehead. Apparently he'd walked too close to a moving swing, and the sharp corner of the wooden seat had struck him just above his right eye.

Long before I'd hit him with the baseball bat, could the corner of that swing have been the real culprit?

I sighed, and walked slowly back to the waiting cab.

Now came the hardest part of my journey, where the memories would be fresher, the scars deeper.

We stopped first, outside a small row house in a block-long string of row houses on Laval Street.

It was one of many such streets, lying in the shadow of Mount Royal, that had, during the sixties, been a scaled-down version of San Francisco's Haight-Ashbury district. This was where many children of the middle class had come to drop out. This was where they'd set up their ramshackle communes and celebrated their hippie lifestyle of freedom and rebellion. This was also where some of them had died.

I placed a red carnation outside the front door, and with shaking hands, snapped off a picture.

If I'd hoped to leave quickly, memory forbad it. A single memory, that, unbeknownst to me at the time, had, secretly and stealthily, laid down the roots for my future guilt. Now, that memory took me over and carried me back. Until I was no longer where I was, but where I'd once been.

Safe. With him.

Saved. *By* him.

*   *   *

I'm huddled, shivering, at the foot of my brother's bed in a spare and shabby room, dimly lit. Pain writhes, snakelike, inside me. No sun can possibly warm so deep a cold or ease so pervasive an ache. I stare at the bare, ring finger of my left hand, and catch the imaginary gleam of the diamond no longer there.

Our parents in Europe, I was alone, an empty echo rattling through an empty house. In my agony, and praying for death, I built a pyramid of sleeping pills, tranquilizers, antihistamines, and aspirins. Intending to wash them down with vodka and tomato juice. The most lethal of Bloody Mary's.

Instead, I placed a frantic phone call to my brother. So frightened was he by the death wish in my voice that he came, not on a horse, like a prince in a fairytale, but on a motorcycle, to rescue me from myself.

He leans toward me now with love in his eyes and sympathy gentling the sharpness of his narrow features. He holds out his hand, and I see the thin, misshapen stick of white paper, twisted tightly around its pungent contents.

"No, I don't — " I shake my head and push his hand away.

"Trust me. It'll stop the pain, take you to a higher place, where all you'll feel is peace."

Peace. The word is foreign to me now.

I should never have been so dramatic. For what my fiancé had precipitated, I, with one grand, dramatic gesture, had effectively concluded, by hurling his diamond ring back in his face.

And now I fear the emptiness, the yawning hole of nothingness. The penalty I'll have to pay for such a grand, dramatic gesture. With the shortened foresight of youth, I whimper, "If I don't marry him, I'll die."

To which my brother replies, "No, you won't."

"But it hurts ... it hurts."

"I know. That's why I want you to try this."

"I'd rather have a glass of wine."

"We have no wine. It's not pure."

"And grass is?"

"It's God's own weed."

I stifle a laugh. Or rather a bolt of fresh pain does it for me. My brother extends his hand further. The ash is growing, the white paper shrinking. As if reading my thoughts, he says, "You're wasting it."

With a sigh, I put out a trembling hand and accept the joint. I'm prepared to cough as I slip it between my lips. He knows this and coaches me through my first, tentative pull on God's own weed.

I'm immediately enveloped by an acrid haze reminiscent of burning autumn leaves. The rising smoke scalds my eyes, the swallowed smoke sears my lungs. I draw God into a system trained to resist false gods, and struggle not to belch its polluting cloud back out.

"Again," he counsels as I exhale with a coughing whoosh. And I immediately obey.

I feel the vapour spreading through me. It fans outward from my constricted chest in ripples of cooling calmness. And as it spreads, I feel myself opening as if I were a rusty lock just sprung. Walls of resistance crumble, years of natural caution melt away, as gratefully and willingly, I embrace my brother's God.

"Again."

I'm weightless, rising upward in a soothing spiral. I float, like a bubble, on my cloud of burning autumn leaves, and steer myself higher, then higher still. I'm exhilarated, and in my exhilaration lies my release. My freedom.

My brother lights a second joint, inhales deeply with practiced ease, and joins me on my joyous carpet ride. We fly together, climbing and dipping, soaring and spinning, travelling outward to the very edges of infinity. We pass the magic baton of God's own weed back and forth between us, until nothing remains but a tiny, blazing nub, which he reserves for himself.

Time has ceased to exist. Without its boundaries to define it, I expand to fill the void, until the me I know, no longer exists. Deep in the fog that obliterates my pain, a whisper chants, "He's saved my life ... he's saved my life ... he's saved my life ... "

He returns with me to our parents' house, where, night after night, he stands quiet and protective watch. Loving's faithful guardian.

I plead with him to mediate between my fiancé and me. And he agrees. We three meet, and talk, and ultimately, we two pledge to begin again.

I bless and thank my brother for saving my life, and sign my name in blood on an IOU.

* * *

My head snapped back as if someone were shaking me. The memory receded; the guilt rushed in to fill the vacuum.

I returned to the cab and burrowed, like a stricken animal, in the backseat. The minutes passed, the metre continued its subtle ticking. Finally, I found my voice.

I gave the driver the address of my brother's next — and last — home. It was only a few blocks away, and I could see it as clearly as if it were yesterday. A sprawling, multi-roomed flat, located above a Greek restaurant, in an old, rundown brick building.

We arrived at the designated corner and I gasped in disbelief.

The building was gone.

Seven

*T*he entire structure — the restaurant, the flats above and below it — had vanished. Even the civic number no longer existed. In its place, stood a tacky, white brick building containing several stores.

I got out of the taxi and stood there on the sidewalk, staring and shaking my head. I blinked several times, hoping that when I opened my eyes again, the building would have disappeared, and everything would be as it once was.

"Give me a minute?" I asked the driver.

"Take all the time you need," he said, opening his newspaper.

I leaned against the cab, my camera in one hand, a single, red carnation in the other, and looked up. Narrowing my eyes, I directed my gaze at the white brick eyesore across from me, watching its façade fall away to reveal the original, red brick and stone building underneath. Black, wrought-iron stairs spiralled upward across its face, while inside, a narrow, dimly lit staircase climbed steeply past the second-storey restaurant to the third-floor landing. And the spacious flat where my brother had lived out the rest of his brief life.

I concentrated then, on another, single memory. And when I tasted bile, I knew I'd succeeded. Succeeded in summoning up the devil.

*   *   *

I've crossed the River Styx and disembarked on the shores of Hades.

In the alien darkness, candles flicker, thin sticks of incense perfume the tepid air, and frayed black curtains hang limply at windows, whose frames are painted black. I'm seated cross-legged on a lumpy cushion on the floor of a large, black-walled room, where even the ceiling is black.

"How much longer?" I whisper to my brother.

"Ssh!"

"Look, if you don't answer me, I'm leaving."

"Any minute now."

"You said that ten minutes ago."

"He knows when the need is greatest."

"When the need is greatest," I scoff. "We've been sitting here for nearly an hour. Are you sure he's not out somewhere getting stoned?"

"How dare you speak that way!" hisses my brother. "It's blasphemy."

"Blasphemy?" I'm incredulous. "Who do you think he is, God?"

But I already know the answer. After all, isn't that why I've agreed to come here? To see for myself, the man my brother deems his own, personal god.

There are eight of us clustered together in this black, cryptlike room: seven devout believers and one skeptic: me. The girls are distinguishable from the boys only by their lack of beards. Otherwise they're identical: with their ragtag shirts and jeans, matted hair, and bare, dirty feet.

All around me, joints flare and dim. Like tiny feral eyes, they gleam, reddened pinpricks in the semi-darkness. And in the glow of the candles, seven pairs of human eyes are glazed, their expressions vacant.

"No, thanks." I refuse the joint my brother hands me and pass it to the young man on my right.

My brother's eyes are closed, his head rolled back, and he's holding the bitter smoke in his lungs longer than should be humanly possible. I have to call his name twice before he opens his eyes. He looks at me, not really seeing me. I fight the sudden clamminess crawling across my skin, and shake him, once, gently. His eyes finally focus, seem to brighten, and he smiles.

"Listen," he murmurs, "he's coming."

I glance over my shoulder. "Where? I don't see him."

"I can feel him near us."

Suddenly, a collective chanting begins. I turn again. God is standing in the doorway.

He doesn't look like a god. He's small, with short, curly hair and a tiny beard. He's wearing a long, blue robe. On his head is a cap adorned with silver crescents. To me, Basil Harcourt Hawthorne is a combination gnome and Elijah Muhammed.

As the chanting grows louder, the little man makes his way through the room, pausing to rest a hand upon each person's head. I watch with mounting distaste as he moves in my direction. Bracing myself, I try to calculate his arrival so that I can duck. But his hand is on my head before I know it. I shudder, and gooseflesh rises on my arms and neck.

He approachs a large, high-backed chair, performs some complicated gestures with his right hand, then sits down. His seven disciples, still chanting, wriggle forward on their cushions, and group themselve at his feet. I remain behind, ignoring the message beamed my way from his small, dark, evil eyes. But I'm not one of the converted; his gaze holds no power over me.

He raises his hand. The chanting stops. He begins to speak in the soft, lilting cadences of the Caribbean.

"My children, once more my mission brings us together here. I have returned from your southern brothers with a message of peace, and bring from them the proof of their love for you."

He continues to speak, but I've stopped listening. I'm fixated instead on what he's doing. From inside his robe, he withdraws a bulky leather pouch. Opening it, he carefully removes a cluster of small packets. He nods now as he speaks, and, one by one, the believers rise, receive a packet, a whispered message, then sit down again.

My brother takes his turn. Bas seems to favour him. My

throat constricts in revulsion. I move my pillow closer to my brother's.

"What did he give you?" I demand.

"As he said, love."

"Love?" I saw the clear plastic packet before he could hide it in the pocket of his shirt. It was filled with grass. Their god is obviously a dealer.

Is he the only one? I ask myself. Or are they all dealers, my brother included? I'd always assumed he was no more than a recreational user. Naiveté on my part, I wonder fearfully, or wishful thinking?

Bas stands and drifts slowly out of the room. The chanting begins again, trailing behind him like the folds of his cloak. I feel displaced. Snatched from a downtown flat in a cosmopolitan city and dropped into a tribal village on some primitive island.

I must get out of here. Get out and take my brother with me. I cannot, will not allow him to remain in this satanic blackness. In this house of evil. With this devil-god.

My brother's on his feet. I call up to him. But either he doesn't hear me or he's chosen not to, as he follows after Bas.

I'm frantic, yet my movements are clumsy as I struggle to stand. My legs are asleep from having sat crosslegged so long, and I can barely feel my toes. I make my way into the hall. My brother and Bas are nowhere in sight.

The flat is large. I go from room to room searching for them. Signs of the zodiac are painted above the doors and astrological charts cover the peeling, black walls.

Suddenly, I hear Bas's low voice coming from a small room off the kitchen. I tiptoe toward the sound and see my brother kneeling in homage before his god. Bas lays his hand on my brother's head in benediction, and my brother stands.

I call his name and both men turn to look at me. My heart stops. While Bas's eyes gleam with dark malevolence, my brother's merely stare. I clutch his arm, feel how thin it's become, and give it a tug.

"I'm leaving now," I tell him, "and I want you to come with me."

"What for?"

"I want to take you home."

"This is my home," he says, staring through me.

"Please." My voice and grip grow more insistent. "We'll talk. The four of us. Please."

"They've made it clear I'm not welcome there."

"You're wrong. They're hurt and they're frightened. All three of us are."

A strange smile spreads across my brother's face. "Frightened of what? Of me or the truth?"

"The truth?"

"Yes, the truth."

I shake my head is if to clear a space for what he's saying. "The truth," I repeat. "What truth?"

He doesn't reply; he simply continues to smile. Then he gently frees his arm from my grasp. And as he does, I feel him slipping away from me. Forever. I'm powerless against this greater, darker power that holds him in its thrall.

I cast one final, pleading glance at him, then turn and run. As I clatter down the stairs, I carry in my nose the smells of the house: air and incense; candles, bodies, and grass.

But overriding them all, is the smell of my own terror.

* * *

The red carnation had snapped in two in my hand.

Its head lay on the sidewalk at my feet, leaving only its stem behind. I dropped the broken stem and opened the taxi door.

"The Mount Royal Crematorium," I told the driver, and he started the engine.

My forehead was pressed against the window as we drove through the gates of the enormous cemetery that covers so much of the mountain. We followed a long, winding road, up, down, and around. And on and on. Past small, carved headstones and imposing marble mausoleums. Through lush, landscaped grounds, rich with spreading shade trees and luxuriant flowerbeds.

How benign it all seemed on this warm, sun-drenched summer day. How very different from the foreboding bleakness of that damp, chill autumn day so long ago.

I held my breath as we pulled up to the large Gothic building, which, on that terrible day, had loomed, like some ghostly mansion, out of the swirling fog of a Charles Dickens novel. Now, suddenly, I was struck by the beauty and elegance of the place. It was no longer the same, frightening spectre, whose image had been etched so indelibly upon my brain.

Then I noticed the pair of high, wide, arched doors, and felt my stomach drop.

With a clenched jaw, I placed a red carnation between the two doors, and took a picture. Then, once again, I forced my thoughts back in time. For if I was ever to lay this particular demon to rest, I had to acknowledge what had happened here. Every ghastly bit of it.

*   *   *

Like black beads strung on a chain, the black cars of our procession follow, one after the other, along a road that curves between tall, naked trees and barren flower beds. We drive on, forever, it seems. Then, at the crest of a small hill, it rises ominously before us. The crematorium.

A flood of acid fills my throat, and I'm struck by the irony of it. A crematorium. This dread, detested symbol of six million lost Jews about to receive the body of yet another Jew. How did it happen? Did my parents even consult me? Did I agree? I can't remember.

I want to scream, "Stop! It's not right. You're breaking Judaism's laws."

Dust to dust, ashes to ashes, all in nature's own time. Not artificially hastened as if to dispose of my brother's body as quickly as possible.

Is that the reason then? Is it my parents' intent to erase all proof of his existence from this world? Or is it their attempt to purify him in death, as atonement for what they consider his contaminated life?

The back door of the limousine opens, but I can't move. I'm bent over, crushed by the weight of my agony. And my certainty. The certainty that whether my brother's decay is gradual or instantaneous, his spirit will stalk my every step, shadow my every move, for as long as I draw breath. The certainty that no ceremony, sanctioned or otherwise, will ever break the hold his living and his dying has over me. The certainty that we are bound, inexorably, together, forever.

My husband tries to help me out.

"Don't touch me," I plead.

It hurts whenever anyone touches me. My body is like a single, live nerve ending, stripped of its protective sheath, exposed and raw.

I push myself onto legs that barely support me, and move forward like an automaton. My dark glasses shield me as I enter the semi-darkness of the chapel.

We're told to stand. The casket is placed directly in front of us. Sobbing begins all around me. I feel myself crumpling. Then I stiffen, straighten up again, cursing my weakness.

The rabbi reads from the poem I wrote the night my brother died. In it, I recorded not only my grief, but, above all, my guilt.

Oh Peter, my Peter, forgive me. Forgive me for not being able to save you.

Flowers are pressed into my hands. White gladioli, so bright against the blackness enveloping me. My mother moves closer to the casket and places her own gladioli on its burnished top. The casket begins to move. Downward.

Wait! In my panic, I step forward, but my arms are locked. Wait! Please God, wait! It's too soon. I'm not ready.

My father releases his flowers. I hear someone speak my name. The casket continues to move, downward, slowly downward. And still my arms refuse to open. Someone nudges me. I kiss the flowers, command my frozen arms to open. Through stricken eyes, I watch the flowers fall through space, landing, at last, on top of the others.

Horrified, I watch the casket being swallowed up, as if by some great, hungry mouth, as the doors slide shut. He's gone. My brother's gone.

I envision the casket, carrying all that's most precious to me in this world, as it begins its journey along the soundless belt that will deliver it to the waiting fire. I see the flames lick tentatively at the wood that, for awhile, will guard and protect him. I hear them crackle, surge into a roar. I see the casket begin to crumble, then give way completely before the ravenous demands of the flames.

My mind shuts down, refusing to see further.

As I leave the chapel, I sniff the air, and smell the smoke that was my brother.

*   *   *

Closing the door of the cab behind me, I asked the driver to take me back to my hotel. I'd had more than enough for one day.

Eight

*S*unday morning, before checking out of the hotel, I called my home number, and picked up my phone messages. The last one left me gasping. It was from Richard Huard of the RCMP.

Apparently, he'd gotten on the elevator with his boss, who'd seen me, and asked if I was "another nutcase." Huard told him no, and explained what I'd wanted. The man glanced at the three names written on his notepad, and said, "I know *them*."

Rougeau and Fortin, he said, were retired, while Joseph St. Denis was still in law enforcement elsewhere in Canada.

Huard then gave me St. Denis's address and once more, wished me luck with my search.

Fate had handed me a gift. Of all the lucky coincidences. If I hadn't gone to RCMP headquarters ... If I hadn't spoken to Huard ... If his notepad hadn't been open when he got on the elevator ... If his boss hadn't gotten on that same elevator ...

I couldn't wait until Monday. To call and speak to ...

I let out a groan.

To speak to the man who'd arrested my brother.

As far as Joseph St. Denis was concerned, my brother had represented the enemy. One of the bad guys. How could I expect him to talk to me? How could I expect him to even remember my brother?

My initial elation turned sour. I left the room with my stomach in a knot, and my heart in my mouth.

*   *   *   *

The last stop on my trip was the Baron de Hirsch Cemetery. I divided the bunch of white chrysanthemums in two and placed half of them at the base of my father's headstone, the other half at my brother's. Then I finished off the film in my camera.

Kneeling before my brother's grave, I brushed some fallen leaves from the blanket of red begonias that covered it, and stared at the name inscribed on the small, marble marker.

"Help me," I whispered through a rush of tears. "Help me to find the answers I need. Help me to know all of you. Help me to stop missing what I can never have: the you that might have been. Help me, please, help me to finally let go."

I picked up two pebbles, kissed them, and laid one on top of his headstone, and one on top of my father's. Then, as I walked away, I forced myself not to look back.

Despite my trepidation, the first thing I did Monday morning was dial St. Denis's number. My heart was pounding so loudly in my ears, I barely heard the voice at the other end explain that he was out of the office until Tuesday.

I hung up with a huge sigh of relief. Then, following Michael's suggestion, I contacted Tom Gottlieb, who provided me with my first, eyewitness account of life inside my brother's world. Beginning with Bas.

"Phil went to Jamaica on vacation and met Bas, who claimed to have written his own version of the Bible. He supposedly possessed remarkable powers. One of the stories he told was of being accused of sedition and put up against a wall before a firing squad. The bullets missed him.

"I found him to be an understanding, alert, and interesting fellow. He was open, nice, friendly, knowledgeable. He was sensitive to nuances and feelings. He used to walk around barefoot. Nothing affected him, neither hot nor cold. I remember his cooking steaks and turning them over with his bare hands.

"He spent most of the time in the house and did much of his speaking on the porch. People would bring him food and ask him questions. There was a fascination about him because of his connection to the past. To them, he was an alternative, a different kind of role model. He espoused brotherly love and spoke about human relations.

"He would speak about 'righteousness' and preach the Rasta philosophy, saying Haile Selassie was King of the black people. He would talk about Jamaica, about the pastoral life there.

"Being stoned was all part of it, as was the sharing. He was an experienced traveller of the mind, with the culture to back it up. He'd been smoking for a long time and understood the effects. He did LSD as well. He'd talk people through their LSD trips, telling them to light candles, relax, lie down, be calm."

He turned, next, to my brother, saying, "Peter was so impressed with Bas, as a mystic, as a guru. He was influenced by Rasta mythology and even began to look Rasta. He was Bas's confidante. They would argue points of logic and Peter would hold his own. He eventually went into his own line of mysticism, his own cosmology.

"He was concerned with different states of being. He began studying the Kaballah, the Tree of Life, *The Tibetan Book of the Dead*, and adapting them to the psychedelic experience. He was almost in competition with Bas. There was almost an animosity between them. But the drug dealing kept them together.

"Finding grass was hard in those days, it was like trying to find heroin. When it became available at the house, it made it easy for people. It started as minor, then grew into major dealing. Several times a month, people would go down to Jamaica and come back with anywhere from four to ten pounds of grass.

"At first, it was beautiful, part of an era, part of the time. It was all so new. It was a lifestyle built on sharing, on living together, communally. It was us against the others, the 'plastic people.'

"Life took place mostly in the house. It became the centre for spaced-out people, a crash pad with people tripping out. It attracted attention as one of *the* hippie places. Some nights, there could be forty to fifty people there. A mystic thing was happening. The whole world came to you; there was no privacy anymore. It was non-stop joints."

"And LSD?"

"Yes." He paused a moment, then said, "You know, LSD allows you to see things. It opens the gates, lays down the barriers. It allows in a flood of stimuli. You're in another state of mind. You're aware of there being another kind of consciousness out there. You can actually see and experience the flow of your cells.

"You can function on it, but at a different level, because the mind accommodates to it. If you're intelligent to begin with, you can manipulate it. As with grass, you're very open, very sensitive. But with LSD, you're in an eternal present." He let out a long, slow sigh, then turned again to my brother. "Peter became quite famous through the house. He wasn't in it for the money; he believed the money coming in was for everyone to use.

"He was very fast, a cerebral person. He loved adventures of the mind and was far into it. The beauty of thinking thrilled him. He was very sure of himself and always wanted to do things to the extreme. He believed everything should be done from within, on your own. He'd say, 'Do it the righteous way; don't do it on the backs of others.' He spoke of this even before Bas. To him, everything was a celebration of life.

"But as far as he was into his mind, he was also interested in the politics of the outside world: Quebec, the States, Vietnam. I remember one night he came into the room where the TV was on, and Prime Minister Trudeau was speaking. Everyone was making noise, and he said, 'Be quiet, this is important.'

"We did LSD together every Sunday. On trips, he liked to listen to music and go for walks in the park. It never disabled him. When he was tripping, he was really happy with the beauty of the mind. He could see all these connections, see into other people's minds, sense what you were feeling.

"He was on a mission with the sanctity of drugs and espoused the personal freedom to take them. He was out in the vanguard, setting a cultural example. He felt one could learn more *out* of school. He believed in the communal lifestyle.

"He wanted out of the capitalist, materialistic game, and action for action's sake. He felt a chasm had developed, a sense of them and us. It was war to see who was right and who was wrong. He said to stay away from materialism and to explore the mind. Be stoned, spiritual. He wanted to bring the system around to his way of thinking.

"He was anxious to test it all out. He was so high out there. He was a hipster, really radical. A rebel like Abbie Hoffman. He was so far into it, as far as Leary. He was part of folk history."

Hearing my brother rhapsodized this way astounded me. Yet, somehow, it pleased me, too.

"Were you in the house at the time of the raid?" I asked, almost reluctantly now, and Tom said no.

"But Peter often talked of his fear of someone infiltrating them and exposing them. He had a great fear of arrest, jail, and punishment. He would have been frightened by the RCMP. The bust would have been a big thing for them. He tried to protect Bas at the time of the drug bust; he was afraid he'd be deported."

Was that why he'd signed that declaration, to protect Bas?

"He was stoned all the time, you know," Tom continued. "But he didn't fear death; he saw it as just another stage. He believed one is still conscious after death."

I thought back to what both Howards had said about my brother's attitude toward death. Did he truly feel that way? And if he did, when had he come to believe it? *How* had he come to believe it?

Hastily scanning my notes, I underlined several key words: Rastafarians. Kaballah. Tree of Life. *The Tibetan Book of the Dead*. Then, before I could put another question to Tom, he said, rather sadly, "Peter was just too sensitive a person, too intelligent. Things got too heavy for him, he couldn't handle it.

"Things could have been so much better had he lived. He would have done radical things. I could see him being the first environmentalist. He wouldn't let us settle for second best. He'd tell us to get off our butts, tell us to be the best we can be."

My eyes began to fill and I could hardly see the page in front of me.

"He was a great stimulus. It was a great waste. He was very

special, very brave. And he thought he'd go on forever. I still feel a sense of guilt, you know. Why didn't I pull him out by the scruff of his neck and say, 'What the hell are you doing, man?' I still feel a sense of loss. I'm just as upset now as I was twenty-seven years ago. I want him to be my friend; I want him to be here."

He then gave me the name of another friend to call, Allan Lerman, and we said goodbye.

At nine the following morning, I was dialing the number for Joseph St. Denis again. I scarcely had time to swallow before the man himself was on the line.

My mouth was dry, my tongue thick and heavy, as I gave him my name, then asked him, haltingly, to cast his mind back to a night in early September, 1968, when he led a drug raid on a downtown flat in Montreal.

"I remember it distinctly," he said, and I felt my heart stop.

How? I asked myself. How, after twenty-seven years, after all the other raids he must have led, and after all the other cases he must have handled, could he possibly remember?

But to my utter stupefaction, he did. Because the more I refreshed his memory, the more he was able to remember.

"When we arrived," he told me, "I recall seeing some Rastafarians there, and everyone was high on grass. I remember there was a swinging chair mounted from the ceiling in the front room, where this Bas would sit and hold court."

My jaw dropped. Tom had described the very same chair to me. It was a light bamboo chair with cushions on it, where he himself often sat. You could look out over the mountain, he'd told me; it was comfortable when you were tripping.

"My partner and I were surrounded, intimidated, and harrassed. We left and called for assistance and took control of the scene at that time. Bas was agitated and upset when we went in the second time. Your brother was protecting him, taking the heat."

Again that assertion. My brother protecting Bas.

"How did you know about the house?" I asked, recalling what Tom had said about my brother's fear of infiltration.

"We'd gotten some information about it," was all he said. "But when we hit the place, we didn't get the motherlode we'd expected to get."

"Do you recall who conducted the investigation into my brother's death?" I asked him then.

He answered without the slightest hesitation. "The coroner did his own investigation and the Montreal police did the follow-up. They even came to the RCMP and questioned my partner and me, because our names had apparently been in your brother's book."

Book? Suddenly, I recalled my mother's telling me that, among my brother's effects, there'd been a book filled with names and figures, which she'd assumed represented drug deals. She'd thrown it out, along with everything else of his, years ago.

"What was strange, though," St. Denis continued, "was that there was a great reluctance to release the full coroner's report. Other agencies were looking for it, too, but it was being kept close to the coroner's office. We were told it was a very sensitive issue, that it involved a high-profile citizen."

As he said this, I could almost feel my scalp begin to lift.

"Do you think the police took the easy way out," I asked, "and wrote up my brother's death as a suicide, so they wouldn't have to spend time tracking down a killer? In other words, do you think they *really* investigated his death, or was it only cursory, because they thought of him as just one more drug dealer being taken out by one of his own?"

"Absolutely not. I can assure you there was nothing like that, and no cover-up. Besides, the police said he apparently left a suicide note. They found it near his body."

My mouth opened, but no sound came out. A suicide note? Wasn't that what we'd hoped to find, but never had? An explanation. A rationale. Anything to help make sense out of something so senseless.

If there *was* a note, could someone have seen it and never told us? Could that same someone have placed it in one of those old, supposedly destroyed files, ensuring that it was now lost to us forever?

"Are you certain about this?" I asked. "Because it's the first time anyone's ever said anything about a note."

"That's what I heard," he insisted. Then his voice grew gentle. "If it had been my brother or sister," he told me, "I'd be doing the same thing you're doing. And I want to do whatever I can to help you with this, to help you get past the denial. Let me put your suspicions to rest right now; there *was* no police cover-up, there *was* no murder."

Then he said he'd search for the notebooks he'd kept during his years with the RCMP, and that if he found anything pertaining to my brother, he'd call me back.

And he did.

"You know I'm doing this on humanitarian grounds," he said before he began. "Okay then. These are my notes.

"Hawthorne called himself a high priest from Montego Bay and believed he was god. He defied us to touch his hands in order to take his fingerprints. We did, and he said he'd put a curse on us. During our interrogation of him, he said the cure for society was through the use of herbs, meaning grass. He admitted that your brother was one of his followers and close associates. He admitted, too, as did others, that he'd blown his mind on LSD.

"Your brother was very, very upset that his god had been arrested. The date of the preliminary hearing was September 21st, and he didn't show up. Court documents indicated his father, who was influential, had gotten him into the Douglas Hospital.

"On September 25th, he came in to our drug office and talked to me with the purpose of obtaining the capsules of LSD we'd seized. Since we hadn't laid charges for LSD at the time, he thought they should be returned to him. He was very agitated and angry with me for refusing to hand them over, and said he was going to see a lawyer about getting them back.

"I've written here that, on September 26th, your brother killed himself in a house on Coloniale Street, while under the influence of LSD."

Nine

I felt as if I myself were tripping. not on drugs, but on information. My head no longer felt connected to my body. My feet no longer touched the ground. I'd entered a time capsule of my own making and had sealed myself off from the rest of the world. Everything, once so important, now seemed, suddenly, trivial. Everything once familiar, now felt alien to me. My friends. My interests. My life.

I was obsessed, possessed by all things pertaining to my brother. *His* friends. *His* interests. *His* life.

I contacted Allan Lerman and we agreed to meet later that day. In the meantime, I drafted a letter to the Douglas Hospital, the *Centre d'archives de Montréal,* and the Police Archives, applying, under the Access to Information Act, for permission to see my brother's files. I enclosed a photocopy of Fred Kaufman's letter with each one, and sent all three Registered mail.

Then I headed downtown to see one of my brother's oldest friends.

As we settled down at a table to talk, Allan began by saying, "I remember Peter as a prodigy." Then he turned immediately to that last, fateful year. "I lived in the house as a sort of gofer for a few months. Peter had a big motor bike, which he loved. We'd go for walks, take bike rides. Sometimes he played the guitar for us. Once we baked a chocolate cake with hash in it. Boy, talk about high.

"Sometimes we'd roll a spliff and — "

"A what?"

"A spliff. It's a monster joint with about an ounce of grass rolled in brown paper, like the kind bread comes in. Bas would invite us to smoke one with him. We'd roll the paper into a long cone, fill it with grass, and pass it around."

"Speaking of Bas," I prompted.

"I never understood how Peter got involved with him," Allan told me. "I never bought what he was into. But he *was* charismatic. When he looked you over, you felt humbled."

"He did LSD with Peter. He controlled Peter. Peter became Bas's servant. He did everything for him.

"Bas had a penchant for teenaged, white girls. He used to gather them around him on his bed. His bedroom was like the holy sanctuary, and he himself wanted to be glorified. On Sunday mornings, he'd conduct Rasta services, sit in the swinging chair as if it were a throne, and everyone else would sit near him on the floor. They'd burn incense and chant.

"I never had the nerve to ask Peter why he was being sucked in this way. Although I once said some deprecating things about Bas, and got roughed up by one of his supporters.

"Peter was the person in charge, the front man, directing traffic, while Bas was always there in the background. Peter's ambition was to be a big drug dealer."

"Why?" I asked.

"Power probably. They were into drugs big time. Peter was like a broker or a wholesaler. He sold large quantities of drugs to others, who sold them in small quantities."

"Did you ever talk about the future?" I asked.

"No."

"What *did* the two of you talk about?"

"The occult, Leary, Richard Alpert, Gurdjieff — "

"Gurdjieff?"

"He was a Russian occultist. Peter had Gurdjieff's Enneagram painted on the wall above his bed."

I vaguely recalled having seen such a symbol; a sort of corrupted Star of David enclosed in a circle.

"Peter really needed help," he blurted out suddenly, taking

me by surprise. "When he was discharged from the Douglas, I remember thinking, 'He pulled it off.' He had this incredible ability to play both sides, you know."

I didn't, but I was learning fast.

"Were you there at the end?" I asked, and Allan nodded.

"He basically said he was going to kill himself a day or two before he died, and that he was going on to another life."

"What!" My pen slipped from my hand and bounced off the table.

"But he also talked about taking a trip across Canada on his motor bike, so I didn't take what he said seriously. I still feel guilty about that. I still ask myself why I didn't take him *more* seriously, call your father, tell him what he'd said."

For a moment, all I could do was stare.

"I'd slept over at a friend's house the night before Peter died," he went on. "I got a call in the morning to say he was dead. My friend and I arrived before the police. He was lying on the bed in the bedroom. His skin was yellowish; his face didn't look anguished or anything, it looked relaxed.

"One of the guys was sitting on the floor in front of the bed reading from *The Tibetan Book of the Dead*, to make sure that Peter's soul crossed over properly to the other side."

I could feel my lunch make threatening motions in the pit of my stomach.

"Some plainclothesmen arrived, roughed us up a little, and questioned us. Your father and another man came in. Then I guess it was the coroner who arrived, and the body was removed."

As to Allan's conclusions?

"Everyone knew he'd killed himself. They all accepted it; no one questioned it."

It seemed I had another name for my list.

"You know," he said, "in my opinion, I thought Bas wanted to show he could control people. And if he could get Peter to kill himself, what better proof would there be of his authority? There was something hypnotic about Bas. Whether he truly hypnotized people, I don't know; but I feel Bas could have suggested Peter kill himself."

This had been one of my mother's earliest theories. And now I'd just heard it from someone else; someone who'd been there. Whether hypnotized or not, had my brother's death been the ultimate sacrifice for his god?

"Do you recall seeing any letters in the room at the time?" I asked.

Allan shook his head.

"Do you recall anyone ever mentioning that some sort of note or letter *had* been found there?"

He shook his head again. Could St. Denis have been mistaken? I wondered. It was possible. Yet he'd been so clear on everything else.

"The one thing I've always wondered about," Allan said, "was what was in Peter's mind. Think of the power that must have been surging through his body to enable him to do this to himself."

Yes, I agreed sadly, just think.

It was time for some research. I began with a two-part tape on *The Tibetan Book of the Dead* narrated by Leonard Cohen, which I rented from the National Film Board.

As I watched, spellbound and incredulous, I learned that *The Tibetan Book of the Dead* is basically a guide, presenting dying and the afterdeath as one, continuous possibility. It teaches that the physical body may die, but that the consciousness continues. In a constant repetition of life and death, an old body's exchanged for a new one, and a person's reborn over and over again.

There are forty-nine days between death and rebirth, during which time the consciousness of the deceased lingers between this life and another. Because at death, one can still hear, the text's read aloud the first time in the body's presence, to encourage and direct it, then read again every day for the next forty-nine days.

The deceased is told: The light of this world's faded, the light of the next world hasn't yet appeared. Your body's lost all feeling; this is what death is. Let yourself go.

As the days pass, the deceased is told: Listen without

distraction. Don't be afraid. The body you had in this life's becoming indistinct to you, and the body you'll have in your future life's becoming clearer. There's no place for you to rest. You want to be born soon. Look for a good human birth, where you may yet recognize your own, true nature.

The deceased passes through numerous, transitional states called Bardos, as he moves from death to life. If he recognizes everything that appears as a projection of his own mind, accepting them as products of his innate wakefulness, he'll be liberated. Recognition and liberation are simultaneous, which the mind experiences as a piercing luminosity, a radiant, pure white light.

To keep the deceased from clinging to his former life, and to ensure that his loved ones release him from the bonds of their attachment to him, his body's offered to the fire in cremation.

On the forty-ninth day, the mourners gather for the last time. The deceased is instructed to give up anger, attachments, and yearning for relations and friends. He's told to hold his head high and enter the human realm. Then the mourners pray that he'll find a fortunate birth.

I looked at the notes I'd made and applied them to my brother. According to Howard Berson, he'd been absolutely certain he wasn't going to die, but was going to a different place. According to Tom Gottlieb, he'd believed one was still conscious after death. He hadn't feared death, but had seen it as just another stage. According to Allan Lerman, he'd said he was going on to another life.

That someone had been reading from *The Tibetan Book of the Dead* in the presence of my brother's body seemed now, both logical and appropriate. That he'd been cremated, however, was almost too cruel an irony. For if he'd been as devout a believer as his friends described, then my parents had inadvertently assisted him in putting his beliefs into practice.

Had my brother been reborn? I asked myself. Or was he still trapped somewhere between one life and another, because of me? Because I'd never released him from the bonds of *my* attachment? Was this the real reason I'd set out, after twenty-seven years, on my quest? To free *him* as well as myself?

*   *   *   *

In the morning, I began my seige of the Metro Reference Library.

Over the next few days, I went from book to book, magazine to magazine, subject to subject, making photocopies, and taking notes. What emerged was a pattern, an interconnectedness between dogmas, so that my brother's actions in the last year of his life started, finally, to make a perfect kind of symmetrical sense. And with what I learned about the Rastafarians, that pattern became even more clearly defined.

Marcus Garvey, a native of Jamaica, and born in 1887, was revered as a prophet of black liberation. In 1919, he spoke of the coronation of a black king from Africa who would bring redemption to black people everywhere. And so, when, in November of 1930, Ras Tafari Makonnen — the birth name of Haile Selassie — was crowned Emperor of Ethiopia, some thought Garvey's prophecy had been fulfilled. Selassie himself claimed to be the 225th in a line of Ethiopian kings, stretching from the time of the Queen of Sheba, and the only, true lineal descendant of King David.

Unique to Jamaica, the Rastafarian movement, which was founded in the early 1930's, is built around a specific body of myths and doctrines. Among its most unifying powers is a belief in the supernatural, a belief in a miracle man, who will ultimately deliver the faithful from oppression, a faith carried to extreme self-sacrifice, and the claim by its leaders to knowing the absolute "truth." Strong, too, is the belief in mental and physical liberation, and the certainty that all those who believe in Haile Selassie, will be eternal and never see death.

Ganja is the name given to marijuana, which the Rastafarians know as "the herb" or "wisdom weed." According to Rasta lore, the weed was found growing on the grave of King Solomon; hence "wisdom weed." For them, its use is religious, supported by various lines taken from the books of Genesis and Exodus in the Bible, which contend that God, who created all things, created the herb for the use of men. The weed, they claim, helps keep their minds focused on higher things, and enables them to gain clear insight into their problems.

Was this, then, what Bas had preached, as he sat in his hanging chair with his worshipful followers grouped in a grass-induced stupor at his feet? Smoke the wisdom weed and be wise? Believe in Haile Selassie and never die? Know the "truth?" That same, elusive truth my brother was never able to explain to me. Or, according to his friends, to anyone else.

What about the other principles of Rastafarian philosophy? I wondered. The worship of Haile Selassie as a god. The belief that black men are "God's people," and that white men are inferior to them. Had my brother embraced those parts as well? And what about Bas, who alternately called himself the head, the king, and the high priest of the Rastafarians? Wouldn't such claims have been considered blasphemous?

What a power trip for any Rastafarian, who believed himself superior to all non-Rastafarians. What a heady experience for an ignorant farmer from the hills of Jamaica to assume dominance over a group of bright, white, middle-class adolescents, all of them looking for someone with easy answers.

I was seized, then, by a hatred so intense, I actually balled my hands into fists. But, as quickly as that, the fury passed, to be replaced instead, by satisfaction. And a sense of justice. Brutal, perhaps, but most certainly poetic.

For not long after returning to Jamaica from Montreal, Bas, the great, powerful, and invincible Bas, had, reportedly, been hacked to death with a machete.

The false god, dead, like his first disciple, at the end of a knife blade.

Ten

I focused next, briefly, on the Kaballah, which in Hebrew means "received lore" or "tradition." An occult, religious philosophy developed by certain Jewish rabbis in the Middle Ages, it's based on a mystical interpretation of the Scriptures, and hints at a world of ecstasy and contemplation.

Words are denied their literal meaning and letters are given arithmetic values. As a result, every Biblical text, Jewish symbol, and Hebrew letter has a mystical significance that, if properly understood, can hasten the coming of the Messiah.

Like Rastafarianism, it was a response to oppression and misery. With so few satisfactions in their own world, the ancient rabbis created for themselves and their followers the possibility of a newer and better world elsewhere.

I then located a single book on Gurdjieff, Georges Ivanovitch Gurdjieff, the Russian mystic and philosopher, and leafed through the brittle pages until I found what I'd been looking for: the Enneagram.

Why wasn't I surprised that it greatly resembled the Kabbalistic Tree of Life?

The diagram was just as I'd remembered it. A simple, nine-pointed configuration, its junctures numbered from one to nine, enclosed within a circle.

Much like Hansel and Gretel and their trail of breadcrumbs, my brother had left behind a trail to mark the path *he'd* taken. The further along I travelled, the clearer those markers became. And the three most distinctive ones, the three that seemed to have held the most fascination for him were: messiahs; life everlasting; and heightened experiences of the mind.

The next, most logical subject, then, was LSD, and I began with Timothy Leary. For hadn't my brother patterned his life after Leary's own prescription to "turn on, tune in, drop out?" Yet, according to Leary, his famous slogan was meant, not to encourage young people to get stoned and abandon all constructive activity, but rather, to increase intelligence.

What he'd meant by it was: Turn on: go within, become sensitive to the various levels of consciousness. Tune in: interact harmoniously with the outside world. Drop out: become self-reliant, discover your singularity, and be committed to mobility, choice, and change.

I continued with the writings of Leary's Harvard associate, Richard Alpert, who later became a Buddist guru, adopting the name Baba Ram Dass; and Sidney Cohen, MD, Chief of Psychosomatic Service at the Wadsworth Veterans' Administration Hospital in Los Angeles.

I could almost hear the echo of my brother's voice in Alpert's own words, when he wrote that, to him, LSD was less dangerous than a four-year, liberal arts, college education. I could almost hear my brother's justification for dealing drugs in Cohen's suggestion that the wish to introduce someone to the world of LSD was a matter, both, of giving pleasure, and feeling good about the power to do so.

What then, I wondered, was the great attraction of LSD? I found no shortage of answers.

According to Cohen, under LSD, the tripper has the overwhelming feeling that what he's experiencing is the "real" reality. Why? Because the drug acts on the filtering mechanism of the brain. It has a disinhibiting or releasing effect, allowing sensory signals to flood into one's consciousness, and spread freely from one sensory pathway to another.

The tripper loses the capacity to discriminate and scrutinize. Loses, as well, the ability to evaluate the validity of an idea or fantasy. Even the strangest illusions seem true, and the vague generalities of — and here, my eyes widened — *The Tibetan*

Book of the Dead take on enormous significance.

The tripper's overloaded with sensation. There's a sense of oneness with the universe; sensations of awe and power, feelings of bliss, love, and ecstasy. Visions of extraordinary light and beauty may occur, or visionary figures be seen. In short, a good LSD experience is very similar to the mystical experience.

The book that most intrigued me, however, was *The Psychedelic Experience, A Manual Based on The Tibetan Book of the Dead*, co-authored by Leary, Alpert, and Ralph Metzner. It, too, was a guide. It, too, described a mystical journey similar to the one outlined in *The Tibetan Book of the Dead* itself. Only this time, the emphasis wasn't on dying, but on living.

It provided specific instructions for the safe navigation of the psychedelic journey, and even prescribed the precise dosage of LSD for the trip.

According to the manual, the voyager passes through three different Bardos. The first is complete transcendence, achieving and maintaining the primary, clear light at the moment of ego-loss. The second involves the self, either in sharp, exquisite clarity, or in the form of hallucinations. The third, and final Bardo, involves the return to reality and the ego.

The most successful trips, apparently, are those undertaken by voyagers who embrace the notion that their own awareness is limitless. Who remain passive, relaxed, and calm; who go with the flow; and above all, remember that everything they experience, whether pleasant or unpleasant, comes directly from within their own mind.

How seductive, I thought, how tempting. Impossible for an inquisitive mind to resist. Impossible, once tried, to resist trying over and over again. And why not? Who wouldn't want to experience ecstasy?

I concluded my research — for the moment at least — with a sobering look at drug enforcement itself during the sixties. Under the Narcotics Control Act of Canada, the penalty then for simple possession of marijuana was a fine of one thousand dollars or six months in jail, or both. For conviction upon indictment, imprisonment for seven years. For trafficking, up to life imprisonment.

*   *   *   *

One Sunday morning, my mother gave me the name of someone else to call.

I'd forgotten, but my brother had spent part of his last summer working in one of the Classic Bookshops' stores owned by our friends, the Melzacks. I immediately called their younger son Brian, who, like his parents, now lived in Toronto.

"Your father asked my father to give Peter a job," he said, "and he did, at the store I was managing. He always did his work well and seemed to thoroughly enjoy it. He had a gift of the gab; he was able to express himself easily, and enjoyed talking to the customers.

"I recall his being into Eastern religion, particularly *The Tibetan Book of the Dead*. He liked to talk about and justify Eastern culture. He used to borrow books and devour them. His favourite section was theology. He was always up there, cleaning, arranging, dusting.

"He was trying to work out his place in life as he saw it, embracing an alternative lifestyle, and turning away from traditional values. But he never tried to convert me. He was always neatly dressed, but with longer hair than was customary. To me, it was like a badge, a method of expressing that he was different.

"I remember discussing drugs with him as well as our relationships with our fathers. He was angry with yours because he'd wanted part of the small inheritance left to him by your grandfather, in order to buy some land in Jamaica and set up an ashram there. Apparently, your father blocked it."

He apologized for not remembering more and urged me to call his mother Rose.

"When Peter applied for the job," she said, "he told me, 'I don't want to be paid in cash, I want to be paid in books.' I told him that he'd have to be paid just like everyone else, but that he could buy whatever he wanted with the money.

"He always carried a book with him, Gurdjieff, I believe. He'd only been working for three weeks or so, when he came up to me and said, 'I can't work here any more. This place has the devil in it.' And he quit."

*   *   *   *

As the days passed, my mail box assumed a place of ever increasing importance to me. Until, finally, I received my first reply.

It was from Richard LaBranche at the Douglas Hospital, saying he'd render a decision on my request within twenty days. But my heart sank when I read that a copy of his letter had been sent to France Lemieux.

My gloom, it seemed, was well-founded, because the following day I received a letter from France Lemieux herself, denying me in writing what she'd denied me verbally the month before.

I was furious. My brother was dead. What difference could it make now, either to him or to them, if I saw his file? Was I invading *his* privacy by wanting to see it? Or was I invading theirs?

A light flashed on inside my head. Was that it? Were they afraid of what I might find? Were they afraid I myself might institute the proceedings my father had only threatened to institute against them twenty-seven years ago? Wasn't this a potentially embarrassing can of worms better left unopened?

I studied both letters again. Whose decision really counted: Lemieux's or LaBranche's? I decided to ignore hers and wait the twenty days.

In my letters to both the Douglas and the *Centre d'archives de Montréal*, I'd given them each a week to respond. It was time, therefore, to call the *Centre d'archives*.

I was immediately transferred to archivist, Luc Lépine, and when I gave him my name and quoted the number of my brother's file, he said, to my amazement, "Oh yes, Peter David Berger. I've just been looking through the file, and it's very strange. The only document we're legally allowed to give you is a copy of the coroner's report, and it's missing."

"Missing?" It didn't make sense. Norah had mailed me a copy. "Was there anything else in the file?" I asked, recalling what she'd said about the coroner's report being the only paper in it.

"Oh, yes," Lépine replied. "There's a letter from the Douglas Hospital and a copy of a six-page police report."

The police report! My hackles rose and I started to shiver.

"Will I be able to get a copy of it?" I asked, daring to hope.

"No, *madame*. I was getting ready to put it all in a letter to you, explaining why you've been denied access to the file."

"Tell me now."

"It's according to the law, *madame*."

"Which law?"

"'The Act respecting the determination of the causes and circumstances of death,'" he said. "According to section 96 of the law, the coroner's report is the only document of a public nature, and therefore, the only one to which you are entitled. But, in my letter, I'll be informing you of the person to contact in order to see if this decision can be reversed."

More laws, I groaned. More red tape. More delays. Unwilling to give up just yet, I took a chance, saying, "I already have a copy of the coroner's report, which I got from the Court Archives on Bleury."

Lépine was surprised by this, and asked me to read the report to him. When I'd finished, he said, "Let me tell you then, *madame*, that the police concurred with the findings of the coroner."

Pushing my luck further still, I asked, "Did they ever mention the possibility of it's being murder rather than suicide?"

"No, *madame*, they did not."

Then, before I could frame another question, he said, "One other thing, *madame*. In the police report, there are copies of a letter and a poem written by your brother."

I caught my breath.

"And they were found near the ... in the room?"

"Apparently, *madame*."

"Dear God, do you know what this means?" I cried. "Please, *monsieur*, could you tell me what they said?"

"I didn't read them, *madame*, and besides — "

"At least tell me about the poem."

"*Madame* — "

"The letter, then, to whom was it addressed?"

"I cannot say, *madame*."

"But you saw it, you've got to remember. I mean, was it a laundry list or something, or was it really a letter?"

"It was a letter, but more than that I cannot say. As I told you before, *madame*, I'm putting everything in writing, and you should receive it sometime next week."

I was numb as I thanked him and put down the phone. St. Denis had been right, after all; there *had* been a letter. But it was a letter I might never see.

I stared at the coroner's report in my hand, still mystified by what Lépine had told me about the one supposedly missing from his own file. And then it hit me.

I hurried into the study, opened my three-ringed binder to the letter "C," and pulled out the single, thin sheet of paper Norah had mailed me. Then I compared the two reports.

"Unbelievable." I gave my head a shake.

No wonder Lépine couldn't find it. The report which Norah had sent me wasn't a copy at all; it was the *original*.

After debating whether or not to tell my mother about the letter, I decided I would. She was as shocked as I'd been.

"Are you sure Daddy never mentioned a letter to you?" I asked.

"Absolutely."

"Is it possible he might have seen it, felt it was too disturbing or whatever, and chose *not* to tell you?"

"Anything's possible," she said.

"Or Dave," I wondered aloud. Could *he* have seen it?

I phoned him immediately and put the question to him. He reflected a moment, then answered with a disappointing, "I could have, but I simply don't remember."

What I needed, I now realized, was someone with connections. Someone influential enough to cut through the red tape threatening to keep me tied in bureaucratic knots for months, or worse, forever.

My mother's suggestion? The very man who'd urged my

parents not to file charges against the Douglas: Victor Gold-bloom.

I discovered that he was now Commissioner of Official Languages for the Federal government, and had his office in Ottawa. But I decided, instead, to try him at his home in Montreal.

All I got was his answering machine. As I left my name and number, I wondered how long it would take him to return my call. *If* he returned it.

I waited a few days, then tried again. This time, I reached his wife Sheila. They'd been out of town, she explained, but Victor *had* gotten my message, and had taken my number with him to Ottawa, intending to call me from there.

I didn't wait. I immediately rang his office, and left a new message with his secretary.

Then I finally acted on Fred's advice concerning the Access to Information Act and phoned the Offices of the Information & Privacy Commissioner in Montreal. I asked the woman who took my call if either the Douglas or the coroner had the legal right to refuse me access to my brother's files, and was told, "Yes, according to the laws governing both bodies, they do. But you aren't without recourse.

"Within thirty days of a refusal in either case," she said, "you can apply in writing to the Commission asking for the decision to be reviewed. Include a copy of your original letter as well as a copy of their letter of refusal. A file will then be opened and a lawyer appointed to look into the matter. He'll contact both you and the other party to see if an accord can be reached. If not, you're entitled to present your case before the Commission."

"And if I'm still refused access?"

"You may, in some instances, take the matter to court."

"Would it expedite matters if I had a lawyer?"

"No, *madame*, it would not."

To my great relief, Victor called me back that afternoon. After I'd explained everything to him, I asked what *he* remembered of the Douglas episode, and he, unfortunately, replied, "Nothing."

But he did promise to comb his memory to see what he could come up with. Then he said, "I must be clear about one thing. Are you doing this for yourself or for future action?"

"For myself. Why?"

"Because one of the reasons you may be meeting this resistance is the fear of reprisal."

"If my father didn't sue the Douglas back then, I certainly have no intention of suing them now," I assured him. "What I want are answers, nothing more."

He appeared satisfied with my response because he said that he'd speak to the head of the Commission in Ottawa, to LaBranche at the Douglas, as well as to Fred, and get back to me.

Suddenly, I felt a renewed sense of hope. Here, at last, was the contact I needed.

Eleven

I was beginning to ask myself, "What now?," when my mother came up with another name for me: Wilder Penfield.

Not only had Wilder been my brother's roommate at Bishop's, he'd once interviewed me for *The Toronto Sun* after the publication of one of my novels. I gave myself a mental slap. Some sleuth I was.

When I called him, he immediately agreed to see me, and said he'd bring along his journal from 1968.

I found myself bouncing now, a human tennis ball, between two extremes: elation and sorrow. True, the mechanics of the quest — each new lead, new fact, new interview — energized and excited me. But what ripped at my heart was the *reality* of what I was uncovering. It was like taking a crash course in someone else's life, condensed, like Cole's Notes, for the last-minute crammer.

And I realized, that no matter what my mood, one fact remained painfully clear: I missed my brother. I'd taken a fleeting presence from my past and wrapped him round me like a shawl. And now, the two of us were inseparable.

I'd gaze at his photograph on my bedside table and long for him. I'd run my eyes, like fingertips, over his face, pretending I could feel him there with me in the flesh.

How I loved looking at him. His thick, wiry hair tamed and parted, curling over the tops of his protruding ears. His brushy brows wide, his dark, almond-shaped eyes gentle, his nose slender. Below the dark mustache, his mouth — thin, upper lip and fuller bottom — stretched into a sweet half-smile. His narrow chin dotted with tiny, dark hairs, as if he weren't quite sure whether to shave them or let them grow.

Only when the pain became too much, would I blow a kiss to him and turn away.

Wilder and I met in the small restaurant in my building. Over tea and pastries, he said that, yes, he and my brother had been "bogmates" for two years at Bishop's. Then he hastened to explain the term to me.

"It meant we each had our own bedroom separated by a common bathroom."

I nodded and he continued.

"Peter took it upon himself to mentor me as to how the world worked. He was the most fiercely bright guy I knew. He could take you from one point of view to another, get you to agree with each of them, then bring you back to the beginning again, and get you to agree with that. He could quote sources for everything and always talked about things that mattered."

"Such as?"

"The politics of the moment, religion as it pertained to us. What he wanted was good dialectics. There was always a challenge in his stance, as if he were saying, 'Let me know what you think and then I'll convince you otherwise.' He'd use anything for conversational fuel, and he saw all sides of an argument for the *sake* of argument. The more complicated the situation, the better.

"He craved people who'd stand up to him because he craved intellectual exercises. He'd basically say, 'Don't agree, it's so frustrating, so boring.' He had to mix things up, keep them sparking, keep them from becoming dull.

"He was a chameleon, a high-energy person, always active, active, active. There was nothing casual about him. I often wondered if he was manic. But back then, who really knew what manic was?

"I recall being absolutely dazzled by his guitar playing. He loved Dylan, I remember, but he was a better singer. He especially liked blues and accoustical music. Anything really, so long as it was sufficiently weird and abrasive.

"We used to play cribbage for five cents a point. He had an astonishing memory for cards and would often play until dawn. Despite owing everyone money all the time, he said he'd make a million dollars before he was twenty-one. He once told me to buy shares in Xerox, that it was going to be huge.

"He was a binge studier. He was proud of not cracking the books until the week of an exam or term paper, then he'd cram or write it, and assume he'd ace it. The irony was he never performed well at all.

"He was an awesome skier. He got exhilarated, showed a fierce delight, almost an ecstasy, when he was skiing on edge down a hill. He once borrowed a faculty member's car and we drove to Stowe. Needless to say, we made it in record time. He loved speed. Any hazards on the road he met calmly, and considered a challenge he could deal with and triumph over.

"We were doing more than a hundred when an animal strayed onto the road. Peter calmly swerved up on the grass, went round the animal, and drove back onto the road without even lifting his foot from the gas pedal.

"In second year, we didn't hang around as much. After Peter left Bishop's, we met each other on occasion at the New Penelope. Kids would be discreet, but the drugs were everywhere. They'd either go in stoned or go outside for a smoke, then go in again."

"Did you ever visit the house on Mt. Royal?" I asked.

"Once, after running into Peter at the New Penelope. I recall seeing hanging baskets filled with hash and grass and pills. It seemed important to him that I see this, his Eden or Shangri-la, if you will. That fact made me think it wasn't working for him.

"What I remember most is that I could detect nothing joyful or serene in Peter. He was driven, feeding from wherever and going wherever. It's as if he knew he'd be here a short time, and he wasn't going to waste any of it."

"Do you think he committed suicide?" I asked, and Wilder nodded.

"I think his suicide and the way he chose, was entirely in keeping with him."

He opened his journal then. And when he'd found what he wanted, he pushed the book toward me, and pointed to a single paragraph. What I read made my blood run cold.

"Apparently sane," Wilder had written, "a non-participant at a drug party, he went on a religious kick and pierced both hands and both feet with an ice pick. If anyone took much note, they certainly didn't inform any authorities, because he didn't kill himself until Thursday, when, after a long monologue on the danger of control by the powerful, he stabbed himself with a knife to the heart."

Dear God!

My entire being rebelled against this newest, horrifying image. The image of my brother crucified. Could that have been the reason no one ever saw the full coroner's report? Could that have been the real reason for protecting us?

According to Howard Berson, it had been a can opener. Now, according to Wilder, an ice pick. Was either account true, I wondered, or merely apocryphal? Another part of Peter lore? Another part of the myth that had grown up around him? And how would I ever know?

That night, I dreamed I was at a desk going, slowly and methodically, through the Douglas's file on my brother. I remember my elation. My satisfaction at having gotten the first of the files I wanted — no matter how revealing, no matter how disturbing.

Nine days had passed since my conversation with Victor, and because he still hadn't gotten back to me, I left a message for him at his office. Then I left a similar message for Fred at *his* office.

When, by the end of the day, neither man had returned my call, I began to get really nervous. Time was running out.

I decided not to wait any longer, and in the morning,

contacted Richard LaBranche myself. When I asked if he'd reached a decision yet in my case, he seemed genuinely surprised by the question.

"I referred the matter to France Lemieux in Medical Records," he told me.

"But I thought *you* had the higher authority," I said, refusing to believe that I'd wasted so much valuable time.

"It's not a question of higher authority," he explained. "She's responsible for the medical records, and she's following hospital policy."

After that call, panic set in. I'd had thirty days in which to ask the Commission to appeal the decisions of both the Douglas and the coroner. Now, with less than half those days remaining, I still hadn't heard from Victor and I still hadn't received the letter from Luc Lépine.

I tried Fred again, and this time, thankfully, I reached him. But when I asked if he'd spoken to Victor, he said no.

Swallowing my disappointment, I told him of how anxious I was, and of how little time remained. He suggested that I wait for the letter from Lépine, then FAX him everything I had.

Feeling only slightly better, I left a second message for Victor. But he didn't respond to that one either. I decided then, that when I FAXed Fred, I'd FAX him as well.

That afternoon, a letter arrived from my cousin John in New Orleans. He'd once been close to my brother, and so I'd written him, asking for *his* memories of my brother.

"You've hit a very raw chord in me," the two-page letter began. "I'm limiting myself to forty-five minutes, since what I could tell you about my remembrances and feelings on the subject of Peter could take days or longer — emotionally-packed ones.

"I recall his great sensitivity when I first met him (he was twelve-and-a-half), as well as his brashness and forthrightness. And I recall that, at thirteen, he showed a great disdain for violence and violent people.

"I remember his quick, often sarcastic wit, which was

always done with a twinkle in his eye. Very much like your father's twinkle. He really did worship your father."

I scanned ahead to the last time John saw my brother: a month before his death.

"He looked at me disgustedly and asked how I could live in a country that carried on a war such as the one then raging in Vietnam. I explained that we, at the universities, were protesting, rather than running away, but he considered that too slow.

"He was tall, green, his hand was cold and clammy; he didn't look right. Your mother later told me how upset your father was, seeing him in such a state."

As distressing as that image was, the following one was worse.

"Now, I'll tell you of an episode that happened in your kitchen during one of my early visits. Peter asked that I never tell anyone. He was cutting some food with a big knife. Suddenly, he began jabbing the counter with the knife, and I was scared that he might do some damage. He stopped. And I promised. And now I've broken that promise.

"After I learned how he died, I felt guilty for not telling anyone in 1963 or 1964. For a non-violent, anti-violence person, it seemed out of place, yet, maybe he had a rage inside him that would ultimately be uncontrollable. I'm sorry I wasn't smart enough to see something in this episode.

"I've known many people who've died over the years. But only two such people have *never* died for me, because I feel they're always there, next to me: my father and Peter."

As I re-read John's letter, more slowly this time, it was like reading about two different people: my brother as he'd once been, and my brother as he'd become. And, there *I* was, still looking for that singular, defining moment when he'd changed from the former into the latter. Was I being unrealistic? I wondered now.

Were his friends right in suggesting that the changes in my brother's personality and behaviour weren't sudden at all? But rather a *gradual* deterioration due to his excessive use of drugs, coupled with something innate within himself?

If so, then, what *was* that something?

* * * *

At last, I thought, as I opened my mail box, and found the two letters I'd been waiting for. Not surprisingly, the one from the Police Archives apologized for not being able to help me, and explained that all the files from 1968 had been destroyed. The one from Luc Lépine was much as he'd said it would be, complete with the name of the man to whom I should address my appeal.

With leaden heart, I composed two separate letters, then FAXed one to Victor and one to Fred, together with the correspondence he'd requested. But as I watched them feeding through the machine, I knew, instinctively, that I'd get no help from either quarter. That I was, now, as I'd been at the beginning: entirely on my own.

That evening, I called Heinz Lehmann again, anxious to push for whatever else I could get from him.

"In looking through my brother's file," I asked, "did you come across the letter he'd written to my parents when he dropped out of Bishop's?"

According to my mother, she'd given the letter to the Douglas after my brother was admitted.

"I don't recall," Lehmann said. "If I had, I would certainly have stopped to read it. No, I don't think there was such a letter in the file."

I told him about the letter and poem found at the death scene, and he was quite taken aback.

"Then it would seem it was a suicide, after all," he said. "I wouldn't have thought so. If your brother had seemed in the least suicidal, the hospital never would have released him. We had a strict policy about that." He concluded by saying, "I don't think you're going to get anything more from the Douglas. I'd concentrate on getting those letters from the coroner, if I were you."

But you're *not* me, I thought. And when I'm through with the Douglas, I'll have gotten *everything* from them.

Following Lépine's instructions, I called the Ministry of

Culture and Communications in Quebec and spoke with Yves
Laliberté, secretary to the Minister. He noted the particulars of
my request, said he'd discuss the matter with Lépine himself,
and get back to me at the end of the week.

Next, I phoned the Offices of the Information and Privacy
Commission in Montreal and said I wanted to appeal the
Douglas's decision. They told me to send my request to Annick
Reinhardt at the *Commission d'acces à l'information du
Québec*, and gave me both her address and telephone number.

I decided to speak with her first. She told me to FAX her
the relevant material, which I did. But I included with it, a
two-page letter, giving her enough background information to,
hopefully, arouse her curiosity and set my request apart from
everyone else's.

When, by the end of the week, Laliberté hadn't phoned, *I*
phoned *him* again. He told me that he'd talked to Lépine, who'd
merely quoted the law to him, stipulating which documents
could and couldn't be released.

"But," he said, "I'm meeting with one of our lawyers this
afternoon to see if we can find some way to bypass this law, and
I'll call you back at the end of the week. Don't worry, I haven't
forgotten about you."

Nearly a month had passed since my initial phone conversation with Victor, and I had yet to hear from him again.
Surprised and stung by what I considered his rudeness, I called
his Ottawa office a third time, and was told — a third time —
that he was in a meeting.

I promptly gave the woman at the other end my name and
said, "I've left messages for him twice and FAXed him once,
and I'm still waiting for some sort of answer. This is a personal
matter, and he said that he'd try to help me with it. What I need
to know is whether he means to help me or not. If he has no
intention of doing anything, or if there isn't anything he *can* do,
I think the least I'm entitled to is the courtesy of a reply."

The woman apologized and told me that she would "convey the message to him."

My response was to slam down the phone.

During my conversation with Tom Gottlieb, he'd mentioned someone else in Montreal who'd also known my brother. He couldn't remember his name, but promised he'd try to find it for me. When I rang to remind him, he said he was still working on it.

Two nights later, I dreamed I was sitting with my brother in what appeared to be a camp of some sort. I asked him what had happened to Phil, and he told me that Phil had committed suicide.

I decided to give Victor one last chance. I tried his home again, and spoke, once again, to Sheila.

"Victor wouldn't be there, by any chance, would he?" I asked.

"No," she said, "he's in the Gaspé."

Hurriedly, I outlined my predicament to her.

"He's been very busy," she told me.

"I can appreciate that. But he said he'd make some calls on my behalf — "

"I did hear him speaking to someone about you on the phone over the weekend, but I don't know what it was about."

"All *I've* been trying to find out," I persisted, "is whether he thinks he can help me or not. But I haven't even been able to find out *that* much. What I need, really, is a simple 'yes' or 'no' answer."

She seemed, finally, to get the message, and promised to let Victor know that I was asking for a progress report.

I thanked her, calmly and politely, knowing full well I'd never hear a thing.

And, sadly, time proved me right.

Twelve

I kept up the pressure. I spoke again with Annick Reinhardt in Quebec, and asked about the status of my appeal. She assured me that she'd received my documents, that a file had been opened, and that a lawyer would contact me soon.

That same afternoon, I received a letter from the Commission confirming precisely what she'd said.

That night, I dreamed I was seated with a psychiatrist, asking her a series of questions about my brother, and writing down all the answers in my notebook. As to whether or not he'd committed suicide, her answer was, "yes."

I woke with a start, and remained awake until morning.

In the morning, on impulse, I went to the bank, opened my safety deposit box, and took out the ring my brother had bought me for my Sweet Sixteen. Had it ever fit the fourth finger of my left hand? I asked myself as I slid it, now, onto my pinky. It was a charming, old-fashioned ring with a round, fiery opal surrounded by eight blue sapphires in a high, platinum setting.

Suddenly, I saw it as both a link to my brother and a talisman. And I knew it would remain on my finger until the completion of my quest.

I quickly realized that such an unusual ring wouldn't go unnoticed. Had I done this on purpose, I wondered, as part of my healing? As some sort of test? I was about to find out. Seated before Sue, my manicurist, with all ten fingers splayed, I braced myself in preparation.

A few weeks earlier, when she'd asked about my writing, I'd told her, superficially, about my project, and her large, blue eyes had popped wide.

"Jeez, Nomi," she'd said, "I've known you for what, nearly six years, and this is the first I've heard of your having a brother."

Now, when, predictably, she inquired about the ring, as ready as I thought I was, I still felt myself stiffen. It was now or never. I could take the easy way out and lie, or I could take another step toward healing, and tell her the truth. I chose the truth.

I began with my trips to Woolworth's as background to the story, and as I talked, the smile on her face grew wider and wider. And when she started to laugh, I amazed myself by laughing, too.

How good that laughter felt. How warm. How natural. I'd taken a chance and hadn't been punished for it. Sue hadn't recoiled. She hadn't pointed an accusing finger at me or tsk-tsked me or shaken her head at me in disgust. She hadn't judged my brother; nor had she mocked or vilified him.

She'd heard an endearing story about a loving, young boy, and had simply reacted accordingly. Why *shouldn't* she have smiled?

Who *wouldn't* have smiled?

I could almost feel the layer of ice that had safeguarded my brother's place in my heart for so long, beginning to crack. Giving me just that much more room to breathe. I immediately looked for ways to widen the split. And so, I went to my mother and asked her to tell me some stories about him.

"I know I've probably heard everything before," I said, "but I want to hear them again. Only the good ones, though. Ones that'll make me smile."

And she obliged me.

"When Peter was five," she said, "we took him to a seafood

restaurant. He asked the waiter what the specialty of the house was, and the waiter's jaw dropped. People at other tables turned to stare at this precocious, little kid.

"Since he couldn't read, he had your father read the menu for him. When he came to frog's legs, Peter told him to stop. 'That's what I'll have,' he said. 'I've never had it before.'"

Typical of him, my brother had always taken a chance on something new, while, typical of me, I'd always stuck with the familiar. For years, no matter what the restaurant, no matter what the menu, I'd ordered only club sandwiches with French fries.

"At the age of nine or so," my mother continued, "when company was expected and we weren't ready, Peter would say, 'Don't worry, I'll entertain them.' And he would. He'd greet everyone at the door with a handshake, ask how they were, and how their children were, then offer them drinks, and chat with them until we came down."

I, on the other hand, was notorious for running *away* from company. On one occasion, I even went so far as to hide under my aunt's piano bench when one of her friends rang the doorbell.

"When Peter was ten, he got a morning paper route. He was too small to carry the heavy bag, and because he didn't want to ask your father for a wagon, he found some wheels in a neighbour's garage, and made his own.

"He was up every day at five, driving your father frantic with worry as he heard that wagon go squeaking down the street. When he'd made a hundred dollars, Peter came to me, wiped his hands, and said, 'Well, I can quit now. I've just proven to myself that I can be independent.'"

Once again, all I could see were the differences between us. My brother had gotten a paper route and saved up his earnings. And what had I done? Sneaked into his room from time to time, and pilfered some of those earnings from his piggy bank.

By the time I returned to my apartment, I was emotionally spent. But it wasn't a negative feeling. On the contrary, it was actually comforting.

*   *   *   *

With still no word from Laliberté, I called him again. And again, he assured me that he hadn't forgotten me. Their lawyer, he said, was now scheduled to speak with someone in the Justice Ministry as well as the Chief Coroner's Office. Then he startled me by asking, "If the letter says some bad things, will you still want to see it?"

I didn't hesitate. "Yes."

"Well," he said, and I could hear a smile in his voice, "you've waited twenty-seven years; surely you can wait a few more weeks."

Thankfully, that waiting was eased by Tom. When he phoned, finally, with the name I wanted: Peter Brawley.

"We met as teenagers," Brawley told me. "We all used to hang out at the Swiss Hut and New Penelope. Some were middle-class kids, others were street kids, drop-outs.

"Those were the heady days of the hippie movement, when everything was possible. It was exciting. We were innocents, nothing was done with malice. We thought we were rebels of the highest order. We thought we'd turn the world on to peace.

"We felt very deeply about the war in Vietnam. We really cared, followed the movements in the States, read the underground papers. We talked religion, art, politics; we prepared meals; we shared. It was the ideal of the communal living style.

"We weren't in a constant stage of drug lethargy, though. We'd go out onto the street, give away food, help people (there was a growing number of street kids and homeless), buy groceries, go to bookstores, go for walks, go to movies, go hear music.

"Your brother was a sweetheart of a guy, but then," and his tone hardened, "he found the Jamaican witch doctor. At first, it was like a Rasta cloud of love, with Peter Tosh records playing and grass being smoked. Peter and Phil were the leaders, they made the money; Bas had the contacts in Jamaica.

"He was well-intentioned at the beginning. He was a sweet, nice guy, spinning visions of Ethiopia and serving up hot, spiced coffee. But he was smoking us out of our brains.

"After awhile, some of us felt he was trying to be the spiritual leader of the group, preaching old-fashioned morality and advising people on their relationships. He realized how much money they could make and how much power they could have, and it dazzled him.

"We thought it was going to be more fun, but it got too serious for us. It was like being at a Baptist Church meeting, the way Bas would gather his little group of believers around him and pontificate. He turned into a megolomaniac, a really bad guy, haranguing a few of us for not giving enough of ourselves to the 'movement.' And a schism developed.

"Peter bought into the mystical trip that Bas was indestructible. The guy came on like Jesus Christ. There's this 'faux Jewish thing' in Rastafarianism, you know, because of Haile Selassie's claiming to head the lost tribe. Even the Kaballah's filled with warnings not to get involved young.

"He kept saying that Bas would save us all, that he'd take us to Jamaica. And I said, 'Paradise in Jamaica, Berger, really. Let's go to B.C.' What was Bas, really? A little guy, a bullshit artist from the mountains of Jamaica. He told us, 'You be the bad people.' We tried to get Peter away from him, to go to Vancouver with us, but he wouldn't do it."

"Why not?"

"He got involved. He really did buy it. He was riding this dream. But he must have had some heavy anxieties if he felt responsible for the raid and for Bas being arrested.

"Peter's death was the first, real shock, the first thing that went bad in Montreal. Everyone knew about it. It was the end of a dream, the end of the money, and it brought a lot of people down. We were all horrified when we found out."

"Do you think someone might have murdered him?" I asked.

"No, why would they? Everyone liked him. We were told he did it right out of the blue. We heard they ran into the room and found a letter, absolving Bas of blame, saying his death would make the whole thing right, and apologizing for the whole thing."

My heart skipped a beat. Finally, one of my brother's friends who knew about the letter and what it said.

"We came back from Vancouver a few weeks after Peter's death to confront Bas. He had a bungalow on the West Island, with a few followers, hippie kids, still around him, and some women to make the pots of hot, spiced coffee. We were going to push him into the St. Lawrence River.

"He tried to bamboozle us, saying, 'You're my brothers,' and we said, 'We're not your brothers, man.' He said he was haunted by Peter's ghost, but that he was safe because of the letter Peter had written.

"We told him how bad it was Peter had died, and that he was to blame. We said, 'You're lucky to be alive.' There we stood, five big, young, white guys, and told him to get out. He turned into a wreck and started snivelling.

"A few years later, when I was really down, I ran into someone who said he had some news that would cheer me up. Then he told me Bas had been murdered in Jamaica. And you know what, I did feel better. To me, his death was a balancing out."

I asked him then, the question I'd begun asking everyone: Did he know what had happened to Phil?

"Phil?" He snorted. "He was Peter's best friend, but *I* didn't think he'd been a good friend to him. I was angry because he'd let it all go too far. I heard he became a heroin addict.

"The last time I saw him was about 1980. He was still on drugs and looked washed up. He was also a babbling idiot. Peter was the end of Phil. He could never forget about it; he always wanted to talk about it. Who knows if he's even alive?

"I know in retrospect," he went on, "that it all looks dippy. It's easy to see that we were working under some naive, anthropological delusion. We were a bunch of well-meaning yo-yos. All of us were talented, middle-class kids, whose creative spirit was never positively reinforced. It was like a game, with all of us role playing. We were innocents, trying to make the world a better place. But when you're a kid, you want to prove you can do it."

Then, as our conversation wound down, he gave me the name of John Shore in Vancouver, and wished me luck with my search.

John, to my delight, was most eager to speak with me. But he was in the middle of a birthday party for his wife, and asked me to call back the next evening. I was just about to hang up when he said, "Have you spoken to Sandy Rhéaume?"

Sandy? I let out a gasp. Sandy was the name of Kathy's brother.

"No," I told him. "Do you have any idea where he is?"

"Sure, he lives in Quebec City now."

"Can you spell his last name for me?" I asked and he did, adding, "Don't ask Information for Sandy, ask for Alexandre."

There were two Alexandres listed. I asked for both. Then I called the first one, and crossed my fingers. Bingo!

His voice was deep, lightly accented, as he said, "I remember you."

Then he told me, "Peter was very extraordinary. His head was such a high-powered instrument; the force of his mental power was incredible. People who experienced him are still holding pieces of him.

"He was very special to me. I suffered some of the same ills he did. I loved him very much, like a brother, and still do. But I let go of him a long time ago, so that he could get to another place."

When I described the possible reasons behind my journey as they related to *The Tibetan Book of the Dead*, I could almost hear Sandy nodding.

"I've felt contact from Peter over the years," he admitted. "His presence is quite clear. From what you're saying, it's as if he's been inhabiting you for the last few months, as if he's been telling you there's something you must do for him. And you're doing it."

"Yes," I said. "That's what I believe, too." Then I asked him to go back, and begin at the beginning.

"I met Peter and Phil in the winter of '68, after I'd dropped out of McGill. They were living in a dump on Laval. Peter said he could hook me up with acid. It seems he was heavily involved and knew how to get drugs.

"Eventually, Peter, Phil, Allan, John, my sister Kathy, and I took the place on Mt. Royal. Phil, who'd set up communications with Bas in Jamaica, arranged for a small amount of weed to be sent up. Then Bas himself came up.

"The man possessed an evangelical kind of power. As a Rasta priest, he had the Rasta fervour. Listen to some of Bob Marley's music, and listen, really listen to the words. It's all about going back to the original revelation of truth. That was the kind of spirit the Rasta religion was able to convey. The whole idea of some incredible, powerful spirituality handed down and passed on. You can find that same find of fervour among Orthodox Jews, in Moslem mosques, at Christian revival meetings, whatever.

"Your brother was cynical about society. He had a desperate need to find some truth to believe in, an alternative to what the world offered. He wanted to experience other things, to turn himself into other things. His need was the door by which evangelicals enter; they step into the vacuum with their own message of truth.

"You have to think about what was weak about him to make him cling in such a desperate fashion. He messed up, his potential was never appropriately applied. He could have been anyone: prime minister, messiah, dictator of the universe."

"What do you think happened?" I asked.

"I think he was pissed off with your parents."

At this, I stiffened defensively.

"Peter was very particular about what he revealed, very reticent about giving details. But then, he was going through the stage when it was normal to be pissed off at one's parents. I think he felt he never measured up to what he was supposed to be, and that was to be great."

When I asked for his thoughts on my brother's stay at the Douglas, Sandy said, "I think he was able to go through the tests and project whatever image he chose to project. He could control the perceptions of the doctors to suit his own purposes. He could have been a raving lunatic and appeared sane."

"And his death?" I asked. "Suicide or murder?"

"Forget about it being a plot being fabricated by anyone. No major drug dealer had any beef with him. It was his reaction to a whole series of pressures. He would probably laugh, but I think he felt guilty about Kathy, who was underage, and had been arrested, and was being held in a detention centre."

"Did you see him ... you know ... dead?"

"Yes. I saw him before the police arrived. I'd gotten back from the Yukon the night before, to find my sister in detention and the whole scene in an uproar. Allan and I were staying at our friend Tommy Sise's place in Westmount, and he woke me early in the morning to tell me Peter was dead. We went down to Coloniale Street immediately."

I tensed in anticipation of what was to come.

"He was in a pose of total peacefulness," was all Sandy said, as if sensing my discomfort.

"Did you see any letters from him?"

"I vaguely remember some stuff around. But I found a piece of paper, and scrawled at the bottom of it, in his handwriting, were the instructions: 'Read *The Tibetan Book of the Dead.*' So I did; we all did."

My heart did a sudden flip-flop. Which version was right, Sandy's or Brawley's?

"What he did, in my opinion," Sandy continued, "was give the finger to everybody. It was a wilful act of defiance to the universe in general. A deliberate act, as if he was saying, 'I can leave here and you can't stop me.'

"I also think he was trying to take responsibility for everything, trying to be a *mensch* and maintain some honourability. He was trying to move beyond what he considered drab and empty-headed. Beyond the unresolved frustration of being a disappointment to your parents."

"What about Bas's involvement in his death?"

"Bas didn't do it. What Peter did, he did because he wanted to. Drugs didn't cause his downfall; *he* used *them* to cause his downfall. He pushed that limit in an irreversible fashion. For all

I know, he could have had schizophrenic tendencies which the LSD triggered."

"What, if anything," I asked, "do you know of Bas's death?"

"Years ago, a friend of mine met a Rasta in Jamaica who said, 'Bas went to Montreal and was the cause of someone else losing his life, so we took *his* life from him.'"

"Why?"

"Because Bas was recognized as being one of those who spread the light. He had a spiritual responsibility toward others. His murder was seen as an affirmation of that responsibility."

I swore then, that I could hear Sandy smile.

"Your brother's the head of a cult now, you know. The 'Peter adoration cult' is alive and thriving. If you gave a party to celebrate him, everyone would come. We were the opposite of the punk kids out there today, whose slogan is 'no future.' Back then, we were looking for something to believe in, but everything disappointed us."

As I added Sandy's name to my list right after Brawley's, I asked if he knew what had happened to Phil, and if he knew how Phil spelled his last name. (At that point, I'd tried him under four spellings, each slightly different, and all with the same, frustrating result: nothing).

He said he didn't, and gave me yet another version to try. I dutifully called Baie Comeau Information again. And again, nothing.

Thirteen

*L*ate the following night, I was back on the phone with John, who told me, "I came to Montreal in the fall of '67 to attend night school at Sir George Williams, but I eventually dropped out. Dropping out was the thing to do then. Education was useless; you got your education on the street.

"I got a place on Prince Arthur, met Sandy through a cousin, and we shared the apartment. It was Sandy who first met Peter. He was funny, always had something to say, and a sharp tongue to say it with. I can still remember his flat. It was at the head of a flight of stairs. There was a table there, with cash and drugs lying around on it.

"He was a master con artist. He talked a woman out of some money and bought a motorcycle. He really knew how to make things happen, knew karma, knew manifestations. We communicated a lot using material from P. D. Ouspensky's book, *In Search of the Miraculous*. And acid made a big difference; we could really communicate psychically.

"Peter was also a weekend junkie. He shot heroin, just to try it. He was introduced to it by Phil, but he never got hooked. To him, it was just lots of fun."

Heroin! My mind rebelled. Grass and hash and LSD, yes. But heroin?

"We both agreed that we wanted to make a scene happen, get a big place that would be cool, where people could drop in, and perhaps make a difference in their lives. Peter started looking for a place, and found the flat on Mt. Royal. Do you know how we financed it?"

"No."

John chuckled. "I'd been given a one-thousand-dollar bond by my father, and Peter knew about it. He told me to get a loan on the bond, which I did, and we rented the flat."

"In whose name was the lease?" I asked, recalling St. Denis's testimony that the RCMP didn't know who'd rented the flat.

"Mine. Peter said, 'Tell them you're really wealthy.' I never even met the landlord. This was all done over the phone.

"After that, we just started hanging out. It was relaxed; an easy, nice, domestic scene. Sandy made deliveries. We really didn't have to make an effort, the word got around easily enough. Peter and Sandy knew a lot of people, had lots of connections. It was easy to unload the stuff.

"I dated Kathy first. She was young, pretty straight, and didn't do much in the way of drugs. Then I fooled around with someone else, and she found out. She dropped me and moved in with Peter.

"Things started getting serious after awhile. Peter and I fought verbally all the time. We were each trying to work out our own point of view, trying to work out our own way to unity and harmony. I began fading from the scene, and met some other people who had a place, where it was more fun, more relaxed. I went out of town, came back, and Bas was there.

"I only met him once. He was sitting in this hanging basket chair, which had been my idea, and holding court. I didn't like him or the whole scene. But Peter was ecstatic about Bas, and he stopped talking to me then. Pretty soon, the energy of the group began to change as people dropped out and others came in. The dynamics changed. There was no way to get through to anybody at that point because of Bas and his influence.

"Peter thought Bas was even better at mental power trips than he was. We were naive about Bas and his part in everything. He was always saying, 'I'll take you flying,' and talking about 'astral planes.' There was this whole thing about 'be right, be strong.' He really ground it into you.

"According to Gurdjieff, we develop along two lines: knowledge and being. The art is to keep the two balanced. When I moved out to Vancouver, I'd call the house a lot. Once Peter said to me, 'My knowledge is doing great, but my being isn't doing so well.'"

"How did you hear about my brother's death?" I asked.

"Tommy Sise called to say Peter had killed himself."

"Do you know where I could reach this Tommy?"

"Sorry, but I don't."

"Did you ever hear anything about Bas's death?"

"I was told he'd been beheaded."

"Why?"

"Because of the death of a brother. He was discrediting Rasta by taking power from people and trying to sweep them off their feet into a 'Bas clan.' He acted irresponsibly with all his talk about astral planes and so on."

Yet another version of Bas's bloody end. And I was left to wonder, yet again, which, if any, was the real version. Then John chilled me by recounting two incidents that had occurred shortly after my brother's death.

"At Christmas, a group of us dropped acid and threw the I Ching. For the first time ever, we all got the same trigrams. We all received this incredible energy.

"The wind chimes in the room started ringing, and this black cat came out of nowhere, and started climbing over everyone. I felt a pain like none I'd ever felt before. It was a total out-of-body pain. I felt loss, despair, and a feeling of 'where am I?'"

"Are you saying that you felt my brother was there in the room with you?" I asked.

"Yes."

As to the second incident?

"Brawley kept saying 'Someone's got to have a baby, someone's got to have a baby.' My girlfriend Marlene got pregnant very quickly. We had a son, Steven. He was hyperactive, he wouldn't sleep, he wouldn't sit still. He was totally brilliant. I fought with him all the time."

The message was clear and it gave me goosebumps.

"Are you trying to tell me that you believe your son was the reincarnation of my brother?"

Another yes.

I gave my head a shake. It was as if I were on some bizarre, surrealistic voyage. Much like Alice in the Lewis Carroll story of Wonderland, and the one in the Jefferson Airplane's song, *White Rabbit*. But, unlike those two Alices, I'd taken neither a pill nor a magic mushroom.

There was much about these men's *own* life voyages that seemed too fantastic to be true. Much about the experiences they'd shared, and the times in which they'd shared them, that seemed to glow with a special flame undimmed by the years.

They'd all been riders on the same, electrifying carpet ride, participants in that same, mad, mystery tour called the sixties. But, unlike so many of their icons and contemporaries, and unlike my very own brother, they were among those who, albeit scathed and scarred, *had* gotten out alive.

I was so caught up in my thoughts that I barely heard John asking, "Have you spoken to David Fowler yet?"

"No," I answered.

"He lives in Toronto now. He had the house where your brother died." There was a brief pause, and then, "He was the one who found your brother's body."

In the morning, I located David Fowler.

"I was living on Coloniale Street with the late Katherine Arnold," he explained. "We were den parents to lots of kids, runaways, draft dodgers. We knew the members of the English artistic community. Brawley brought a few guys around, and one of them was your brother.

"They started telling us about this man from Jamaica, who had strange powers. They told us about some of the things they'd witnessed, such as his making stones rain from Heaven on the roof. They said he was a spiritual master, and that they were going to bring him to Canada. The house on Mt. Royal was almost a natural set-up to support a guru, and everyone in it was involved for his or her own reason.

"Bas possessed some sort of kinetic energy that you could

feel with or without drugs, a personal power that's hard to imagine unless you witnessed it for yourself. I even believed I once saw him walking two inches off the ground in that place.

"Although Katherine was very impressed with him at first, I didn't think Bas was very nice. Then, when he made sexual advances toward her, she changed her mind about him.

"He could read your mind, you know. And one day he was insulted when he read *my* mind and knew I was thinking that he wanted to have sex with Katherine. He rounded on me and said, 'Don't you realize I can have the ultimate sexual experience just sitting here?' It was as if he were above everything, at such a high level, and he was insulted that someone would think he'd want to have sex with a mere mortal."

"But he did."

"He did. I remember a young runaway, a small, pretty blonde girl, had to be hospitalized for mental problems after Bas seduced her."

What a monster, I thought. How then, could my brother have allowed him*self* to be seduced, figuratively, by someone so monstrous?

"Despite my fear of Bas," David went on, "we believed he had enough spiritual power to keep us from ever getting caught or busted. He used to tell us all the time, 'Don't worry, I'm keeping everybody safe. I'm keeping the narcotic agents away through my power.'"

"And just how did he exercise this power?" I wanted to know.

"He said he was doing his work in the astral plane, keeping the bad guys away from us, the good guys. He'd communicate with the unseen world and arrange things in our favour; he said he talked to the spirits about this."

"Did anyone see him talking to these spirits?"

"Oh no."

What a surprise.

"No one was allowed to witness it; he'd do it alone in his room."

Eager to change the subject, I asked, "What do you think happened to my brother at the end?"

"In my opinion, he'd tapped into a source of willpower of some sort. He wasn't able to control it, and it eventually destroyed him. It was as if there was a conflict between his sense of what was good and what wasn't. He'd acquired a lot of magnetism toward the end. It caused him to believe it was time to be free of these mortal bounds.

"He came to us after the Douglas, you know, and took over the master bedroom. There was a second couple at the other end of the house, so we moved into a room off the sun porch."

When I asked if my brother had ever talked about the raid, the time he'd spent in jail, or his confinement at the Douglas, David said, "If he did, I can't remember. I think the shock of having been the one who found him caused me to blank out a lot of my memories."

"After the Douglas," I inquired, "was he the same or different?"

"He was definitely different. I felt he'd crossed some line into madness. He'd taken on the role of spiritual mentor, taken on Bas's role, and he was pontificating all the time."

"How did he seem?"

"He was distraught a few days before his death. He talked a lot."

"What about?"

"Like the truths of the universe." Then, almost as an afterthought, David said, "Bas would send messages to us through him."

"How, over the phone or mentally?"

"Both."

I rolled my eyes.

"Peter would say, 'This is what Bas wants you to do.' Then he'd tell us how to feel about things and why.

"A day or so before his death, he looked at us with an intensity in his eyes that you wouldn't believe and said, 'Don't you understand, I'm not what I used to be; I'm the most powerful being in the universe. And I'm going to prove it.'

"We were short of food, and Peter said, 'I'll show you how powerful I am. I'm going to Moishe's and get them to donate six of their best steaks to us.' So we went with him. He marched into the boss's office, gave him the case, said he wanted him to make the right decision, and make a donation of the food. We walked out of the restaurant with the steaks."

He chuckled as he said this, but I remained mute. Oh, my brother, I thought sadly. To think what you could have done ... to think what you might have been ...

"Could you tell me about the day he died?" I asked David then, and steeled myself for his reply.

"I woke up suddenly, and heard something that resembled a groan. I'm convinced I probably heard him do it. The door to the master bedroom was open a few inches; none of the doors in the house closed properly. I went into the bedroom to get some clothes and saw him.

"At first, I thought it was a joke. You know, one of those gags you can buy in a store, a knife with blood on it, sticking out of you. And I thought, 'What? Why did he do that?' I stood, paralyzed in the doorway. I had the strangest feeling he was still there, but he was obviously dead. I got Marshall — "

"Marshall?" I interrupted.

"Marshall Hopkins. He lives in Vancouver now."

I scribbled that down.

"Marshall came in, sat on the floor by the bed, and started reciting the prayers for the newly dead from *The Tibetan Book of the Dead*."

"Who called the police?"

"I did."

"And my father?"

"I don't remember who called your father, maybe it was me."

"Did you believe, without a doubt, that my brother's death was a suicide?"

"Yes."

"Why?"

"I think it's possible Peter suffered because of some of the things Bas had done. He might have felt responsible because he'd introduced Bas to us. I think there was guilt and confusion over the general bahaviour pattern they'd fallen into, that is, the drug-importing business.

"I think it was, in part, that he believed he was able to transcend death, the same way an LSD trip transcends actual human existence. I think he chose to escape the entire conflict, and passed from life into death, consciously and deliberately.

"It felt like the scene was staged. He was dressed in a combination of his and my clothes, even wearing my black leather winter coat. And he'd used one of our kitchen knives.

"He was sort of propped up on pillows, just as if he were presenting it directly. I honestly think it was to make it ceremonial; to show that he was finally in control of what was happening."

Enough! my heart cried out. It was too much. Too graphic, too clear. David had, with his words, created an image as explicit as any photograph, and I couldn't bear to look at it.

"Do you recall finding a letter written by him," I managed, "or perhaps a poem?"

"There were lots of his writings around; sometimes he'd scribble his rantings down. He was a huge idea and feeling machine, but the material was feeding through him too fast."

"What happened after he died?"

"We took Bas's wife and three kids under our wing for awhile; they really couldn't cope. Then the house broke up."

"Did you ever see Bas again?"

"I spoke to Bas once more. When I told him I was the first person who'd found Peter, he said I should have told him immediately, and the fact that I hadn't, was really serious. I still don't know what he meant by that. Perhaps I was being paranoid, but he hinted that something had inhabited Peter, and that it was now inhabiting me."

"What were his feelings about my brother's death? Did he say he felt, in any way, responsible?"

"No. He felt anything bad that happened to someone else was what they'd done to themselves. He took no responsibility for Peter's death. To him, death wasn't something to feel remorse about. To him, Peter had decided to change his mode of existence and had acted accordingly."

He ended our conversation, saying, "You know, when Kathy died in the plane crash, I had the feeling that she and Peter were still linked somehow."

Fourteen

*H*ow odd, I thought, as I dialed Marshall's number in Vancouver. I was spending more time talking to strangers than my own friends. It was as if we'd formed a loose network of otherwise disconnected souls, of which I was its temporary centre. The thread holding us together now, just as my brother had then.

We were all voices from the same shared past, united in the present. Not only in recollection and commemoration, but in closure as well. For, to my amazement, many of them had admitted that my brother and his death were issues as yet unresolved in their own minds. That the trauma of it was a wound that had never completely healed.

And so, it seemed my quest was no longer solely for me; it was for all of us.

Unfortunately, Marshall's memories were few.

"There was a bunch of scary stuff going down at the time," he told me. "I remember sitting in the hammock on Mt. Royal and listening to music. I also remember Bas bawling me out once for kissing a girl. The irony was, he was trying to kiss her, too.

"I was frightened, I remember, about all the spliffs they were smoking. They had all these names for pot, one of them being 'the Lord's breath.'"

When I asked if he could recall anything about my brother's death, he said, "I woke during the night to go to the bathroom, and heard a gurgle or a cough coming from the master bedroom. I wondered, afterward, if he'd had difficulty breathing, and I'd passed by."

Night? I thought my brother had died in the morning.

Then Marshall startled me by saying, "I heard Peter left a note saying he'd done it as a sacrifice to Bas."

I now had one more person who'd "heard" about a note. But, to me, it was still just hearsay. I wanted proof. I wanted that letter and that poem. And I was still waiting. Waiting to see whether the greater powers in Quebec would be able to force the lesser powers in Montreal to turn them over to me.

Suddenly, I was tired of waiting. Despite what I'd been told by the Commission, I contacted Norah, and asked her to find me a lawyer who was an expert in the Access to Information Act.

It was the Jewish New Year. And, traditionally, the worst time of my own, personal year. What was once a holiday shared by four, had, since my brother's and, in 1989, my father's death, become an agonizing reminder, not of what remained, but, rather, of what was missing. And of all the New Years since 1968, this one promised to be even worse, because the anniversary of my brother's death fell on the second day of observances.

As I lit the ritual *yuhrzeit* candle in honour of his memory, I could almost feel the weight of my present journey compounding the weight of my perennial grief. Then, just as I had at his gravesite, I began to speak to him, softly, through my tears.

I told him that I loved and missed him. I told him of the pain that never went away. Of the loneliness that never abated. Of the hole within me that would never be filled. Then I told him about his friends, and how his leaving had left them less than they'd been when he was with them.

As I spoke, I could feel his presence in the room, alive in the small, flickering candle flame. And I knew that for the next twenty-four hours, his spirit would burn more brightly than on any other day of the year.

*   *   *   *

That night, I felt as if I were on guard. On a death vigil. And I shuddered, recalling the night before my brother died. When I had the premonition.

I was sitting in bed, reading. My husband was in the den. Suddenly, the bedroom turned cold. *I* turned cold. I looked up from my book and saw a shapeless blur of white, like a gauzy shadow, flit across the room and disappear.

I began to shiver. Icy prickles of gooseflesh coated my entire body.

"Someone's going to die," I whispered. "Someone's going to die."

The following morning, my brother was found dead.

In a second, brief, phone conversation with Peter Brawley, he'd said that he'd given my number to another of my brother's friends, and that he'd be contacting me "soon." But eight days had passed since then, and I was getting anxious.

"I still haven't heard from your friend," I told him.

"He said he'd call you when he reached Toronto."

"And when will that be?"

Brawley's answer was a laugh.

"Could you at least give me his name, so I'll know him when he does call?"

"Sure. Paul Mallory."

A few days later, Norah provided me with the name of Montreal lawyer, Mark Bantey.

I reached him easily, gave him some background information, then briefly described my current situation. He told me of a case of his, in which they'd tried to get what was termed "annexed documents" from a coroner, and how difficult it had been. He couldn't recall the outcome, but said he'd check on it for me.

In the meantime, he suggested I send him all my documentation, and that, as soon as he'd read it, he'd let me know if there was anything he could do to assist me, and what his fee would be.

As chance would have it, I stopped by my mail box on the way to the post office, and what did I find? A letter from Yves Laliberté informing me that my case had been referred to the Office of the Coroner in Quebec.

He'd written that, according to section 101 of the "Act respecting the determination of the causes and circumstances of death," it was possible, "with the permission of the chief coroner or a permanent coroner, to convey certain documents." I would, he assured me, be contacted shortly.

I made a photocopy of the letter and mailed it off with everything else to Bantey.

A few days later, I sat at the computer, staring gloomily at a single name on the screen: Paul Mallory. I still hadn't heard from him and wondered if I ever would. Just then, the phone rang.

It was Paul Mallory.

"I met Peter in '67 or '68," he said. "I was living on a farm in Nova Scotia and made about twenty-one trips to Toronto that year, stopping about sixteen times in Montreal. I saw him whenever I was in town.

"I knew him only in a positive form. I just loved him; we were great friends. He was such a great human being, very eclectic. We had great fun together, rambling around, going out to dinners and attending concerts. Then he bought into what Bas was selling.

"There was a dark side to him, you know, leaving him open to that kind of spirituality. He was on the edge, in a treacherous sort of dreamscape. But the sixties themselves were very, very dark. They cast a bright light, but also dark shadows. I suggest you read *Meeting the Shadow*. It's a collection of short stories by various authors, describing the dark side of human nature."

I jotted down the title, then waited for him to continue.

"Peter was searching for answers in the wrong places; he got in too deep and became the wrong person. The sheer amount of his drug use would have accounted for what happened. It was very high quality, Jamaican weed. Phenomenal mind experiences, combined with the phenomenal amount of drugs, is a recipe for chaos.

"Besides, what Bas was into wasn't Rasta; it was a corruption of Rasta. He had this evil energy, and Peter's death was a manifestation of all that evil energy. He took a lot of the focus of it."

"Do you think his death was a suicide?"

"I think he was highly suicidal, in that he had a different take on things. Due to his feelings about death, the ticket to the journey was killing himself. It *was* a very unusual way, though," he admitted, "fraught with all kinds of variables. But over the years, numerous friends and even my own brother have committed suicide, so I'm never shocked by it." Then he added, "People who kill themselves don't think of who they're leaving behind; it's not contained within the context of their thinking."

When I told him about my brother's last words to me, and the anguish they still caused me, he said, "Peter was part of the flashing landscape, part of why you couldn't have done anything about it anyway. That time was like no other time in history. Peter's death became the symbol of how crazy it was. He was the first."

Then, almost casually, Paul dropped the bomb.

"Did you know," he said, "that a few years after Peter's death, a retired RCMP narcotics officer published a book about drugs? To me, it was all distortion and propaganda, but in it, was a photo of Peter with the knife in his chest."

My heart stopped, then restarted with a jolt.

"We all saw it and passed it around. We couldn't believe it."

When I could work my mouth again, I peppered him with questions about the book, most of which he couldn't answer. All he remembered was that it was small, a paperback, and had a glossy, "shock-value" kind of cover. But I wanted to know more.

What was the name of the author? When was it published? Where was it published? Who was the publisher? Was it written in English or French? Was it still available or out of print? Would libraries have it?

I was so stunned, so horrified, I could barely sit still. But I had to. I had to continue. Quickly then, I asked him about Phil.

"I heard Phil disappeared into heroin," was all he could tell me. Then, after a long pause, he said, "You know, this whole episode with your brother has been unresolved for so many people. What you're doing is very relevant in terms of the sixties. People are still haunted by them.

"Back then, it was like being on an ocean liner that wasn't supposed to sink, but it did. Anyone who took a heavy amount of drugs and is alive today, is simply lucky."

I was still so rattled, I almost missed it when he gave me the names and numbers of two other people, who'd been living in the house on Coloniale at the time of my brother's death.

"They both said you should call them," Paul told me. "I think they'll give you the recall you've been searching for."

To say that I felt sick thinking about that purported book, would be an understatement. I was horrorstruck.

Who was this man? What right did he have to publish a book using a deathbed photo of my brother for his own personal ends? What right did he have to violate my brother's privacy in that way? What right did he have to desecrate the memory of someone else's loved one as he lay helpless in death?

I was seized by a rage so great, I knew, at that moment, how it felt to want to kill. Frightened by the intensity of my anger, and desperate to tell someone, I called Norah. Her response to my hysterical tirade was a hushed, "Good grief."

Then she agreed, without hesitation, to begin the search for the book on her end, while I began it on mine.

Fifteen

*D*espite a tortured and sleepless night, I forced myself to call the first of the two names Paul had given me: Heather McLaren in Gatineau, Quebec.

"I didn't know Peter that well," she said. "But what I do remember is his bright face, curly hair, and beautiful skin. He was riding a wave when he was around that house.

"We, on the other hand, were poverty-stricken hippies living in a commune, boiling fishheads for our meals. Peter would sweep in, bringing food. He was very generous. Once he brought sirloin steaks. That was such a treat. What a gift to experience."

Could those have been the steaks from Moishe's? I wondered.

"My boyfriend Marshall was the singer in a rock and roll band. I was the only one in the house with a real day job; I was a secretary."

Marshall. The connections were tightening, the web closing.

"There was great energy, great cohesion among us, the bond between people. There was great strength in that for us. We thought about a better world. We took the choice that love, not hate, provided."

"Tell me about Bas," I urged.

"I was never caught up in Bas. At the top of the stairs in our place was a table, and on the table was a photograph of Bas with a candle burning in front of it, like a shrine. It was put there by Katherine, who adored him. I had a hard time going by that picture.

"When I met Bas for the first time, he was like a godhead among the people who circled him and looked after his needs. He came up to me, and he had these penetrating eyes. He looked at me as if assessing me to see what I was made of.

"I was wearing this sort of see-through, Ghandi, white shirt. He grabbed both of my breasts and twisted them painfully. It was an invasion, an insult. Katherine didn't seem surprised. She said he just came on a bit strong. I wasn't ready to sock him in the face, but I thought, 'No matter what his spiritual line is, he's not going to get me in his camp.'"

"Were you there," I asked, "when my brother died?"

"Yes."

"What do you remember about it?"

"Certain things stand out about that day. I'd never experienced anything like that before. Peter picked out a serrated bread knife that was one of mine. We were all huddling in the kitchen, fearful. It was terribly shocking, we didn't understand.

"Your father came in, pushed past the police, saw him, and gave out such a scream, it turned our blood cold. Then he came into the kitchen and started to scream at us, saying we were all guilty of killing him as far as he was concerned.

"The police interrogated us. We spent the next few days shaking in our boots. I remember the mattress with all the blood on it. The house broke up after that; no one could go on living there."

The explicitness of Heather's description nearly made me gag. I could hardly wait to get off the phone.

When I did, I sat in my chair, trembling. My poor father, I thought wretchedly. My poor, poor father. I could see him in that room of death. I could hear his agonized scream. And the sound of it tore me apart.

I cursed myself then for ever having started this quest. For bringing such pain back into my life. For being so insatiably curious. So dogged. So obsessed.

And I considered calling a halt to it there and then. No explanations. No apologies. Simply ... no more.

But when I thought of all the loose ends still waiting to be tied up, I knew I couldn't even *think* of stopping.

Two days later, I regretted my decision.

I proved too good a sleuth.

At the Metro Reference Library, I tracked down the book. It was much the way Paul had described it. Rigid with dread, I lightly fanned the pages.

It was only a millisecond, but I saw it. And I gasped. My heart began pounding so hard and so fast, I was afraid it would leap out of my chest.

I dropped the book and jumped from my chair in a single movement. I took a step back, then a step forward. A jerky step back again. Then another one forward. Several people at a nearby reading table glanced up at me, curious.

My entire body was shaking so violently, I could barely stand. I stumbled to my seat and sat down again. I tried breathing normally, but it was impossible. My heart continued its rapid pounding, my body its shaking.

I had to get out of there, I knew. But could I even walk?

Struggling to my feet, I fumbled with the book, my purse, and my jacket, nearly dropping everything in my haste. My legs were so unsteady, I tottered like a drunk as I made my way to the cart beside the Retrieval Desk. With fingers I no longer felt, I let the book fall, clattering, onto the top shelf. Then, as if to prove that I *could* walk, I made myself take the stairs, rather than the elevator, down to the main floor.

I didn't realize what I was doing until I heard myself singing softly, just barely above a whisper. And then I understood. I was trying to distract myself. While trying, at the same time, to hold onto my sanity. But behind my eyes, the photograph, that damning, soul-destroying photograph, had already taken root.

I tried everything from willing it away to blinking it away, but it remained, stubbornly and permanently, implanted there. And so, I was forced to continue my whispered singing, nonsense words to a tuneless tune, as I threaded my tortuous way back home. I sang softly all the way up to my apartment, then increased the volume as soon as the door closed behind me.

I poured some wine into a glass and gulped it down. It didn't help. With a fresh glass in my quaking hand, I paced the floor of my apartment, all the while, jumping and twitching and splintering inside. In my agony, I didn't know where to put myself. No sooner would I sit down someplace, than I'd leap up again and continue pacing.

Gradually, the initial shock began to wear off. In its wake, however, trailed a numbing kind of fatigue. While inside my head, the photograph burned on, a dark, poisonous flame, impossible to extinguish. What had, previously, been only words — from the coroner's to Heather's — now, suddenly, had a tangible shape. And I'd seen, as a ghastly still-life, what my father had seen, in the flesh, twenty-seven years ago.

Now, like my father, that deathbed image of my brother would be the last thing *I'd* see each time I closed *my* eyes at night. If I even *dared* to close them now.

On legs like jelly, I tripped into the bedroom and left a message for Norah on her machine.

"I found the book," was all I said, and asked her to phone me. Then I listened to my own messages. One was from Richard Huard in Montreal. I frowned, curious as to the reason for his call, and promptly called him back. He told me that he'd had no success in locating Phil.

"Without a date of birth," he said, "you can't get a lead on anyone's driver's license."

In the state I was in, I had no recollection of even having asked him to try. Then, suddenly, it all came pouring out of me. I told him about the book and about the photograph.

"My first reaction when I saw it," I said, "was that it had to be murder."

He asked me why, and I described my brother's pose to him.

"Have *you* seen any homicides?" I asked, and he said yes. "Is it possible to stab yourself that way, and then assume such a tranquil pose?"

"It is. You don't die immediately. You'll still have time,

even if it's only seconds, to compose yourself. Some will fold their hands across their chest, while others — "

I closed my ears to the rest.

That evening, I was supposed to meet a friend for dinner. I wanted to cancel, but the thought of staying home alone with only the photograph for company, kept me from backing out.

I managed to survive the dinner on sheer grit. No one would ever have known that behind the bland façade, the forced smile, and fake laughter, was a woman on the verge of collapse. But when I arrived back at my apartment building, the mask abruptly fell away.

I wanted my mother. I needed my mother. I needed her to put her arms around me and hold me before I died of the pain. And so, I buzzed her once, quickly, on the intercom and asked if I could come up.

As soon as she opened the door, I flung myself at her and burst into tears.

"Did something happen?" she asked, a tremor in her voice, and I gulped out, "Yes."

In between sobs, I managed, somehow, to tell her, revealing no more than the barest of details. Then, while she held me, I kept repeating, "How am I ever going to close my eyes again?" like some frantic, broken record.

It took some time, but the storm eventually played itself out, leaving me limp and exhausted. With her arm around my waist, my mother led me over to the table in her kitchen, where we sat, tightly holding hands.

"Do you want a tranquilizer?" she asked.

I shook my head. "Later. I had wine before and with supper."

"So? Take one now."

"Later, mommy, later." I wadded a paper napkin and pressed it to my eyes. Then I burst out, saying, "Oh, God, I'm sorry! I'm so sorry to be doing this to you. I'm so sorry to be dredging all this up again."

She tried, once more, to comfort me, as only a mother can comfort a child. But I was, for the moment at least, beyond consolation. We talked awhile longer, then I left.

Near midnight, Norah called. I told her what I *hadn't* told my mother, while she listened in grim and sympathetic silence. Then, because the book had been published in Montreal, I asked her to find out if the company still existed, and if so, could they put us in touch with the author. She said she would, first thing in the morning.

As I stared out at the sleeping city, I thought with fury of the man who'd so ruthlessly violated, not only my brother's privacy, but my family's as well. Obviously, the photograph had come from my brother's *police* file. How, then, had an *RCMP officer* gotten hold of that file?

How had he even known about my brother's death?

Could he have taken part in the drug bust?

Had he been given authorization to use that photograph? If so, whose? And if not, hadn't he, as an officer of the law, *broken* that law by using it?

Over the next few days, I fought off the gruesome image by filling every moment with activity, and every silence with either whistling or singing. And I developed a mantra. Each time the image appeared, I'd say, "Go 'way."

And it would. Until the next time. When, once more, I'd have to say, "Go 'way."

"Go 'way."

"Go 'way."

Sixteen

*I*t was Friday the thirteenth. And in my fragile state of mind, I dreaded the day. I expected almost anything to happen, all of it bad. But to my relief, nothing did. And on the positive side, I hired a lawyer.

Mark Bantey called from Montreal to say he'd read through the documents I'd sent him, and that I should, definitely, appeal the Douglas's decision. I didn't even think twice.

As for the Office of the Coroner, he advised me to wait a few more weeks. If, by then, I still hadn't heard anything, he'd contact them on my behalf.

When I told him about the photograph, he said I might have the right to sue. No photograph of that nature could be used, he maintained, without the permission of the family.

I gave him the name of the book, the author, the publisher, and the date of publication, and he said he'd try to track down a copy of it.

On Sunday morning, after several failed attempts, I reached the second person Paul had suggested I call: Gordie Fulton in Kitchener, Ontario.

"I met Peter," he told me, "one night in early '68 in a place on Park Avenue. Everyone was on acid. He was kind of power tripping, not in a negative way, but he wanted to see how people would react to him, to his questions, and his actions.

"I'll give you an example of what I mean. He asked us out

to eat, and we all piled into his car. It was one of those wicked, winter nights, and as we drove across the Jacques Cartier bridge, he started pulling spins.

"The next time I saw him was closer to the end. I was living with the people on Coloniale, and we'd go up to Mt. Royal and buy smoke, listen to music, and so on."

"Did he seem the same to you then or different?" I asked.

"I did notice a little change in him. He wasn't like before. He wasn't as strong. He was calmed down, more reflective about what he said and who he was dealing with."

"Was he depressed?"

"I wouldn't say he was, just more introverted. But by then he'd gotten into what I called Bas's 'ganja voodoo.' There were a number of Bas's 'experiments' out there."

"Experiments?"

"Kids he really messed up. He was like a Charlie Manson, only less violent. I didn't like him at all. He was a capitalist through and through. He wasn't about peace and love and religioso stuff."

"When was the last time you saw my brother?"

"The night before he died, he brought over bags of groceries, and we had a big dinner. He was very generous, with his money and with groceries. One of the things he talked about was that the doctors at the Douglas were very interested in him, and wanted him to speak to them about LSD."

At last! Someone else to corroborate what we'd been told twenty-seven years ago.

"This interested him," Gordie said, "and he looked forward to it. I remember thinking, 'This is a person who knows what he's talking about.'"

But if he was looking forward to it that much, why would he have killed himself?

"What else do you remember about that night?" I asked.

"Nothing much. We were drinking, smoking joints, talking. Nothing out of the ordinary."

"And then?"

"Everyone went to bed. David was sick. I was up early to go to a job interview. Peter was up, and he sat with Katherine,

David, and me in the kitchen, drinking coffee."

I recalled my mother's telling me that my brother had gotten dressed and eaten breakfast that last morning. It had been one more reason why I'd never accepted his death as a suicide. For who gets dressed, eats breakfast, then goes off and ...

"What was his mood like?" I asked.

"He seemed comfortable," Gordie said, "everything was fine. Katherine and David went back to their room, and Peter went back to the master bedroom. I got my bike and walked to the door, when I heard a choking sound, like a gurgling, very light. I didn't think anything of it and went downstairs.

"When I got back from the interview, there were police everywhere, and Marshall came up to me and said, 'Peter's committed suicide.' I ran into the room. I think your father was there. Detectives were there. I glanced onto the bed, and there was Peter."

"Do you remember how he looked?"

"There was no line of pain on him at all. I went into the kitchen, the police took my name, asked what I did, and so on."

"Did everyone assume it was suicide?"

"Yes."

"Couldn't someone have crept in, killed him, and crept out again?"

"I doubt it. There were the others in the house. And besides, there was no cry of anguish. Only a low gurgle and a wheezing from his throat."

"Did the police give any indication as to what *they* thought might have happened?"

"No, never. At the police station, it was all straight forward. I told them pretty much what I just told you. If it was murder, they would have pursued it harder than they did, believe me."

"Do you recall anything about my brother's having left a note or a letter?"

"I heard he wrote a letter, which was what got Bas out. I always understood that he did this for Bas. Peter was very strong mentally."

"But he'd already signed a declaration at the time of his arrest, stating that everything in the house belonged to him. Why kill himself then?"

"Why he did it is still puzzling. Maybe it was the experience of jail, the drugs. LSD will cripple you, eventually, you know." Then, in his gentle voice, Gordie admitted, "It's kind of nice to talk about it, it helps a little bit. We were all affected by it a lot.

"I didn't like Bas, and I certainly didn't like the police officer, who brought out that book. He called Peter '*un victim de LSD*.'"

So he knew about the book, too. How many of the others had known, and hadn't, for one reason or another, mentioned it to me?

"Did you ever see Bas again?" I asked.

"Once. Katherine, David, and I went to Bas's place after he'd gotten out of jail. He was sitting on the bed, smoking a joint, passing it around, and blabbing away. I found it hard to think. I didn't like the feeling I was getting. He kept intruding in my thoughts. I eventually got up, walked into the living-room, and listened to some music."

I asked him, finally, about Phil.

"The last I knew was that he'd worked for CN or VIA Rail in the early eighties."

It may not have been much, but at least it was something. I jotted the information down, then added Gordie's name to my expanding list.

When I told Norah about Phil, she mentioned that a friend of hers worked for VIA Rail, and that she'd see what he could find out.

"Now, as to the publisher of that book," she said, "the company's still in existence, but the book itself is out of print. And as to any information about the author, you'll have to put your request in writing, and address it to them."

I chose a different, more direct route. I called up a friend of mine, who was, himself, a publisher in Montreal. He described the other publishing house as "low brow," and suggested I contact the Policemen's Brotherhood to see if they had any records on the author of the book.

They didn't, and told me to try the Personnel Department of the MUC. But when the phone rang and rang, and no one answered, I simply hung up.

In the morning, I awoke with a severe case of the chills. A few hours later, still shivering, I tugged a long, brown envelope out of my mail box.

When I noted the return address, *Bureau de Coroner*, I let out a cry and raced, trembling, to the elevators. Even before the doors had closed, I was tearing at the envelope's gummed flap. I slid out a letter and several, long sheets of paper.

He'd done it! The Chief Coroner had released the letter and poem to me.

After so many months, I'd won. I'd gotten some of what I wanted.

But was I ready? Was I prepared for what I might find?

Yes, I thought, yes. No matter how painful, I had to know. I had to know *his* truth, my brother's truth. In his own words, in his own hand. Giving me his own reasons. So that I might finally have the chance to put some of my demons to rest.

"What!?"

I nearly dropped the papers and everything else I was holding.

"I don't believe this!"

Thankfully, I was alone on the elevator, as I laughed out loud, a bitter, incredulous bark of a laugh.

"It can't be," I said, "it just can't be."

I was dumbfounded, shaking my head in utter bewilderment, all the way to my apartment. But when the door closed safely behind me, I let out a shout, "Dammit to hell!"

Then I flung the papers onto the countertop in my kitchen and covered my face with my hands. After all the waiting, all the anguish, and all the hoping ...

It was cruel, too cruel. Like some great, cosmic joke. The absurdity of which was almost too much to absorb.

Peering out from between my fingers at the two photocopied documents on the counter, I knew, with sickened certainty, that I'd never find the truth I wanted.

For the letter, typewritten, unfinished and unsigned, had, obviously been written by David Fowler. As for the poem. It was handwritten, in bold, fat script, most decidedly not my brother's, and signed, "Love, Allan." Allan Lerman.

Why had these two documents, both unrelated to my brother, been kept in a coroner's file for twenty-seven years? And why had Luc Lépine told me *and* written me that their file contained "two letters written by Peter David Berger?"

I was livid. This had all been for nothing. Nothing.

What about the paper Sandy saw? Or said he saw. Wouldn't that have been the one to keep?

I felt as if I were on a seesaw. For every statement, there was a counterstatement. For every certainty, an uncertainty. For every answer, another question. And ifs. There were still too many ifs.

But, strangely enough, the chills were gone. And I was reminded again of the cold I'd felt the night before my brother died. Had I turned cold *this* time because I'd sensed the arrival of the envelope?

Was the psychic connection between us still that strong? Even after death?

I believed, in my heart of hearts, that it was. Just as I believed, more devoutly now than ever, that *because* of our very connectedness, I'd started down the painful path toward our *mutual* liberation.

An hour later, I made two calls. The first was to Allan, the second to David. Both men were stupefied. When he heard the poem, Allan said he probably *had* written it, but asked me to send him a copy to be sure. David, after hearing part of the letter, confirmed that it was indeed his.

Then he and I decided to meet. At the library. He wanted, he said, to see the photograph.

I hesitated at first, uncomfortable with the mere thought of it. Although I'd intended to make photocopies of certain relevant pages of the book, I never had. I hadn't so much as set foot inside the library since that awful day. Nor had I even begun to recover from the shock of what I'd seen there.

"I'll make the copies for you," David volunteered when I
mentioned this to him, and we agreed to meet the next day at three.

Included in that same mail delivery, was a letter from Mark
Bantey. I'd asked him, among other things, to check on the age
of majority in Quebec in 1968, and now I knew.

It was twenty-one. Not eighteen, as Khalil Geagea had
claimed. In releasing my brother without my parents' authorization, the Douglas had, in fact, released a minor.

Just then, the telephone rang, and with the letter still in my
hand, I ran to answer it.

It was a man named Roberto Iuticone from the legal
department of the *Commission d'acces à l'information du
Québec*. He said he'd read through my file and that it would be
a waste of my time to proceed. When I asked him why, he
explained that the law governing a public body's right to keep
information private superceded the Commission's right to get
them to make that information public.

He then asked *me* if I wanted to close the file and I said
no. I'd discuss it with my lawyer and get back to him.

Bantey's opening words, when I reached him, were, "I
have two dates for your hearing before the Commission. You
can have either the thirteenth or the fifteenth of December."

For a moment, I was too taken aback to speak. But after
I'd managed to tell him about Roberto Iuticone, he snapped,
"That's ridiculous, everyone's entitled to a hearing."

He then said they'd located a copy of the book, and that he
was having it delivered to him.

No sooner had I gotten off the phone with Bantey than I
called Yves Laliberté. He said he'd been FAXed his own copies
of the letter and poem, and that he was as surprised as I was. He
promised to speak with Luc Lépine and ask him why he'd told
me the writings were my brother's.

But that wasn't good enough for me. I quickly banged out
a letter to the Office of the Coroner, demanding that, as compensation for their error, I be granted access to the sole, remaining document in my brother's file: the police report.

Seventeen

*I*n reviewing the notes of my conversation with Gordie, I came up with several questions I hadn't thought of before, and called him again. My focus now: the last six days of my brother's life. Beginning with his discharge from the Douglas on Friday, September 20 and ending with his death on Thursday, the 26th.

In an effort to clarify what was still a hazy picture for me, I asked Gordie, among other things, if he'd been present the night when, according to my mother, my brother had delivered an eloquent and impassioned talk on death.

There was a pause, and he apologized for sounding confused and perhaps mixing things up, but, as he reminded me, it was all so long ago. Then, after another pause, he asked, "Do you know Gerry Merchant?"

I told him I didn't.

"He had a place on Esplanade. And I remember his telling me that Peter had started talking about death, and that he'd put his feet together, you know, like in the Crucifixion, and started piercing himself with an old-fashioned can opener."

I swallowed hard. Here was yet another version of that same, macabre story. And when I got off the phone, I had someone new to call.

I was almost glad, though, when I got, not Gerry, but his answering machine. I left a brief message and hung up.

The following afternoon, I focused all of my energy on

meeting David. But I dreaded what I was about to do, and my anxiety level rose accordingly. My trepidation had as much to do with the book as with the man I was going to meet. A man tied more closely, and more personally, to my brother on that fateful day, than anyone else. For my brother had died in *his* flat, in *his* bedroom, on *his* bed, in *his* jacket. And *he* had been the one to find him.

My knees were wobbly, my stomach queasy, as I neared the building I'd carefully avoided for the past eleven days. Pretend it's a blind date, I told myself, and almost managed to laugh.

By three-oh-five, I was convinced he wasn't coming, and began to "what if." What if he'd changed his mind? What if he'd called after I'd left my apartment, and the message was waiting for me on my voice mail? What if the book wasn't there? What if someone had taken it? What if it had been reshelved incorrectly?

By three-ten, I was getting ready to leave. Obviously, he wasn't coming. Then, suddenly, he was there. A tall, slim man with longish, brown hair.

"David?" I held out my hand and he took it, smiling.

I gave him a copy of his letter and we sat awhile inside the lobby, simply talking. Shyly and awkwardly, with all those jagged stops and starts that punctuate the conversation of newly-met strangers. Then we headed for the elevator.

"Are you okay?" he asked as we stepped inside, and I nodded. When all I really wanted to do was run, I forced myself to stand, silent and still, beside him.

Within minutes, we were seated at one of the few, empty tables, the treacherous, little book filling the narrow space between us. Thanks to the tranquilizer I'd taken before I came, my body's responses had slowed to the point of sluggishness. Slowed so much, in fact, that my head no longer felt attached to my body.

"How's your French?" I asked, and David made a face.

I kept my own face averted as he pulled the book toward him and started, slowly, to turn the pages. As he turned them, I asked him various questions, all of which he answered, cautiously and quietly.

"It's probably in the chapter headed LSD," I said, and he continued turning.

"It's on the righthand side, the whole page."

My face was still averted, but I knew. "Do you have it?" I asked, feeling a pang despite my artificially-induced calm.

"I have it."

"Is it him?"

"It's him."

I sucked in some air. "Does the room look familiar?"

"Yes. I can even see the religious sticker that Katherine put on the headboard. But," and he sounded puzzled, "there aren't any sheets on the bed."

"Were there any, or do you think he might have stripped the bed to ... you know ... to keep from ruining them?"

Out of the corner of my eye, I watched him shake his head. "All I remember," he said, "is putting the mattress outside afterward and leaving it there. Finally, we just threw it away."

I ordered my stomach to be still.

"I wonder if they've reversed the picture," he murmured. "I seem to remember him turned the other way ... " His voice trailed off.

"You said he was wearing your jacket, is he?"

"Oh, it's here, all right."

"Do you see a copyright or a credit anywhere near the photograph?" I asked, looking straight ahead of me.

"No, nothing."

"What about on any of the other photos?"

I waited, while he thumbed through the rest of the book.

"No. They all obviously came from police files."

"Is there a bibliography or a list of photo credits at the back of the book?"

Again I waited.

"No."

"Is there anything written under the photograph?"

"Yes."

"Would you read it to me?"

He translated the caption slowly, and the angry bitterness in his tone matched the angry bitterness I felt.

"Bastard," I muttered. "How could he know what was in my brother's mind? How dare he presume."

I waited for the anger to recede, and when it did, the two of us sat together for several minutes in silence. In quiet contemplation. And then, as if from nowhere, I heard myself saying, "I think I can look at it now."

Almost reluctantly, David turned the book around and slid it over to me. I drew in a long, deep breath, and then I looked down.

I felt none of the shock of that first time. None. I was detached, distanced, floating high above what I was seeing. It could have been a picture of anyone. I was, at least for the moment, safe.

I allowed my eyes to travel the page, searching for clues. Murder or suicide? Suicide or murder? Tell me, I implored the figure in the photograph. Tell me and lay the matter to rest once and for all.

To my untrained eye, I had to admit that what I was seeing, did not look like a murder scene. And yet ...

I turned, then, to the front of the book, and read both the brief introduction by the author, and a lengthy interview with him. I appreciated his reasons for writing a book like this. I even approved of its anti-drug message, aimed, as it was, at parents, in the hopes of helping them protect and save their children. But, in using my brother's deathbed photograph, the man had acted indecently and irresponsibly. In the name of doing good, he'd succumbed to sensationalism and sunk as low as any tabloid. In the name of helping some, he'd succeeded only in hurting others.

My brother, misguided though he may have been, hadn't existed in a vacuum. He'd had a life. He'd loved and been loved. He'd had a family. Friends. Schoolmates. Teachers. A wide circle of acquaintances.

To see that photograph was to be scarred forever. And this, I found both indefensible and unforgivable. For how many people had this man, unthinkingly and thoughtlessly, left permanently scarred?

"I think I'll make some photocopies," I said, all but forgetting, in my newly rekindled rage, that David was supposed to do it. I happened, then, to look over at his face. "Are you okay?" I asked.

"Better than a few minutes ago." Smiling wanly, he pushed himself to his feet, and followed me to the nearest machine.

When we were through, we returned to the table and talked awhile longer. Then, on impulse, I reached into my purse and took out my wallet.

"Here," I said.

David glanced at me, questioningly.

"As an antidote to what we've just seen." I held out two small photographs. Both of my brother. "This," I explained, indicating the first one, "was taken when he was in the second grade. Apparently, the teacher said, 'Smile,' and he did."

David looked at the photo and immediately started to grin.

"This one was taken on my wedding day."

"That's the way I remember him," he said, a wistfulness creeping into his voice.

As I slipped the photos back into my wallet, we smiled at each other and shrugged. Then we got up to leave. With the promise to stay in touch, we separated as we'd met, just outside the library's main entrance.

"Wow, a bit of a mind blower there."

That was the message Gerry had left, together with his work number, on my voice mail. But when I called him back, all I got was *his* voice mail. It seemed our game of telephone tag was destined to continue awhile longer.

Digging deep into my own mind for another name from the past, I came up with Ruth Schlossberg. A psychologist and former co-worker of my mother's, she'd conducted a series of psychological tests on my brother when he was sixteen. And, according to my mother, she'd tried — and failed — several times to reach those at the Douglas in charge of my brother's case.

She was extremely sympathetic to my project, and when I asked if she could recall anything about her findings on my

brother, she said, "He showed no signs of psychosis or schizophrenia. He was very bright, but what troubled me was his lack
of judgment and his daredevilishness. He would," she added,
concurring with what others had said, "have run circles around
the people at the Douglas."

As to the way he died, she said, "It wasn't only angry, it
was bizarre."

After speaking with Ruth, I called and left a message for
Joseph St. Denis, telling him about the book, and asking if he'd
known the man who wrote it. I was just putting down the
receiver when the thought suddenly came to me. As crazy as it
seemed, it was as if the photograph had, after twenty-seven
years, made my brother's death real for me. As if seeing him
that way was the first, official proof I'd ever had that he was, in
fact, dead.

In thinking back to how different he'd looked in his coffin,
I could see how easy it would have been for me to believe it
wasn't him. But now, because of that photograph, I'd been
forced, finally, to concede that it was.

Later that afternoon I received a message from St. Denis.
The author of the book, he said, "*was* known to me at the time.
He'd been seconded to the RCMP Drug Unit from the Montreal
police, then went back to the police."

He didn't, however, recall his being there at the drug bust,
and didn't know if he'd taken part in the investigation into my
brother's death. He closed with, "God bless and all that stuff."

I smiled at that, and played the message again, taking care
to record everything he'd told me. Then I took a closer look at
what I'd written down. And what I saw made me gasp. The man
had originally been a Montreal police officer. Could that have
been the connection? Could that have been how he'd known, or
at least known *about* my brother?

My hands tightened into fists. I wanted this man, God, how
I wanted him. I wanted to see him sued. I wanted to see him
punished. But first, I had to find him.

I picked up the trail where I'd left off: with the Personnel

Department of the MUC. Only this time, I waited until someone answered.

I explained to the woman who took my call about the police officer I was trying to find, and gave her whatever data I had on him. To my relief, she decided to be helpful.

Moments later, however, my relief turned to incredulity. According to police records, the man I wanted had died in 1976.

I sat there, appalled and stunned.

"Did he have a family?" the woman asked.

"Yes," I told her.

She suggested I call the Association of Retired Policemen, and gave me their number.

To my utter disbelief, the Association records showed the same thing. He was dead.

I couldn't believe it. My first thought was: good, the bastard, he deserved it. My second was: the poor guy, to have died so young. He was only forty-three.

When I'd recovered somewhat from the blow, I put in my own call to Luc Lépine at the *Centre d'archives* in Montreal.

"What I don't understand," I said when I reached him, "is why you told me the two documents were written by my brother, especially when one of them was signed, 'Love, Allan.'"

"The police obviously thought they were your brother's," he replied, and apologized for his part in the misunderstanding. Then he added, "You know, in getting those documents released, you've made jurisprudence."

Jurisprudence? I'd set a precedent? That gave me pause. And a certain degree of satisfaction. Although *I* may not have gotten exactly what I'd expected or wanted, perhaps now, others would.

Eighteen

I suddenly found myself vacillating. Should I proceed with the hearing before the Commission or let the matter drop? I turned to Norah for advice, who virtually insisted that I proceed.

"Even if nothing comes of it," she said, "you'll never be able to accuse yourself of not having tried *every*thing."

In the end, I agreed with her. I FAXed Bantey my decision and told him that I'd prefer the hearing be held on December 15. Being a Friday, it would give me the weekend in Montreal to tie up some final, loose ends there.

No sooner had I returned from sending the FAX than Allan rang, confirming he *had* written the poem, and that he'd taken it from one of the Psalms. But he couldn't recall *when* he'd written it or how it had even come to be in the room where my brother had died.

I located my copy of the Bible and scanned each psalm until I found it. Psalm 142. A Prayer of David's, when he was in the cave. I compared it with Allan's version, and although I found some differences between them, they weren't marked ones. I put away my Bible and sat down to re-read what Allan had written; only this time, I used a mental magnifying glass to highlight each and every word.

I cry with my voice to the Lord
With my voice, I make supplications to the Lord.

I pour out my complaint before Him

I tell my trouble before Him.

When my spirit is faint
Thou knowest my way;
In the path where I walk
They have hidden a trap for me.

I look to the right and watch,
But there is none who take notice of me;
No refuge remains to me,
No man cares for me.

I cry to thee, O Lord;
I say, Thou art my refuge,
My portion in the land of the living.

Give heed to my cry,
For I am brought very low.

Deliver me from my persecutors,
For they are too strong for me.

Bring me out of prison
That I may give thanks to Thy name;
The righteous will surround me;
For Thou wilt deal bountifully with me.

Certain key phrases glared up at me as if illuminated in irridescent red ink. Could they have been describing the final days of my brother's life? I wondered. And if so, could they also have alluded to his escape from it?

After several more days of telephone tag, Gerry and I finally connected. But it would be a conversation I wished we'd never had.

"I met your brother," he told me, "in the spring of '68. I lived in the Town of Mount Royal, went to Sir George, and hung around downtown at places like the New Penelope and the

Swiss Hut. We were all hippies.

"I remember being so impressed with Peter. I remember reading a paper he'd written on the I Ching for school. It was incredible, and he'd only been seventeen at the time."

I shivered, thinking back to John's strange story about the I Ching.

"Bas was an exotic attraction in this whole scene. He was establishing a kind of white Rasta cult. All these kids were busy putting up pictures of Jesus on the walls of their houses.

"It was intriguing, an adolescent adventure. I went up to the house to smoke, buy some grass. Going over there was like entering a whole different world. But I thought Bas was getting quite weird, setting himself up like an emperor. He surely had them wrapped around his little finger."

"What did he talk about?" I asked.

"He preached Rasta, talked about the herb being the sacrament, and how they had to have it. He also taught that women were submissive. I felt he was basically conning them into smuggling drugs. They were so self-confident; they made no effort to conceal it.

"I was growing pot behind the Fina station in the Town of Mount Royal. I remember one time, when Bas's people had no herb and they were desperate to get some. I offered them some of mine and Bas really appreciated the gesture. He looked at me like I was an indigenous head of Canada."

Girding myself for what was coming next, I said, "Could you tell me about my brother after his release from the Douglas?"

"The word on the street was that he'd escaped. There was a protective barrier around him. Everyone respected him; he was so brilliant.

"I saw him again for the first time, two days before he died, at Peter MacNeill's apartment on Esplanade. I went to see Michael Colvey, and your brother was there."

"Peter ... Michael?" I interrupted, as I scribbled down their names.

"Yeah, Peter's an actor; Michael od'd and died some years ago."

I crossed out Michael's name.

"I didn't know what had happened to your brother," Gerry continued. "He'd been hyper before; he'd had a higher energy level. But when I saw him that night, he seemed to be in a trance, in a very contemplative, melancholic state. It was the day before Bas's birthday and his mission was to get a cake to Bas with herb in it."

Here I stopped him. According to my mother, she and my father had arranged to meet my brother for a picnic, but that he'd kept them waiting for hours while he visited Bas in jail — with a cake — for his birthday. But that had been on Sunday. What Gerry was describing had occurred on Tuesday.

"He wanted us to design a cake to conceal an ounce of dope without it looking like something was inside. He demanded we help him. No matter what we said, he said it wouldn't work. He got frustrated with us, and we were getting frustrated with him. Michael and I went to the kitchen, leaving him in the front of the house, and he came in, and said, 'I need something sharp.'

"He must have noticed our looks, because he said, 'Don't be afraid.' He picked up a paring knife and said, 'I want you to see that I can control my bleeding.'

"I said, 'What do you mean?' He took the knife and nicked his wrist on the bony part, saying, 'Watch.' He held his wrist, and when he released his hand, a little trickle of blood flowed out. He kept repeating, 'Don't be afraid,' and went back to the front part of the house."

I could feel my stomach beginning to churn, and all my muscles tighten.

"Michael and I looked at each other, and I said, 'This is weird. He needs help. What should we do?' It was pretty serious. I didn't know what he was going to do next. We thought the others would come, but they didn't.

"He came back into the kitchen and said, 'I need something sharper.' I said, 'What for, what are you going to do?' And he said, 'Don't be afraid, I'm not going to hurt you.'

"Michael told him to calm down, that everything was cool, but he kept saying, 'Don't be afraid.' I said, 'I'm not afraid,' and he said, 'Yes, you are, I can see you're afraid.'

"There was nothing sharper. Then he said, 'I need something pointier,' and grabbed a manual can opener. I was terrified. For all of us. There was no back door off the kitchen. Michael and I were sitting at the table and Peter was standing. I thought, what the hell is he doing? He went down on one knee, put one foot forward, and put the can opener between his big toe and his second toe, and hammered it in."

I winced and bit down hard on my bottom lip.

"I heard this bang and heard the skin breaking, and he said again, 'Don't be afraid. I am the son of God, don't be afraid.' We kept silent."

"What did he do, take off his shoes and — ?"

"No, he was barefoot, he was barefoot the whole time. Part of their ritual was that you had to take off your shoes before entering the house. The women often helped you do it, like Rasta geishas.

"I thought, I've got to get help, I've got to get out of here. But the phone was disconnected; the bill hadn't been paid. Michael and I stood up. There wasn't much blood. Peter said, 'I feel no pain. You must listen to me.' I said, 'We're listening.' But I thought, is he going to turn on us? He said, 'Don't go. Stay. You must listen to me.'

"We manipulated ourselves around the table and stood in the doorway, and looked at him. We didn't know what he was going to do. He said, 'I can tell by your eyes that you're afraid.' 'I am,' I said, 'I don't understand.'

"He pulled out the can opener and a flood of blood poured out of his foot. It was very melodramatic, him down on one knee and a light bulb shining on him. He said, 'It doesn't hurt' and put the can opener between his next two toes, saying, 'You must listen to me, the children of Canada must listen to me. They smoke too much pot. They interrupt the perfect astral fields. Don't be afraid. I am the son of God. You must listen to me, you must follow me. These tears you see are not tears of pain, they are tears of pleasure. You must listen to me. Don't be afraid.'

"It was like a mantra refrain, the way he kept repeating, 'Don't be afraid.'"

I wrote as quickly as I could, forcing myself not to think, not to hear, not to ingest any of what Gerry was saying.

"Michael and I said, 'What are we going to do?' to one another. Peter then said, 'No, wait.' He stood up and went ahead of us to the front door of the house, and stood there bleeding from his foot. The guy who lived on the third floor started coming down the stairs. Peter looked up at him and smiled, and said, 'Hello.' The man turned around and went back upstairs.

"We said, 'You need help,' and he said, 'I know you're afraid. Don't be. Don't worry about me.'

"We left and tried getting in touch with various people, but nothing happened. I went back the next day and I saw the bloodstains on the steps. Someone said you could follow his footprints all the way to Coloniale Street, there was so much blood.

"He'd obviously flipped out; the question I still ask myself is, how did he snap like that? And that was the last time I saw him."

"Did you tell anyone about the incident?" I asked, still trying to separate truth from hearsay.

"Yes, I told Gordie, Brawley, and other friends."

"What about the people on Coloniale?"

"I didn't really know them."

We talked a moment longer, then said goodbye. I was so shaken, I refused to even look at what I'd written. Refused to let this newest horror shape itself into yet another image for me to combat.

Later would be soon enough.

As I transcribed Gerry's monstrous story onto my computer, I was again astounded by the vividness of his recall. How shocking, how traumatizing the experience must have been for him if, after twenty-seven years, he was still able to relay, word for word, what my brother had said to them that terrible night.

Clearly, something had happened to my brother in the last six days of his life. Something dreadful. Dreadful enough to have altered him completely. Powerful enough to, perhaps, have even driven him mad. But what?

I was reminded of the five "W's" and one "H" of journalism. Who, why, what, when, where, and how. All I knew, so far, was the "who" in this particular situation: my brother. Still missing, were the why, what, when, where and how.

Like the journalist I'd trained to be, I opened to a fresh page in my notebook and drew up a list. Why did he change? What caused him to change? When did the change occur? Where did it occur? How did it occur?

I skipped a few lines and began a second list. Was it a gradual process or did it happen suddenly? Was it due to the accumulated effect of the drugs? Had he, perhaps, taken tainted drugs? Had he experienced a psychotic episode or a series of psychotic episodes? Had he suffered a complete psychotic breakdown? And if he had, was it a factor of his own brain or was it caused by LSD?

Had he become so immersed in mysticism, that he firmly believed whatever he did and said was the real and absolute truth? Was it a combination of the mysticism and the drugs, one aiding and abetting the other? Or was it something far more sinister?

Had he been on the road to madness during his twelve-day stay at the Douglas? If so, why hadn't anyone picked up on it? Or had he succeeded in conning the experts into thinking he was fine? What had happened to change him from someone Lehmann had described as a polite young man, neither psy-chotic, nor suicidal, into some sort of demonic and deluded messiah?

As I re-read what I'd jotted down, I felt a sudden chill. After my brother's death, I'd written several short stories in a vain attempt to exorcise some of my demons. In one of them, a young woman learns the guru who held her brother in thrall has been murdered. She goes to him with the news, certain she'll now be able to convince him to come home with her.

But when she tells him that his god is dead, he looks at her with vacant, staring eyes, and says in a voice as distant as infinity, "*I* am god now."

How could I have forgotten that story? Had I known, or at least suspected his madness then, and unconsciously sup-pressed it?

I hastily re-scrolled the notes on my computer screen.

According to Gerry, my brother had said, "These tears you see are not tears of pain, they are tears of pleasure."

The words were hauntingly familiar. And then I realized why. They were reminiscent of a poem I'd written about my brother, based on something he'd once said to me. I'd entitled it, "And so goodbye."

> do not weep for me —
> share my praise
> with heaven
> and with hell;
> my life begins —
> bring no flowers
> to the grave of my mistakes;
> smile —
> and watch me
> as I begin
> my descent.

Another clue, remembered and suppressed?

I continued with my list of questions. Was it less a case of madness — if indeed he *was* mad — than a rapid process of disintegration, either exacerbated by, or initiated by, the raid, his two days in jail, and those twelve days at the Douglas? Or had the turning point come two days *after* his discharge, on that fateful Sunday afternoon, when he'd met with my parents for the last time?

My mother had described him to me as, "appearing stoned. He was wild-eyed and rambling. He was dirty, his clothes were torn; he looked as if he'd been in a fight."

Was it possible then, as she'd once suggested, that Bas had used my brother's visit to plant in his brain the notion of killing himself? The more I thought about it, the more agitated I became. I immediately rang up Gerry again.

"You said the incident with the can opener took place two days before my brother died, which would have made it a Tuesday, and that the next day was Bas's birthday."

"That's right."

"But according to my mother, my brother brought a cake to Bas in jail on Sunday."

There was silence at the other end of the phone.

"Is it possible that you saw my brother on Saturday, not Tuesday, night?"

"No," Gerry answered. "I wouldn't have been down at MacNeill's on a Saturday night. I would have been out."

"Could it have been Sunday night, then?"

"It could have been, but I doubt it."

I tried to think. In Wilder's account of what was most likely the same incident, my brother had delivered an impassioned talk and supposedly pierced himself with an ice pick on Tuesday night. On Wednesday night, he was eating dinner with the group on Coloniale Street, calmly and contemplatively. On Thursday morning, he was dead.

What didn't fit was the business about the cake. Until Gerry said, "Maybe his attempt to get a cake in to Bas on Sunday had failed, and he wanted to try again."

"Possibly," I admitted. But the precise timing of the incident still remained crucial to me.

If it had occurred on Saturday, it would have been *before* my brother's visit to Bas. That meant the change in him would also have occurred *before* the visit. On the other hand, if it had occurred on either Sunday, Monday or Tuesday, both the incident and the change in him would have occurred *after* the visit.

If, as Gerry was convinced, it had, indeed, happened *after* Sunday, then that infamous visit with Bas was the precise turning point I'd been looking for.

To my mother, at least, it made perfect sense.

"Bas was a man," she said, when I discussed it with her, "a hoodlum, a drug smuggler. How could he take the chance that a nineteen-year-old kid, despite having signed a piece of paper for the RCMP, wouldn't crack under questioning, and turn him in?"

Plausible, I thought. Better to be deported to Jamaica than to face prison in Canada.

If this scenario was true then, my brother would have been launched on his voyage toward death that Sunday. He may have struggled with it at first, causing the agitation and rambling that David had described, then accustomed himself to the idea, and, as Gordie had said, become introverted and *apparently* comfortable.

I agreed it was all plausible, all possible. But was this the way it had actually happened?

Nineteen

*T*he following morning, I placed a call to ACTRA, and asked for their help in locating Peter MacNeill. To my surprise, he now lived in Toronto. I promptly phoned the agency that represented him, and left them my name and number, adding, "Tell him, please, Gerry Merchant suggested I speak to him, and that I'm the sister of ... " and here I hesitated, "Pe ... Pe-ter Berger."

Fifteen minutes later, Peter MacNeill was on the line with me.

"When I first met your brother," he said, "he was a really happy, super guy, really bright. We all went in and out of each other's circles. We could trust each other; we knew none of us was 'the man.'

"Then, all of a sudden, there was Bas, and things were different. The very first time I met Bas, I believed he was evil incarnate. I'd always thought your brother and some of the others had minds of their own, that they were independent thinkers, and wouldn't be susceptible to that kind of thing. They were cynical, and I assumed it would extend to someone like Bas. That's why I was shocked to see them becoming so subservient to him.

"The way they behaved toward him didn't make any sense. He'd snap his fingers and they'd jump to do his bidding. I recall his saying 'beer,' and one of them running to get him a beer, opening it, and giving it to him. He took a sip and threw it on the ground, and someone immediately cleaned it up.

"I was into photography then, and Bas wanted me to take some pictures of him. I said I would. He wore these African kind of robes for the pictures, which I took, but never gave him."

"Why not?"

"Because I couldn't stand him, couldn't stand his arrogance. When I heard about the incident with the can opener, I was angry with Bas; I thought he'd pushed the kids too far."

When I mentioned the possibility of Bas's influence in getting my brother to kill himself, he said, "Absolutely. When I learned about Peter's death, I laid it squarely in the lap of Bas."

That afternoon, I received official notification from the Commission as to the date and time of my hearing: Friday, December 15 at 2 p.m.

I felt an immediate surge of adrenalin as I readied myself for battle. I not only wanted to be prepared, I wanted to be perfectly prepared. Because I not only *wanted* to win the appeal, I *intended* to win it.

I sketched out some introductory remarks on the computer, then began listing the myriad questions to which I needed answers. Answers that could only be found in that all-important, and oh-so-secret file.

The puzzle of my brother's life may have been coming together, but I was beginning to come apart.

I was now, literally, uncomfortable in my skin. Both inside and out. I felt as if I were infested with invisible mites, all of them crawling and scratching and biting at me. I felt frayed and fragmented. Brittle.

Every sensation had become exaggerated, leaving me overly sensitive and overly reactive to almost everything. Half the time, I wanted to lie down and sleep; the other half, I wanted to run. Run from the collection of ghastly, frightening images in my mind. And what they represented.

As a writer, used to living inside my head all day, I'd always needed the evenings to re-establish my connection with the outside world. That need now bordered on the fanatical. I made certain I was busy every night, either culturally or socially.

And although my activities did keep me busy, they didn't keep me occupied.

For no matter what I did or where I went, I never had more than a few minutes respite at any one time. Between the temporariness of each distraction lay one gruesome image or another, waiting to spring. I couldn't escape them, nor, it seemed, could I escape myself. I was trapped.

Trapped by what I'd seen and heard. Trapped by what I'd learned. Trapped inside my own waking nightmare. Trapped by the sound of my voice as it continued to repeat that same, desperate mantra, "Go 'way ... go 'way ... go 'way."

I needed help, and I knew of only one place to get it. From Paul, my therapist. It was time, finally, to let someone in — all the way in — or I'd never see my journey through to completion.

In a series of ongoing sessions, I confided everything I'd been keeping to myself. In return, I received the gentle voice of reason, insight, and support. And although I kept referring to him as "my brother," Paul made a conscious effort to call him by his proper name.

"One way of keeping loved ones alive," Paul told me, "is to talk about them, not hide them."

"That may be," I said, "but I could never do that with my brother."

"Why not?"

"Because I felt that I had to protect him. If I couldn't save him when he was alive, the least I could do was keep him safe in death. You know, my mother always accused me of building a shrine to him. Do you think she was right?"

"Yes," Paul nodded, "I do. Since you weren't prepared to accept the Peter he'd become, you chose to preserve him as the Peter he used to be."

"And now?"

"You've decided that you're finally ready to come to terms with *all* of Peter — the good *and* the bad — not just the parts you'd prefer to hold onto. What you've begun is a process I like to think of as the evolution of conclusions and acceptances."

"But there's one conclusion I'm still having trouble accepting."

"And that is?"

I looked up at the ceiling. "That my brother was a drug dealer. It's so alien to me, so unthinkable. How many sisters from nice, upper middle-class Jewish families, with a long line of rabbis and lawyers behind them, have had to admit something like that?"

When Paul didn't answer me directly, I continued. "I think part of the reason I could never talk about him was because I felt that by talking about him, I was betraying him. Holding him up to contempt, to judgment. Talking about him would have meant talking about what he'd become, and I could never do that to him."

"But you could have said that you had a brother without mentioning that he was a drug dealer, couldn't you?"

I answered with a shrug.

"Don't you think you're confusing things?" Paul continued. "Why would you have been betraying Peter, when it was *you* who'd been betrayed. *Peter* made the choice to take drugs; he also made the choice to sell drugs. If he'd really cared for you and your parents, he wouldn't have done that. His choices may have suited *his* needs, but they didn't suit his family's or society's needs. Now, did they?"

I wanted to rise to my brother's defence, but I simply sat there, saying nothing. What *could* I say? Paul was right. And knowing he was right, made it hurt all the more.

November first was my brother's birthday, and I braced myself for a day of mourning.

At intervals, I was assailed by brief crying jags. Out of nowhere, the pain would build, my eyes would fill, and the tears would stream down my face. The first assault was the worst. And I used it to vent my pain, my grief, and my anger at him directly.

"Damn you," I sobbed as if he were there in the room with me. "Damn you for all the years I've spent mourning you. Damn you for all the years I've spent missing you. Damn you for depriving me of a brother. Damn you for robbing me of a lifelong friend and companion. Damn you for cheating me out of a family, out of a sister-in-law, out of nieces and nephews.

"Damn you for doing this to us. Damn you for hurting our parents, who did nothing but love you and try to help you. Damn you for taking from me the one person I loved most in this world.

"Damn you for abandoning us. Damn you for choosing *him* over us. Damn you for taking the easy way out. Damn you for never thinking of the people you'd be hurting and the mess you'd be leaving behind. Damn you for never saying goodbye. Damn you for never letting us know why. Damn you for condemning me to live the rest of my life without you."

I cried until I'd worn myself out. Then, as I waited for the pain to subside, I thought about what I'd just said. And there it was. Like the lines connecting the dots in a child's puzzle book, this particular diagram was nearing completion. But I knew that both the diagram and I still had a ways yet to go.

I went back then, over all of my interviews, looking for discrepancies as well as similarities, and searching for any holes that hadn't yet been plugged. Then I wrote down the names of those I needed to call again, for the sole purpose of clarifying the time frame of my brother's final, six days.

I began with David.

"Can you recall," I asked, "precisely when my brother came to stay with you? Was it immediately after the Douglas, or just for the last, few days?"

"I think it was just those last, few days; he felt safe with us."

When I asked him about the incident with the can opener, he said, "That does sound familiar. I remember sitting in the dining-room and Peter coming in and raving about his indestructibility. He was tying it in with the business of the stigmata. I remember thinking he'd gone too far for my comfort level. But then, when he did away with himself, he *really* went too far."

"Do you recall seeing any bloody footprints anywhere?"

"No."

"Any blood between his fingers?"

"That sounds familiar."

When I presented my theory about his having snapped that Sunday, David disagreed.

"I suggest the change in him started earlier, *before* the Douglas. He'd become more vocally self-centred, everything was 'Bas and I,' as if they were leading a spiritual revolution of sorts."

"And then it became 'I.'"

"Yes. He took over from Bas, and I don't believe it was a responsibility he particularly relished." Then he added, "I wish my memory was clearer on everything. I know it's all there somewhere; I'm sure if I was hypnotized, I'd get to it, but ... "

He left the thought unfinished.

The following day, I spoke to Bantey about the hearing.

"At first glance," he said, "it doesn't look good. But we're looking for loopholes in the law."

I felt a sinking in the pit of my stomach. "Did you see the book?" I asked.

"I did."

"And? If the author was still alive, would I have grounds for legal action against him and his publisher?"

"You would, but, at this late date, I wouldn't advise proceeding with any kind of suit. It's not like it is in the States. Now, basically, you'd just be putting money in your lawyer's pocket."

I swallowed my frustration, but none of my outrage. I wasn't finished with either matter. Not by a long shot.

I spoke with Gerry again, and we worked to determine when, precisely, the incident with the can opener had occurred.

"It could have been Sunday night," he admitted upon reflection, "because it was so quiet."

"Were you on LSD at the time?" I asked him.

"No."

"Was my brother?"

"I can't say about him. All I know was LSD scared me. Once, when I took it, I thought I was an Indian for two days.

"When I saw Peter that night, I thought he was that way

because he'd been busted, and because the whole Bas thing was disintegrating. I thought he'd had a breakdown. I didn't know he was on all kinds of drugs."

When I commented on his astonishing recall, Gerry said, "I have a pretty acute memory for lots of things. But it was such an impressionable event, especially the violent part. It was very serious and very dramatic, like watching a play that you're trying to be the audience for, but can't be, because you're drawn into it."

As to my brother's seemingly normal behaviour at the Douglas?

"I call it multi-tracking. That's when some people are capable of turning off one part of their mind and acting normal, even on drugs."

While I was transcribing this latest information, Roberto Iuticone called a second time, and asked — again — if I wanted him to close his file on me.

"Absolutely not," I told him, puzzled by his persistence in trying to get me to abandon my appeal. Then, rather smugly, I added, "As a matter of fact, I've been given a hearing date."

"I didn't know that," he said, sounding surprised. He then proceeded to explain — for the second time — the uselessness of proceeding, and said if he'd felt there was the slightest chance, he would have spoken to the Douglas himself.

"Then why don't you do it now?" I asked.

"Because, as I told you, the law is on *their* side, not the Commission's."

"My attorney's looking into the matter," I said, "and he'll let me know whether he thinks I should proceed or not. But even if he thinks I have no hope of winning, I might proceed anyway."

"Why?"

I found myself echoing Norah's words. "So that I can never say I didn't try *every*thing."

"And that is your decision then."

"As I said, I'm waiting to speak with my attorney."

Annoyed and slightly suspicious now, I called Bantey and told him about Iuticone's call.

"The man's supposed to be impartial," he said. "He shouldn't be badgering you like this. If he calls again, refer him to me."

"Do you think you should speak with someone at the Commission," I asked, "perhaps even lodge a formal complaint?"

"No, I do a lot of work with them. I don't want to antagonize anyone."

"Maybe if they knew I was being harassed, they'd look more favourably on my appeal ... you know, show me some mercy."

But Bantey just laughed and said, "I'm afraid it doesn't work that way."

Over the weekend, I continued with my phone calls.

Heather, to our mutual regret, offered little further in the way of help. She had no recollection whatsoever of what I'd always termed my brother's "do not fear death" talk or the "can opener" incident. Nor could she recall whether she'd seen any blood on my brother's hands or feet.

Sadly, she said, "He was an extraordinary being; he gave off a lot of energy. What I do recall is one evening his holding court, all of us sitting around after having eaten, all of us having a warm and wonderful time.

"It was such a trauma. Probably, as you get separated from the event, you fill in things that didn't happen. I remember just being mystified as to why he'd do such a terrible thing to himself."

Gordie concurred with David, saying that my brother had stayed with them on Coloniale for only two or three days. When I questioned him about the "can opener" incident, he said he'd learned of it only years afterward from Gerry. As to the "do not fear death" talk, he couldn't be specific, saying only, "He would have talked about it. Given the time, everyone was on *The Tibetan Book of the Dead* wagon."

I waited until eleven, then called Marshall in Vancouver.

Once again, he had very few answers for me, but he did offer me some further insight into the scene at the time.

"I wanted to be in the inner circle of people who knew Bas," he said, "but he never seemed to notice me. I remember feeling threatened by him, though. There was this whole Jesus connection. Bas claimed to be Jesus and all those around him were like little Jesuses.

"He bought into the notion of Jesus, that you became one with the lamb, with Jesus, by smoking ganja. 'Lamb's body,' 'lamb's breath' were names they used for it.

"There was the feeling that the body ties you down and that the earth's a suffering place of existence."

As for my brother's death?

"He made that choice himself. To him, it was a freeing of the spirit, which could live without the body.

"The sixties was a time to create new ways to go about being, travel to India, go to the forests, go inside your head. We were the children of peace and love, up until Charles Manson. I felt I talked about serious, philosophical things. How foolish it all is now, looking back. At seventeen, I thought I knew everything. That's the artistic ego for you."

"You mentioned waking up in the night," I said, "and hearing a gurgle coming from the master bedroom. But my brother died in the morning. Can you explain that?"

"Because I played in a band, it could have been the morning. I used to get up several times a night to go to the bathroom."

"You also mentioned hearing that my brother had left a note saying he'd done it as a sacrifice to Bas. Do you think whoever told you this was confusing the note with the *declaration* my brother had signed at RCMP headquarters?"

"Possibly."

That wasn't quite the answer I'd been hoping for, but it was all I got.

Twenty

I'd come to think of my quest as a leaky hose. Plug a leak in one section, and a fresh leak springs up in another. Plug that one, and another springs up somewhere else, and so on, and so on. What I wanted now, was to seal as many of those leaks as possible.

I began with the biggest one: the book. And the connection between my brother and the man who'd written it.

I studied the photocopies I'd made and found a clue. The numbers of the two police stations where he'd once worked.

If my brother had lived — and died — in either precinct, it seemed logical, as well as logistically feasible, that the author of the book *could* have participated in either the drug bust or the investigation into his death. Or both. If nothing else, it would at least have put him closer to the source of those police photographs.

I'd simply phone both stations, and ask if anyone remembered working with him or knew of someone else who might.

But when I spoke to the Personnel Department of the MUC, I was told that one station number no longer existed, while the other now combined two different precincts altogether.

Dead end.

It had been two weeks since I'd sent that second letter to the Office of the Coroner in Quebec. I decided it was long enough. I left my name and file number with the secretary, who said the Chief Coroner would call me in the morning.

He called that afternoon.

Pierre Trahan had a strange voice, hoarse with a pronounced rasp, but his tone couldn't have been gentler, his manner kinder.

He'd spoken with Luc Lépine, he said, who'd confirmed what I'd already told him about the two documents, and that he'd asked for a copy of the police report to be sent to him.

My hopes soared. "Then you'll release it me?" I cried.

"Oh no," he said. "I don't have the authority to do that."

"But you released the letters to me."

"That was within my jurisdiction. Only the Minister of Public Security has the authority to release the police report to you."

My hopes were already sinking when I heard him say, "You mentioned that you had a copy of the coroner's report?"

"Yes."

"I'll tell you what to do then. Send me a copy of the report, together with a letter to the Minister. Tell him that you were never satisfied with the findings of your brother's death, and that you're investigating it. Just a few sentences to let him know why you want this particular report. And I'll send it on to him."

My hopes rebounded instantly.

"It may take several weeks," he cautioned, "but he *will* answer you."

"When you receive the police report, are you going to read it?" I asked.

"Oh yes, I'm very curious now."

"Will you tell me what the report says?" I asked him.

"Oh no, *madame*, I cannot do that."

I immediately changed tactics. "Will the report contain the names of the investigating officers?"

"Oh yes."

"Could you do me a favour, then?" I told him about the book and the illegal use of my brother's photograph. "I want to know if the name of the man who wrote that book is on the report."

I must have touched a chord in him because he said, "Give me his name and I'll let you know."

For the first time in a long time, I hung up after a conversation with a tiny bubble of joy inside me.

As much as I dreaded it, I finally discussed the matter of the photograph with my mother.

"If an RCMP officer was writing a book and needed photographs," she said, "he'd know where to get them. How many suicides could there have been like that in those days? Not very many. Don't forget, it was the *beginning* of the drug act. Besides, how large would the narcotics division have been then? It would have been small, not like today.

"I think you're wasting your time on this. What difference does it make *how* he got that photo. You're doing this because you feel punitive, but I don't know what purpose it'll serve."

"I have a right to feel punitive," I replied, more heatedly than I'd intended. "I'm angry, damned angry. My brother was violated, and I'm his only defender. If that man was still alive, I'd have grounds for a lawsuit. There's not much I can do with a dead man, though. All I *can* do is what I'm already doing. And that's using my ingenuity to find ways of getting the answers I want."

"Which are?"

"Was he involved in the drug raid? Was he involved in the investigation into my brother's death? If he wasn't, how did he know about the photos? Did he just announce that he was writing a book on drugs and needed some ghoulish shots of a dead hippie to make his case, and someone simply handed them to him?"

"It was probably something like that."

"Then I want to know *who* he asked, and *who* came up with the file. I want to know how he could have dared use that photo without our written consent. Wasn't he afraid of reprisals or did he think that because he was an RCMP officer, he was above the law?"

"And what will those answers give you in the long run?" she asked.

"Just that. Answers."

"Is this for you or the book you're writing?"

"Both, mom. I *am* the book."

Like a dog with a bone, I refused to let it go.

I phoned the Personnel Department of the MUC again and asked if they had a Public Relations Department. They did. When I told the young woman who took my call that I needed information dating back to 1968, she laughed and said, "I was born that year."

Then she suggested I speak with Jean-Marc de Nobilé, Captain of Detectives, who'd joined the force in '69.

Within moments, he was on the line, open and affable. He admitted having heard of the man who'd written the book, but could tell me nothing more. I asked him then, about the drug squad itself.

"In 1968," he said, "the drug squad was under the responsibility of the Youth Section."

"Would they have assisted the RCMP in any drug raids?"

"If the RCMP wanted help in a major raid, they could have called them. But if it was a small bust, they might have just called a patrol car for back-up."

"Could you explain the procedure that's followed when the police receive a phone call reporting a suspicious death?"

"When a body is found, patrol officers from the nearest station arrive on the scene. They don't touch anything. One of them calls homicide, who immediately sends over an investigative team."

"Who takes the photographs?"

"Photos and fingerprints are taken by someone from the ID section."

"And what happens with papers, personal effects, and so on?"

"They're picked up from the scene by ID and homicide."

"Where do the photographs go?"

"To homicide, where they're put in a file. Copies are sent to the coroner's office."

"What happens to the file?"

"It's kept in the Police Archives."

I gave him the location of the house where my brother had died, and asked which police station would have investigated the death. After thinking about it a moment, he said, "Station 17."

"How do you think this man may have gotten hold of the photograph of my brother?" I asked.

"He may have had a friend in the coroner's office. There was always a liaison between the police and the coroner. Or he could have just asked if there were photos on a drug-related death. He would have had access to the information bank."

"What's that?"

"Whenever someone was arrested or accused of a crime, a card was made. An officer could call up, give the event and the arrest number, and find out about the person. Then he could call the investigator involved, question him about it, and get all the information he needed."

He then recommended I contact Assistant Police Director Dalzel, who'd been on the force in '68, and gave me his number.

When I asked the Assistant Police Director if he knew the author of the book, he replied simply, "He's dead."

"Do you recall how he died?" I asked.

"I think it was in a car accident."

"Did you ever work with him?"

"I worked in the unit next to his at Police headquarters."

My heart gave an expectant leap. "In what capacity was he working at the time?"

"He was acting as liaison between the Montreal Police and the RCMP Narcotics division."

Similar to what St. Denis had said, but clearer now. Bringing him closer, that much closer, to my brother.

When I mentioned his use of my brother's deathbed photo in his book, Dalzel said the photos would have been police property, and that, in his opinion, they weren't to be used for personal gain.

Fueled by the facts I was gathering, I pressed on. Once

again, I found myself calling the Association of Retired Policemen in Montreal, this time to ask if the man's widow was still
alive. She was. I said that I wanted to discuss her late husband's
book with her, and left them my name and number.

What are the chances she'll ever call me? I mumbled to
myself as I returned to my computer.

Within the hour, my telephone rang.

The woman identified herself as the man's daughter
Louise. Her mother, she explained, spoke no English, and had
asked her to call me.

I hadn't even rehearsed what I'd to say to the wife, let alone
the daughter. I'd simply gambled blindly. And now ...

Picking up my clipboard, I tried to keep the quaver out of
my voice as I hastily put together a story that was as close to
the truth as possible. I explained that I was writing a book on
the sixties in Montreal, with emphasis on the drug scene from
both sides of the law, and that in my research, I'd come across
her late father's book.

"I understand your father acted as liaison between the
Montreal Police and the RCMP Narcotics division," I said,
treading carefully. But Louise seemed more than willing to talk.

"He took a degree in drugs in the U.S.," she explained,
"and because of his background, he was the first to see the need
for a drug team in Montreal. If you're interested, we have press
clippings on him from 1956 to 1976."

There was such pride in her voice, I felt like a heel. But I
continued nonetheless. When I asked about the sources for his
book, she said, "They were all people on whose cases he'd
worked or people he'd arrested."

"Did he get the photographs for the book from police
files?"

"Yes."

"Did he get permission to use them?"

She laughed and said, "I hope so. But I don't know about
the law concerning the use of photographs back then."

My heart was racing now, and I had to close my eyes to
get the next words out. "I'm particularly interested," I said, "in
the chapter on LSD. In it, there's a photo of a young man lying

dead on a bed. Would you know if this was a case your father had worked on?"

"No, I don't."

Tears of disappointment stung the backs of my eyelids. "I'm curious about the press clippings on your father," I hurried on, not knowing how else to proceed, "especially any that may pertain to his book."

"You'll have to come to Montreal to see them," Louise replied. "My mother won't let them out of the family."

"I'm working with someone in Montreal. If I sent her in my place, would she be able to make photocopies of the relevant material for me?"

"Oh yes."

I gave her Norah's name and number, then quickly turned the conversation around again. "Tell me, did your father have an agent?"

"No, he did this on his own."

"Was the distribution for the book Canada-wide or only in Quebec?"

"I don't remember. I was thirteen at the time." Then, after a slight pause, she said, "He had a partner who worked with him on the road, but I don't know if he's still alive. I'll try to find someone who worked with him back then."

I thanked Louise for her help and hung up feeling slightly giddy. And just the tiniest bit guilty.

In the evening, I relayed everything to a duly impressed Norah, who said, "I never would have thought of going to the family."

"Are you all right with this?" I asked. "Because if you're not, I want to know. I need you to be honest with me."

"I'm fine, really. My only concern is that I might blurt something out. And," here she hesitated, "I have some misgivings about misleading Louise."

"As to the first, let her talk about her father; don't volunteer anything. As to the second, believe me, I'm not out to hurt her or her mother in any way. They had nothing to do with what *he* did. All I want from her is information."

"All right then, what is it you want to know?"

"Did her father have a file on my brother? Did he work on either the drug raid or the investigation into my brother's death? How did he gain access to the photograph? Did he get anyone's permission to use it? If so, whose? Or did he knowingly use it without permission? Is any of this documented anywhere? Did he keep notes on his book, research, jottings, those sorts of things?"

"What if she has to check to see if there *is* a specific file?" Norah asked. "She'll need a name. I'll have to give her Peter's. Won't she be suspicious then, when she realizes it's the same last name as yours?"

I hadn't thought about that aspect of it; I hadn't had time.

"I'm sure she's already suspicious," I said. "Don't forget, I did mention that particular photograph to her."

I could feel the wheels in my brain turning as I was forced to think about everything now.

"All right, then. If she says something, you can admit that he was my brother, and that his death, together with the prolif-eration of drug use among today's youth, were the reasons for my writing my own book. Then, all we can do is pray that she won't get defensive and refuse to help us."

It was, we both agreed, the only way.

Three days later, Norah called to say that she'd spoken with Louise, and that they'd agreed to meet for lunch in a few weeks.

"We're both busy until then," she explained apologetically.

"Not to worry," I assured her, in spite of my disappoint-ment.

"I asked if she had any copies of the book to sell and she said no, she only has hers. Then, when I mentioned I'd want to ask her some questions, she seemed rather surprised."

I could feel the ice beneath our feet growing thinner.

"Oh well," I sighed, "I guess we'll just have to wait and see what happens."

Twenty-one

"*A*re you able to call him Peter yet?" Paul asked at our next session.

I shook my head.

"Why not?"

"Because his name still conjures up only the blackness. All the dark and awful things. All the horrors. I'd gotten too close to him toward the end, too close to the situation, and I was too much on his side.

"I was caught in the middle, you see. Even though I disapproved of what he was doing, and even though it frightened me, we were siblings, part of the same generation. My parents were part of that other generation. The classic 'us' against 'them.' And I truly believed my first loyalty was to my brother. It may have been wrong, but I couldn't help myself. I loved him too much."

That loyalty, according to my mother, was the reason they hadn't told me about their plan to commit my brother to the Douglas; they thought I'd warn him.

I recalled with graphic clarity, my shock when I learned of his arrest. Of his hospitalization. Of his release.

I recalled my frantic attempts to reach him by phone at the house on Mt. Royal, and how I never got an answer.

I recalled my mounting panic as I repeatedly bombarded my poor parents with the same, desperate question: "Where is he? ... Where is he? ... Where is he?"

"You know," I told Paul, "I'd never thought of myself as an angry person. But after my brother died, I became angry. And it seems I've been angry ever since."

"You should have directed that anger at Peter," Paul said, "for what he did to you, to your family, to your family's reputation, but most of all, to himself. It was a terrible waste of a life that didn't need to be wasted.

"But you shut off your anger prematurely. There should have been a natural evolution to the process, but you put on the brakes to protect yourself psychically. In order to heal, you would have had to accept the dichotomy of him, accept that part of him was good and part of him was bad, and you simply couldn't do that. So, you froze everything. You closed down the entire healing process and went into denial."

"But tied up with the anger," I said, "is the mourning." I told him then, what I'd always told my mother. That I'd have taken my brother any way I could — in prison, in a mental institution, anything — if it meant his still being alive.

Paul, however, disagreed. "What you're mourning is the *fantasy* of what life would have been like had Peter lived. In your fantasy, you'd have taken care of him no matter what. You'd have gotten him off drugs and gotten him to straighten out. Then, once that happened, you'd have gone on to have a good life together.

"But that wouldn't have been the *reality* of it had Peter lived. If someone's that tortured, that much on a one-way path to self-destruction, no one can save him. Would you really have wanted to go through the agony of seeing someone you loved, alive, but tortured?"

"No." I shrugged. "I guess not."

"Do you have any idea what it's like for the family of a person who bounces from one crisis to another? Would you truly have wanted to live like that, or have your parents live like that, going from one upheaval to the next?"

"Logically, the answer is no," I said. "But emotionally, there's this little voice that keeps whispering, 'Yes, God, yes. Anything to have him with me.'"

* * * *

A few days later, I got a call from Pierre Trahan.

"I've received the copy of the police investigation report," he said. "The name you asked about does *not* appear on the report. It was signed by a Sergeant Detective R. Lévesque."

I quickly started making notes. Then I took a chance. I began asking him questions, which, to my utter astonishment, he proceeded to answer.

"The report," he told me, "mentioned the two letters, but never said they were your brother's. It said they were found on the desk near the bed, and that he was sleeping in David Fowler's bedroom. One letter was written by David Fowler, the other by Allan Lerman. They took them and gave them to the coroner thinking that maybe your brother had read them, and had been influenced by them. I don't know why *monsieur* Lépine said they were written by your brother."

"Did the report mention anyone's finding a piece of paper with the instructions, 'Read *The Tibetan Book of the Dead*' on it?" I asked.

"No."

"And the conclusion of the report?"

"The conclusion was suicide. It said the position of the body, the knife, and the hands were an indication more of suicide than murder."

"Was there any mention of a toxicology report?"

"No."

He then told me about the declarations given to the police by everyone at the house at the time of my brother's death. The ones that most concerned me, I said, were Gordie's and David's.

"According to Gordie," he read, "at 7:30 a.m., Peter Berger had breakfast with him and Thomas Garan, and that he looked normal. After breakfast, Peter went back to the bedroom. When he, Gordie, left the house, the door was open, and Peter was sitting on the bed, looking '*soucieux*' ... "

"Anxious or worried."

"Yes, worried."

"So, at that point he was still alive."

"Yes."

"And David's statement?"

"He got up at 9:55 a.m. and went to the bedroom. The door was closed. He opened the door and saw Peter dead." After a brief pause, he added, "You know that he was supposed to appear in court that morning."

"Yes, I know. I suppose that could have been a reason to kill himself."

Trahan agreed. Then he told me that he'd be sending off my letter and a copy of the report to the Ministry of Public Security.

"I feel certain they'll release the report to you," he said, "although I'm not so sure about the declarations. But call me again if you don't hear from them soon."

Could he hear the depth of my gratitude in my voice? I wondered, as I thanked him, not once, but three times.

He must have, for his final words to me were, "I'm just doing my job, *madame*."

To my surprise, I received a call that same evening from Marshall in Vancouver. He told me that he'd run into another friend from the old days, Oscar Sanchez, who'd said I should contact him because, in his own words, "he knew the whole story."

I couldn't believe it. Another witness. I thought immediately of my image of the leaky hose. Plug one leak and up springs another.

After a half-hour of busy signals, I finally reached him.

"I always thought Peter was his own man," Oscar said, "an in-charge kind of guy. His attitude was almost megolomaniacal though, because he was making all this cash. Once he burned a one-hundred-dollar bill to show how powerful he was.

"I remember being in a car with him and doing doughnuts on Decarie to prove he was fearless. He was always challenging. Everything was always a fencing match, back and forth, back and forth.

"Bas was one of those with a persona and intensity that one can see as mysticism or spirituality. He had a deep, orating voice, and the ability to see right through you. He was a 'downtown' Rasta kind of guy, trafficking in weed because it was cash, and," he added, his tone sarcastic now, "the herb of wisdom."

"Do you know anything about the drug bust?" I asked him.

"I heard they'd imported some furniture stuffed with grass, but hadn't received it. Bas and some others went out to the airport and raised a ruckus, spouting curses, saying the Lord would strike them down, and talking about Babylon, and so on. This attracted the attention of the police, who checked the furniture out, and that was the reason for the bust."

I frowned; I'd never heard this particular version before.

"Who told you about the furniture?" I asked.

"Phil."

The one witness I really wanted and couldn't find.

"He was the pick-up guy," Oscar said. "But they were always inflating what they did, making out like they were big and bad."

And then, out of nowhere, he stated, "I heard Bas turned on Peter."

"What!"

"When he was questioned, he blamed Peter, ratted on him, fingering him as the mastermind of the operation. I heard Peter was heartbroken, disappointed, furious with him. He couldn't believe Bas had turned on him and turned him in to the police. He was distraught. He'd bought into the spiritual package, subsidized the guy and his family, everything. Apparently, he left a suicide note cursing Bas."

There it was again. The note that no one but Sandy had ever seen. The note neither mentioned in the police report, nor contained in the coroner's file. Now with a different twist. Not an exoneration of Bas, but a curse on him.

"I made a trip to Jamaica, I think it was in January of '69," Oscar continued. "I knew some Rastas who knew Bas from Montego Bay, and they all spoke kindly of him. I asked about him to see if they'd heard about his having pulled a number on this guy. And I was told he'd died the week before of a brain hemorrhage."

I groaned as I wrote this down. What *was* the truth, I wondered, the real truth? Like the game, broken telephone, there were too many people involved, too many filters, too many years gone by.

I asked him then, about Phil, and to my surprise, he said, "I saw Phil around six years ago."

The gap, at least, was closing.

"But if anyone would know whether Phil was alive or dead, and where he might be, it's Jean Vien."

"And where would I find him?"

"I don't know for certain, but he always gets in touch with Brawley. He could probably tell you more."

Once again, I found myself speaking to Brawley, who amazed me when he said that Jean was currently staying upstairs with his landlady.

I immediately tried the number he gave me, and left a message for Jean on the woman's answering machine. We didn't connect, however, until a few days later, when I called again.

"I met Bas twice," Jean told me, "and I didn't like the guy. There was a cruelty about him. But he was an important influence on Peter. His jive was so good, it came off.

"The last few weeks before the bust, the mood around the place was grim. A lot of them didn't like Bas anymore. And there were all these other, small groups around, dealing drugs, very entrepreneur-oriented.

"My partner and I were busted the same night the others were. Phil and Peter and Bas, and my partner and I, were all in the same holding tank together."

My jaw dropped.

"I looked at Phil and he looked at me and I said, 'Hey, Phil, what are you doing here?'

"The atmosphere was that Bas would be innocent, and Peter and Phil would take the rap. Bas would go free. Peter decided Bas couldn't take the beef, he couldn't go to jail. I said, 'What do you want to take the beef for?' And he kept saying, 'He can't go to jail. It's Bas, it's Bas.' Bas even flashed a peace sign at me."

Whose truth was I to believe? I wondered. I mentioned what Oscar had told me, and Jean said it was all part of the rumours he, too, had heard.

"How was my brother's mood?" I asked.

"He was very calm, not erratic; he was just concerned about Bas."

"Would my brother have gone to jail?"

"Yes, for a short time. You got eighteen months to two years, just for an ounce of grass then. Or if you came from a good family, they'd send you to the Douglas, where you'd walk out and mess up again."

I winced at that, but kept on writing. Then, finally, I asked about Phil.

"I ran into him three or four years ago in a bar in Montreal. He'd cleaned up his act, and was working for either Abbott or Sandoz."

"A drug company, how appropriate," I noted snidely. "What did he look like?"

"Tall, thin, mustache, beard, dark brown hair. Arrogant."

"Do you have any idea where he might be now?"

"None. It was just one of those things. He just popped up. But his brother, Mike, still lives in Baie Comeau."

As soon as I hung up, I dialed Baie Comeau Information, and gave the operator six different spellings for Mike's last name. Of the six, only one had any listings under it at all: two Michels and one M.

I tried all three.

The first was a woman. The second was the wrong Michel. The third number was no longer in service.

In the morning, I called the Personnel Departments of both drug companies, and once again, came up emptyhanded.

I phoned Bantey next. He told me that one of the law students in their office had researched the matter, and concluded that my chances of winning the appeal were slim. But he said that he'd review everything, and get back to me.

I fought the sense of frustration building inside me and called Pierre Trahan again.

"Did Thomas Garan give the police a declaration?" I asked.

"Yes. He said that after breakfast he went back to bed. When he woke up again, everything had happened."

"Does anyone, in any declaration, give an opinion as to why my brother might have committed suicide?"

"No."

"Is there any mention of the night before he died?"

"No."

"Is there any mention of the name Bas? Or Basil Hawthorne?"

"No."

"Is there any mention of my brother's having given a talk on death?"

"No."

"Does it mention the number of Sergeant Detective Lévesque's station?"

"Station 17."

De Nobilé was right; it *had* been Station 17.

"In the report, Lévesque says he interrogated seven people: David Fowler, Gordie Fulton, Thomas Garan, Marlene Vaughn, Heather McLaren, Marshall Hopkins, and Allan Lerman."

I'd talked with five of the seven: David, Gordie, Heather, Marshall, and Allan.

Marlene was John Shore's wife. Should I have spoken to her when I'd spoken to John? I made a note to myself to consider calling them again. And as for Thomas, no one had ever even *mentioned* him to me.

"If this had been your case," I asked Trahan, "would you have concluded it was a suicide?"

"I've seen other deaths like this over the years," he replied, "although it's not a common way to die. In one instance, someone even stabbed himself five times."

And on that grisly note, we ended our latest conversation.

Twenty-two

I placed another call to the Association of Retired Policemen and asked them about a Sergeant Detective R. Lévesque, who'd worked out of Station 17 in 1968. I was told they'd check through their old cards, and let me know.

No sooner had I put down the phone than Bantey called. *His* opinion of my chances of winning the appeal?

"Sixty-forty in your favour," he said.

I let out a whoop. "I'll take it!"

He laughed. "The burden of proof is on the Douglas as to why you *shouldn't* get the file." Then he added, "The aspect of the law we're trying has never really been tested before."

"And what's that?"

"It would have been better if your mother had filed the petition," he explained, "but if she gives you Power of Attorney, we'll argue that your parents held parental authority over your brother when he died, because he was a minor. And that their parental authority entitles them to have access to his file.

"I'd be very happy to represent you," he continued, "but you don't really need a lawyer at the hearing. The Commission usually bends over backwards for citizens without lawyers. Or I could send someone else from the office, who's younger and less expensive."

"And less experienced," I said. "No thanks. You're known to the Commission, and since I've come this far with you, I don't want to do anything to mess up now. I want *you* to represent me."

We agreed then, to meet at his office an hour before the hearing, which he said shouldn't last more than a half-hour or so.

"What's the procedure?" I asked, already anxious. "Who's there? Is it just a few of us? Big room, small room ... ?"

"It's you, myself, the Commissioner, and the lawyer for the Douglas, seated around a table in a small room."

"Does the Commissioner rule on the matter then and there, or take everything under advisement?"

"Everything's taken under advisement and a decision rendered. It could take anywhere from a few weeks to a few months."

"And if we lose?"

"We can appeal, given the permission of the court."

"I think I need a drink," I told him.

Bantey chuckled. "It's not even noon yet."

"That's okay. I'm a writer, remember? We're supposed to have a licence to do these kinds of things."

He said that he'd courier me a draft of the letter he wanted my mother to write, as well as the notes from the staff researcher, and we hung up.

On wobbly legs, I went to the refrigerator and poured myself some white wine.

"To winning." I raised my glass in a toast, then took a sip, as tears welled up in my eyes.

The journey was drawing to a close. Just a few more hurdles to leap — and conquer — and we'd be there.

"To us, my brother." I took another sip, and the tears rolled slowly down my cheeks.

That evening, as I was getting ready to leave for a concert, the telephone rang.

It was former Sergeant Detective Lévesque!

I sat down hard in my slipper chair, and grabbed a piece of paper from the pad on the console table.

"I understand you wanted to speak to me," he said, and I nodded dumbly, as if he could see.

He confirmed that he'd worked at Station 17 in 1968, and

may have investigated my brother's death, but couldn't recall a thing about it. He apologized as I fed him various details, but said he still couldn't remember. I then asked if he'd known the author of the book.

"I had business with him at times, but never worked with him."

Still looking for that vital, missing link, I asked, "Would the RCMP have anything to do with the death of someone they'd recently arrested on drug charges?"

"They would have been called," Lévesque said, "or at least advised."

And that, unfortunately, was that.

The documents arrived from Bantey, and I immediately sat down to read them and make notes. Then I booked a train to Montreal — leaving Thursday morning and returning Saturday night — as well as a hotel room for Thursday and Friday nights.

Over the weekend, I phoned Gordie again, and told him that, according to the police report, he'd had breakfast that last morning, not with David and Katherine, but with a Thomas Garan. To my disappointment, he said he couldn't remember anyone by that name.

Next, I called David. I told him about the hearing and asked him for the precise location of the house on Coloniale Street. Then I asked about Thomas Garan. Like Gordie, he didn't remember him either, and I instantly became suspicious.

Who was this Thomas, and why didn't anyone remember him? Could he have had something to do with my brother's death?

The image of someone creeping in, doing the deed, then creeping out again, resurfaced in my mind and refused to fade. Was it that unlikely a scenario? I asked myself. There *had* been a window of opportunity between the time Gordie left the house and the time David discovered the body. And there *were* several conflicting versions as to when, precisely, my brother's last gasps of life had been heard.

How could I be expected to accept his death as a suicide

if these kinds of questions kept popping up?

And speaking of questions ...

I immediately dialed Sandy's number again. *He'd* been at the house that morning. Why hadn't *his* name appeared in the police report?

"Were you ever questioned by the police?" I asked him.

"No."

"Why not?"

"I left before they got there."

"You're the only one who claims to have actually *seen* a note written by my brother. Some of the people I've spoken to say they just *heard* about a note. Are you certain you saw one?"

"Absolutely. It was on the bedside table near him, with eight or ten lines on it, and scrawled at the end was the part that said, 'Read *The Tibetan Book of the Dead.*'"

"Then what could have happened to it? Why wasn't it even mentioned in the police report?"

"Someone may have picked it up and kept it," he said. "I didn't touch it. I made a point of not laying a hand on it."

"Did you mention the note to anyone?"

"I may have talked to Allan about it."

He then tried, once more, to steer me away from any "conspiracy" theory.

"It was suicide," he insisted, "more a matter of confidence than anything else. Peter felt strongly that his spirit was stronger than his physical incarnation. And he was moving on.

"A few days after first speaking with you," he said, "Peter's presence was extremely strong. It was as if he were really walking around, as if he were deliberately making some things happen. I felt like he was talking to me, that he wanted some help in writing some things, in straightening some things out.

"What was left of him felt he had a lot of karma to work out. That he was ready to leave, that he'd hung around long enough. But that's just me. You don't have to ... "

"No," I said, as his voice trailed off. "I believe it, too. I do, I truly do."

I decided then, to contact Marlene Shore in Vancouver.

*   *   *   *

She told me that after my initial call to John, they'd spent some time discussing it, what had happened, and why it had happened.

"Peter's death was pretty significant in all our lives," she said. "That and all the other stuff going on. Everyone kept saying that someone should be writing it down.

"We didn't share it, though; we all just went away asking, 'Why did it happen?' I'm always amazed when someone commits suicide. I don't understand why, when they feel so low, they don't discuss it with anyone. It just leaves people hanging.

"I've had a lot of friends who died, either from overdoses or doing stupid things. Lots of people went over the edge back then; they couldn't handle it."

"So you never doubted that my brother took his own life?" I asked.

"None. It really spooked me. I felt a strong feeling from him afterward."

"You never thought he may have been murdered because some drug dealer was afraid of what he might have said in court?"

"A drug dealer was out of the question. Didn't he use a knife from the kitchen?"

"Yes, apparently one of Heather's."

We voiced the same thought at the same time; namely, that a killer would have brought his own knife. Then we laughed, hollowly, at our gallows humour.

Unless, I couldn't help thinking, it was someone from *inside* the house.

"Were you actually living in the house on Coloniale when my brother died?" I asked her.

"Yes, I rented a room there and slept downstairs."

"What was my brother's mood like during those last, few days?"

"Mysterious. There was a kind of aura around him. That was the feeling he liked to project.

"And he was aloof. He seemed really into himself. He'd light a joint outside, come in, and give it to someone to pass around, then walk away. That last night, he brought in all this food, steaks, candy, left it with us, and went into his room."

"Do you remember someone named Thomas Garan?"

She repeated the name several times, then said, "No. Unless he was calling himself something else in those days."

She concluded our conversation by telling me, "David always said that Peter was way ahead of his time, and that he just couldn't handle it."

My last call of the weekend was to Norah. After I'd brought her up to date, I told her that rather than wait the few weeks, I'd decided to speak with Louise again, myself.

"I can hear your anger," Norah remarked, "and I think we should talk about it. *I* think you should be grateful to Louise's father."

"Grateful?" I couldn't believe what I was hearing. "That man's traumatized me forever. Why should I be grateful?"

"Because he did something really special. As painful and bloodletting an experience as it was, you saw something you would never, otherwise, have seen. It was another vista, another facet. To me, it's been the absolute highlight, the focal point of this whole thing.

"Nothing else you've done, the people you've spoken to, the clues you've followed, the leads you've tracked down, compares with that photo. It's cracked this wide open. You were finally able to step into that bedroom and see for yourself the truth of what happened there. You've been working toward this calamitous and climactic blend of reality and imagination most of your life, and that photo has almost completed the circle for you."

Her words both jarred and touched me. Some of what she'd said, I'd already thought of myself. But gratitude? It was, I admitted, an interesting premise, one which merited further consideration.

Later.

"Play on Louise's sympathy," Norah advised me now. "Say that perhaps her father can provide you with the answer to the question that's haunted you all your life; namely, why your brother chose to die, and why he chose to die in such an awful manner."

Taking her advice to heart, I drafted a speech for myself, and read it back to her a short time later.

"Too stiff," she said, "too formal, and far too long."

I promptly revised it. But, as it turned out, I didn't even need a speech. Louise's greeting, when I called, was extremely cordial, and I found myself opening up to her as if I actually knew her.

And she couldn't have been more sympathetic.

I talked at length, while she listened carefully, occasionally asking a question, occasionally saying, "okay." In the end, she agreed to go through her father's papers to see if she could find what it was I wanted. She told me to call her again in a week, and we said goodbye.

I leaned back in my chair, limp with relief, and shaking from the effort. What astounded me was the ease with which I'd revealed myself to her. When I'd begun by expressing my reluctance to talk to a stranger about a very painful, personal matter, she'd said, "You can talk to *me* about it."

And when she'd asked, "Is this for you, or for the book you're writing?," I'd answered truthfully, saying, "For both."

I sighed now and closed my eyes. We had much in common, Louise and I. But the strongest link was the saddest: her dead, young father and my dead, young brother.

As the date for the hearing approached, I spent hours at the computer, composing the speech I intended to deliver before the Commissioner.

According to the law, I had to show that my interest directly justified my being granted access to the information I wanted. And I worked and strained and struggled to make my case. The words poured out of me in torrents. Directly from my soul and onto the dark, impersonal screen facing me.

But, as cautioned by my mother, they were words devoid of all anger, all bitterness, all recrimination. And so, while the furies raged on inside me, what appeared in amber print on the black screen in front of me were words evocative enough, I hoped, to tear at even the most inured of bureacratic hearts.

By careful design, I intended to present myself to the Commissioner — thankfully, a woman — as a supplicant, needy and worthy, not only of her consideration, but of her empathy as well.

When I'd completed the speech to my satisfaction, I slipped my brother's photograph from its brass frame, and went out to have a copy made.

My intention was to bring it with me and put a human face on the proceedings. To let the Commissioner see the person we were discussing. To show her the brother I'd lost and hoped now, through knowledge, to regain.

That night, while I waited for the laser printer in the study to print out my speech, I played the CD of the soundtrack from the film, *Carrington*. Michael Nyman's score, dominated by sweet, soaring strings, was exquisite and melancholy. And as I listened, I felt a sudden, welling sensation inside me.

It was similar to the surging restlessness that had led me to begin my quest. Just as forceful, just as insistent. As if something alive in me were straining to emerge. I listened closely, and above the swell of the music, I heard it: my small, inner voice.

Let it out, urged the voice, let it out. Say his name. Hear how it sounds on the air. And I obeyed.

"Pee-ter-rr ... "

I whispered his precious name, drawing it out like a soft, double-syllabled gust of wind.

"Pee-ter-rr ... "

It was a calling up and a calling forth.

"Pee-ter ... "

"Pe-ter ... "

"Peter ... "

As his name spilled out into the room, I heard a loud, cathartic rushing in my ears.

I grabbed a piece of paper and jotted down the feelings that were being released along with his name. They splattered across the page, rambling and disjointed. Thoughts and observations and insights, which, when put together, resembled a manifesto of sorts.

By saying his name, I wrote, I'm giving him back his right to that name.

By saying his name, its magical and protective powers will fade, until it becomes a name like any other name.

By saying his name, I'm validating his existence, acknowledging that, in spite of his poor choices, and in spite of what he became, he's still my brother, and I still love him.

By saying his name, I'm acknowledging his death. I am, in effect, giving him permission, now, to be dead. And to find the peace I've kept from him for twenty-seven years.

By saying his name, I'll be able to keep him with me as a single entity — a union of child and young man, both good and bad — forever.

As I reread what I'd written, something extraordinary began to happen. I could feel the anger beginning to fade, the knots of grief begin to loosen. I felt a lightening in the band of pain around my heart. Even the room seemed brighter.

It's started, I said to myself in wonderment, it's started.

At last, at long, long last, the healing process had begun.

Twenty-three

I'd found a new exercise. Saying my brother's name out loud. To myself.

But somehow, it sounded strange to my ears. Alien and detached. It was a name that no longer seemed connected to anyone I'd ever known. Like a façade with nothing substantive behind it, nothing to either prop it up or support it.

I promptly set the exercise aside. It no longer felt comfortable; it no longer felt right. In fact, it only made *me* feel worse.

As the son of a murder victim had said in a recent television interview, "the business of closure doesn't happen overnight."

How right he was.

And so, as quickly as it had begun, the healing process abruptly shut down.

"I guess part of me is still in denial," I admitted to Paul at our next session, "because I can't get the two halves of him to fit: the brother I knew on one side and the person who dealt drugs on the other. It still feels wrong. And I can't do it, I just can't."

"Why do you think that is?" he asked me.

"Because I still feel I'm being disloyal if I think of him as bad, if I acknowledge what he became. Because I'm afraid that if I accept him as he really was, I might hate him."

"But hasn't this always been one of your problems, the

all-or-nothing principle? All black or all white. All good or all bad. You have to be realistic about this. Back then, there were certain aspects of his life you didn't agree with, right?"

I nodded.

"But that didn't stop you from loving him, did it?"

I shook my head.

"Your mother didn't agree with what he was doing, did she?"

I shook my head again.

"But that didn't mean she'd stopped loving him, did it?"

My "no" was barely audible. "But she was able to say goodbye to him."

"Why's that?"

"Because she'd accepted what he'd become, and had broken her heart over it long before the end."

"Which brings me back to my point. When your brother chose to use and deal drugs, a moral issue became involved. You can disagree with him morally, but that doesn't mean you can't still love him. You can be unhappy about what he did to himself and to your family, but you can still keep loving him."

"I suppose so," I allowed, wondering what had happened to the certainty of only a few days ago.

"But?"

"The guilt. What do I do about the guilt?"

Paul sighed and leaned forward in his chair. "Really happy, well-adjusted people don't get into drugs; they don't look for answers that way. And although those answers may seem profound when they're flying, when they're off the drugs and rational, they recognize them for what they really are: a nonproductive sham.

"Ultimately, what *you'll* have to recognize, is that you're dealing with two different Peters. The good Peter, the one you loved and to whom you built your shrine, died psychologically before the bad Peter, the one who did and sold drugs, died physically. Remember that toward the end, his behaviour was so bizarre, so delusional, his brain cells would have had to have been fried.

"He didn't call you, his sister, when he was released from

the Douglas, did he? No. He went right back to the underworld, right back on drugs. And that in itself was a poor, prognostic sign. It was also a poor, prognostic sign that he'd tried to razzle-dazzle them at the Douglas in the first place.

"He may have thought he was in control, but on drugs, people have no concept of just how *out* of control they really are. And that's the paradox of it all. You must believe me when I say that *you* couldn't have saved Peter; only *he* could have done that."

My mother's words exactly. And I wondered when they'd penetrate deeply enough for me to believe them, too.

Finally! A letter from an advisor to the Minister of Public Security, informing me that my request for a copy of my brother's police report was being forwarded to the Minister for a decision. Although I'd already gotten most of what I wanted verbally, the mere fact that I was still being denied access to the report itself made me want it that much more.

On Saturday, with fingers crossed and pulse racing, I called Louise. But when her answering machine came on, I hung up.

I tried again late Sunday afternoon, and this time, left a message.

By Monday, when I still hadn't heard from her, I phoned her at work. To my dismay, she said that she'd looked through the box at her mother's house, but hadn't found any notes on the book or any photographs.

"What about a file on my brother?" I asked.

"No, no file either."

"Are you sure?"

"I'm sorry. I did my best."

Did you? I wondered harshly. Did you really?

I was stung by the depth of my disappointment. Now I'd never know the connection between them. But worse, I'd never know if she was telling me the truth.

I leaned back in my chair and stared up at the ceiling.

"Okay," I said. "What's the most obvious connection? What's the most logical one I can think of, and then try to live with?"

Her father had worked for both the Montreal Police and the RCMP. That would have guaranteed him easy access to the latest information on any drug busts being made. As de Nobilé had suggested, he may even have had contacts in the coroner's office.

In those early days of the drug scene, the law enforcement network would have been small, people would have talked. Particularly about the arrest of the son of a prominent attorney. And most particularly, about his grisly — and supposed — suicide.

It was possible that he'd never dealt personally with my brother, had only known about him secondhand. And that when he'd decided to write his book, he'd simply gone to the appropriate police files and taken whatever he wanted.

A plausable scenario, I concluded. And a maddening one. For as plausible as it was, it would never be any more than *my* scenario. I could never be certain. I would never, really know.

I FAXed a copy of my proposed speech to Bantey, then asked my mother to write, not one, but two letters for me to bring to the hearing. The first transferred her parental authority to me, the second — which I intended to use to strengthen my case — stated that she was joining me in my appeal for access to my brother's file.

I spoke briefly with Brawley, and arranged to meet him for coffee at my hotel on Thursday afternoon. Then I sat down to reread the case law Bantey had sent me.

And, suddenly, I saw it. Another way to lend weight to my appeal: "the possibility of the subject's having inherited a hereditary disease." It was one of the few reasons for granting a person access to a family member's medical records.

Schizophrenia runs in our family, through some of my first and second cousins. If there was the slightest possibility that my brother had been schizophrenic; despite what I'd been told ...

Within minutes, I was on the phone to Bantey.

"Put it in," he said. Then he told me to FAX him my mother's two letters. "If the attorney for the Douglas calls, I'll

FAX them to him as well. I don't want to surprise him on Friday with the approach we're taking."

My speech, he said, was fine. "But," he warned, "the Commissioner can cut you off at any time and I won't be able to do anything about it."

Just let her try, I thought, just let her try.

I left Toronto early Thursday morning in the middle of a snowstorm, and arrived in Montreal an hour late in the middle of a blizzard.

How fitting, I thought. I'd begun my journey in the heat of summer, and I was ending it now in the cold of winter.

Meeting Brawley later that day in the lobby restaurant of my hotel was much like meeting David outside the library. It was a reconnection with my brother, a reconnection with my brother's past.

We spoke for quite awhile, and then, using my pen and his paper placemat, he drew a diagram for me, indicating the precise location of the entrance to the infamous house on Mt. Royal.

"You're certain it's still there?" I asked.

"Positive."

"Then how could I have missed it?"

He merely shrugged.

As to the house on Coloniale, he said, "They've never been able to keep their tenants over the years."

We left unspoken what both of us were thinking.

"I pass it every day," he added, "because I live just around the corner. It's been converted into a condo and it's currently for sale."

In the evening, I met with Norah. We exchanged Christmas presents, then I ordered dinner from room service, so that we could relax in my suite and talk. Which we did, well into the night.

*   *   *   *

I woke up terrified. Terrified of breaking down during the hearing. Of having a panic attack. Of losing control. Of losing the appeal.

I promptly took a tranquilizer to calm myself. Then, before leaving to meet with Mark Bantey, I took a second one — just to be safe.

My lawyer was attractive and personable, and as we went over our strategy together, I could feel the tranquilizers take hold and my terror begin to lessen. After awhile, I felt almost comfortable. Then he said, "I may not even need to put you on the stand," and I was back on full, anxious alert.

"What stand?" I squeaked. "I thought you said we'd be sitting around a table."

"Sorry. We are. Force of habit, I guess."

I could start to relax again, but not before I'd made something clear to him. Indicating my speech, I said, "I have every intention of reading this, you know. I'm doing it for my brother as well as for me."

As we entered the offices of the *Commission d'acces à l'information* in the Complex Desjardins, I pointed to their logo — an opened lock — saying, "I like that."

And Bantey smiled.

As luck would have it, at the coat rack, removing their coats were the two members of the opposition: Richard LaBranche from Professional Services at the Douglas and a female attorney. As soon as I'd disposed of my own coat, I excused myself and went in search of the Ladies Room.

I smiled at the tall, well-dressed woman combing her hair in front of the mirror.

"Another long skirt wearer," I said, indicating my own long, black skirt.

She smiled back. "It's years old."

"I got mine last year, but I never wear it." I indicated the skirt's high slit. "I have to wear such a short slip that the wool always sticks to my legs."

"Mine's lined."

We both laughed. Then I promptly locked myself in one of the stalls and began taking long, deep breaths. When I came out, she was gone.

I returned in time to see the lawyer for the Douglas motion Bantey into a private room. When they emerged a few minutes later, Bantey quickly motioned *me* inside. Incredulously, I heard him say, "She tells me they're not even going to make any representation."

"What?" My body swayed. Had I heard him correctly?

"They have no objection to giving you the file," he continued. "But because other institutions have gotten into trouble for releasing files, they want the permission of the Commissioner before they do."

"That's it? After all this?"

"Yes."

I was dumbstruck. Mutely, numbly, I followed him into a fair-sized conference room and took the chair next to his on the right side of a long, wooden table. LaBranche and his attorney sat down across from us. I gazed at the files in front of them and wondered which of them was my brother's.

I felt dulled, blunted to the point of near-sedation. Whether from the tranquilizers alone or a combination of the tranquilizers and the stunning and unexpected turn of events, I didn't know. Nor did I care. All I cared about was getting that file.

In came the Commissioner then, and my jaw dropped.

"You?"

She nodded, smiling.

I mentioned our encounter in the Ladies Room and everyone laughed. It broke the tension around the table, and within moments, the proceedings got underway.

Bantey spoke first, handing the Commissioner my mother's two letters, and arguing the law based on her parental authority over my brother, who was a minor at the time of his death. The Commissioner made some notes as Bantey gave copies of the law, both to her and the lawyer for the Douglas, then continued his arguments. When he was through, he announced that I wanted to speak.

"It almost isn't necessary," the Commissioner said, turning to me, "but since you've come all the way from Toronto, you may proceed."

"This is a highly emotional issue for me," I said as I slipped on my reading glasses, "and so, if you don't mind, I'd like to read from a prepared text. But first, I want to put a face on these proceedings." I held up the photograph of my brother for everyone to see. "This was my brother, taken in the year of his death."

I put the photo down on the table and picked up my speech.

I felt nothing now. I was there, and yet, I wasn't there. A dispassionate observer without emotions to cloud her thoughts or mar her speech. Composed and utterly desensitized.

"I want access to my late brother's file," I began, "because I'm a sister who, after twenty-seven years, is finally trying to get to the truth behind her only brother's grisly death at the age of nineteen.

"I've spent the last twenty-seven years believing he'd been murdered. But after six months of intensive investigation, after viewing numerous documents, and interviewing scores of people, I'm nearly convinced that it was, as the coroner concluded in 1968, not murder, but suicide.

"But I'm still not totally convinced. One of the largest pieces still missing from the puzzle is my brother's file at the Douglas Hospital.

"I believe that file holds the clues as to his mental state at the time, and that the information it contains may help me better understand and accept the gruesome manner in which he died.

"The Douglas played a crucial role during twelve of the last seventeen days of my brother's life. He was admitted to the hospital on September 9th, 1968 and released on September 20th. On September 26th, he was found dead in the bedroom of a friend's house, with a bread knife in his chest."

I watched the Commissioner wince at this. It was precisely the reaction I'd hoped for.

"We have a family history of schizophrenia. It's affected several of my first and second cousins. One of them, a brilliant

Cornell student, committed suicide at twenty-four by jumping from the roof of a building.

"I want to know if my brother exhibited any signs of the disease. If so, why wasn't he treated for it? And could it have contributed, in some way, to his death?

"I want to know if the file contains a letter written to my parents by my brother when he dropped out of college.

"I want to know if the file contains a letter from the Douglas to my parents, asking for their permission to release my brother, because he was a minor. A letter my parents received *after* the hospital had al*ready* released him.

"I want to know what the Douglas did or didn't do that caused my father to write to them after my brother's death and threaten them with possible legal action.

"I want to know what prompted Victor Goldbloom to urge my father not to sue, saying, 'this will never happen again.' *What*, precisely, will never happen again?

"There are numerous, other questions I'd like answered: What were the reasons given for committing my brother to the Douglas? Who interviewed him? What kinds of tests were conducted? How extensive were those tests if, according to my mother, within two days of my brother's admission, the hospital was ready to release him?

"Did he receive counselling during his stay? If so, what kind and from whom? Was he treated with any drugs? And if so, what kind of drugs? Why was there no attempt made to interview my parents, when they were the ones who'd committed him?

"Did anyone detect a change in my brother's mood during his stay? From what I've learned from those who spent time with him immediately after his release, his behaviour had changed completely.

"Who was the last to see him? Who signed his discharge papers?" Here I paused and drew a deep breath. "I know nothing can change what happened twenty-seven years ago. I know nothing can right the wrongs, correct the mistakes, turn back the clock. Most of all, I know nothing can return my brother to me.

"What I seek is neither retribution nor compensation. What I do seek, however, is the truth.

"Thank you."

Only then, when I'd finished, did I begin to shake.

After a moment's delay, the lawyer for the Douglas told the Commissioner what she'd already told Bantey: that they were making no representation.

The Commissioner said if that was the case, she'd have her secretary type up the necessary papers, but that I probably wouldn't get the file before the start of the new year.

To my astonishment, the Douglas's lawyer said they had no problem with giving me the file right away, providing they got her permission.

"Fine," replied the Commissioner. "I'll just turn off the tape and leave the room. You can do whatever you want."

I sat there speechless. I couldn't believe it. I reached over and gripped Bantey's wrist, and he smiled at me.

Then, before my startled eyes, the file that I'd prayed for and fought for, was being pushed from their side of the table to ours.

That easily? That quickly?

I thought of the months I'd spent working my way through the system. Of the calls from Roberto Iuticone telling me that I had no chance. Of how I'd persisted and pestered and never given up. And I could have crowed!

I'd done it. *We'd* done it. Norah with her insistence. Bantey with his expertise. Together, we'd done it.

I put out my hand and touched the file, and it was like touching the Holy Grail. For it was more than merely cardboard and paper, it was a part of my brother, my precious brother.

This battle, at least, was over. And I'd won.

Back at the hotel, I made a mug of herbal tea and brought it over to the low, wooden coffee table in the sitting area of my room. Then I curled up on the sofa, with the thick, manilla file folder clutched to my chest. What would I find, I wondered, just what would I find?

I was reminded of the Chinese proverb: Be careful of what

you wish for, for you may get it.

Now that I'd gotten what I'd wished for, I only hoped it would give me what I wanted and needed.

Twenty-four

*I*t was there, all there.

The history of my brother's twelve-day stay at the Douglas. A vital part of his own, brief life's story. As told by others, and finally, by him.

I began at the beginning, with the first of my many questions. And as I worked my way through them, one by one, I was able to check them off, one by one.

What were the reasons for committing my brother to the Douglas?

They were duly noted by Yale Nerman, the psychiatrist, who, at my parents' request, had interviewed my brother solely for that purpose, on a form headed "OBSERVATIONS PERSONALLY RECORDED BY PHYSICIAN," and dated September 6, 1968.

"Push of speech."

What did that mean? I wondered.

"Thought disorder: (a) Delusions of grandeur and a messianic complex; (b) Tangential thinking. Impaired judgment and total lack of insight. Use of LSD and a belief that he is a master of LSD, and the belief that there are no dangers involved for him."

I turned next to a form headed "PHYSICIAN REQUEST FOR CONVEYANCE ORDER," signed by Nerman and witnessed by — and here, my eyes widened — Dave Schatia. But what confounded me was the date on the form: September 7, 1968.

The very day of my brother's arrest. Exactly two days before his scheduled commitment to the Douglas. Simple coincidence? Bad timing? Or something else entirely?

According to my mother, they hadn't quite determined how to get my brother over to the Douglas that Monday. Could some, well-intentioned someone then, have orchestrated the raid with the cooperation of the RCMP as the *means* for delivering him there? Knowing that the presiding judge in the case would, at my father's request, follow through with the already signed papers and *order* my brother committed?

Implausible? Perhaps. But in the light of everything else that had happened, certainly not impossible.

And then, as if lending credence to my theory, I discovered a third form. Headed "ORDER OF CONVEYANCE TO HOSPITAL," it was dated Monday, September 9, 1968, and had been signed by a Judge of the Sessions Court.

Joseph St. Denis himself had been vague when he'd said, only, that "we'd gotten some information" about the house, but that "when we hit the place, we didn't get the motherlode we'd expected to get." And according to Richard Huard, the RCMP never conducted drug raids on a Saturday night.

I clenched my teeth so tightly, they began to ache. I'd always maintained that, if not for the raid, my brother might still be alive. Was it possible then, that the raid had been nothing but a well-meaning ploy gone bad, because no one had figured on my brother's dying? And if so, would anyone even be willing to admit it?

Who interviewed him?

Upon admission: Khalil Geagea, Resident, Burgess Pavilion. After that, among others: Dr. Heinz Lehmann, Clinical Director of the Douglas, and Dr. Helga Ast, Chief of Service, Burgess Pavilion.

As I read the transcript of Geagea's first interview with my brother, I felt a sense of incredulity, together with a saddened helplessness. Back to haunt me, once again, were Allan's tragically prophetic words: "He pulled it off."

And before me, lay the proof of it.

Whether my brother had meant, intentionally, to con them,

or whether he fully believed everything he was saying, I'd never know. But it was apparent that the web he'd woven around himself *and* them, was the key to his ultimate exit out of there.

According to Geagea: "The interview with the patient, on admission, showed a young man with long and untidy hair, beard, mustache, red shirt, tight pants, sandals, long and dirty nails, but with an exceedingly gentle face.

"The patient revealed that he was taking marijuana since the summer of '67, and LSD since the spring of '68, and that he was caught by the police on the 7th September, 1968, with marijuana in his possession in his apartment. He also had hashish and LSD in his possession. He was sent to jail, where he spent two days before being sent to Douglas Hospital.

"During this year, the patient admitted that he took, under the supervision of a master, 6 x 250 micrograms of LSD, and went into only three good trips. The last time he took LSD was in the last week of July 1968.

"The patient believes, actually, that he has experienced all the effects of LSD and does not need to use it anymore, and all that he is now concerned about is love, truth and beauty."

I nearly gagged.

"He is against destruction and is for creation. He cares about love above life; he cares about truth above personal security and liberty; he cares about beauty above bread. He rejects all the violence on earth; for truth, he is ready to go to jail; for beauty, he will often prefer to spend money on more paint or more film; he shares without question whatever food or shelter he has with insiders and any outsiders who venture to ask; he accepts anyone in his apartment with widely differing backgrounds and hang-ups. His ideal is to see a world where more love is possible.

"When asked about his plans to put all this into practice, the patient stayed silent for a while, then said: 'I think that life is very beautiful, but at the same time very difficult.'"

In the report headed MENTAL EXAMINATION, two categories were of particular interest to me.

"Judgment: This seems uneven and unpredictable. At one moment, excellent reality testing based on adult goals and aspirations, and a moment later, impaired reality testing based on persistent, unmastered, infantile longings.

"Insight: This is good. He sees that this year was a reaction against the Bishop's University environment. His plans for the future seem realistic; he wants to go to a school of agriculture, where he can obtain a degree in two years as a farmer. He will then buy a farm, get married, and devote his life to writing."

A writer? When had my brother decided to be a writer? Or a farmer? Although, given the times, being a farmer back then would have made some sense. For wasn't it all part of traditional, hippie dogma: a return to nature, a return to the land? And hadn't my brother wanted to use his inheritance from our grandfather to buy some land in Jamaica?

How much of it, though, was a pipedream, an adolescent fantasy? A teenager's act of rebelliousness? On the other hand, how much of it was truthful or simply playacting? How much of it was said to give *them* what they wanted in order to get *him* out of there?

I glanced then at the next category. Under "Provisional Diagnosis" was written: "Adolescent Reaction" (whatever that meant); and "Borderline Personality," followed by a handwritten question mark.

The final category was "Treatment Plan." The suggested treatment: "Psychotherapy."

At that point, I didn't know whether to laugh or cry, as, with sinking heart, I forced myself to read on.

What kinds of tests were conducted? How extensive were they if, according to my mother, within two days of my brother's admission, the hospital was ready to release him?

As far as I could determine, they were the most basic and perfunctory. Physical tests: chest x-ray, blood, Wasserman, urine, etc. All of them normal. I smiled wistfully when I noted his height and weight. He'd been five-feet-ten-inches tall and had weighed one hundred and forty pounds. Taller, at last than I, and thin. So painfully thin.

The short, little boy had grown, in the end, into a tall, young man.

Psychological testing: WAIS. Body Sway. Rorschach. HTP. Expressive Movement. Again, all normal.

According to the psychological report prepared by the clinical psychologist who interviewed and tested him on September 11: "Mr. Berger informed me immediately that he was a psychology student and had completed two years of undergraduate studies at Bishop's University. He had not studied any testing procedures. He also stated that he saw no reason for his detention in this hospital.

"He admitted to having smoked marijuana occasionally and has used LSD six times, the last time in August. His account of the occurences leading to his admission were organized, clear, and revealed good insight.

"Mr. Berger was fully cooperative, obliging, polite, and at times, witty. Clinically, I saw no evidence for thought disorder or other severe psychopathology."

His summary: "We find no evidence on our tests that this boy, who is functioning in the very superior range of intelligence, is suffering of a psychotic process. Thought disorder or lack of judgment were not in evidence on either test or interview."

His full-scale IQ was listed as 134, "indicating intellectual functioning in the superior range," although, according to my mother, he'd scored higher on earlier tests.

Did he receive counselling during his stay? If so, what kind and from whom?

In the Discharge Summary, signed by Geagea, he'd written, "Patient was interviewed by the Clinical Director of Douglas Hospital, Dr. H. E. Lehmann, Dr. Ast, and myself. Psychotherapy was done in view of improving his judgment and his insight."

It appeared the only area in which they concurred with Nerman was my brother's judgment, which Geagea found "uneven and unpredictable." But they didn't seem the least concerned about it. Or by the fact that, also according to Geagea, he "seems very impulsive."

Was he treated with any drugs? And if so, what kind of drugs?

There was no mention made of this, and none were pre-scribed upon discharge.

Why was there no attempt to interview my parents, when they were the ones who'd committed him?

As I'd expected, there were discrepancies between what my mother had always told me, and what the Douglas, primarily through Geagea, had recorded.

According to the Progress Report, Geagea had seen my brother and my parents on Wednesday, September 11.

According to my mother, that was the day the hospital had originally intended to discharge him. The day she, in despera-tion, had come to them and begged to be seen. And heard. Pleading for some sort of family history to be taken.

Geagea had written that, during the interview, my brother, in explaining his reason for quitting university had said, "the past two years have been a revelation for him because he saw the hypocrisy of the twentieth-century civilization, which gave him the occasion to rebel against his parents, the university, and the social order they represented."

I turned the page, then let out a gasp. For what I discovered were several paragraphs from the very letter I'd been searching for. The letter my brother had written my parents when he'd decided to quit Bishop's. The letter Lehmann said he would have read had he seen it.

According to the typed report, "In a letter which he wrote in November 1967, explaining his reasons for leaving univer-sity, he stated: 'All around me at school, in Montreal, I see only the faces of tomorrow's lynch mobs. You speak always of the progress of North America, you say "look how barbaric they were in the fifteenth century," but the progress of North America is one-sided, it is simply a modernization — a better frigidaire, a faster car, a better-heated home.

'Western man has forgotten the process of the mind. We are all ready to use Einstein's great mind as a tool for physical progress, but we still kill as barbarically as before. Western minds are sick and full of hate. I want no part in it.

'I have gone to school to learn Shakespeare and Milton and so that I could get a degree, to get a job, to get a car, to get a place in the middle class, to pay my taxes, to allow this insanity and sickness to continue. I refuse to contribute any longer to a society which I believe is basically tyrannistic, evil and un-healthy.'"

I sat back, stricken. By my brother's anger, his bitterness, and his contempt. By his total rejection of that which had given him life, nourished and protected him, nurtured and encouraged him.

He may have lied to the staff at the Douglas about the extent of his drug use, but, unhappily, regrettably, these words of his rang true. I'd heard them before, or at least words like them, hurled accusingly at my parents — and in a milder form, at me — all those many years ago.

My brother, the hippie. I almost smiled. But it hurt too much. I read what he'd written again and despaired. At the idealism and the cynicism battling for possession of his soul. At his youth. His naiveté. His wishful thinking. For who, when he's young, *doesn't* want to change the world. *Doesn't* want to make a difference.

And yet, said the objective observer in me, look at the way *he* chose to change things. Look at the way *he* chose to make a difference. But the loyal and loving sister in me, merely gritted her teeth and read on.

On Thursday, September 12, according to Geagea, my brother's case "was presented to Dr. Lehmann, in the presence of nursing staff, social worker, ward doctors, and psychologists. The psychologist's report was discussed thoroughly, as the Department of Psychology reported there was not found evi-dence of a psychotic process. Thought disorders were not in evidence. These findings were in agreement with the clinical impression of Dr. Ast and myself. The patient has been inter-viewed repeatedly.

"Dr. Lehmann felt that, in view of the clinical findings and the psychological testing, we are not justified to keep this patient in Douglas Hospital against his will. He suggested that the parents be seen and that decisions taken in the meeting be discussed with them."

On Friday, September 13, my mother forced another interview with Geagea. He, in turn, brought in Ast. It seemed that my mother's information had conflicted with my brother's, and he was, subsequently, called in to join them.

No details of the meeting were given, but its tone was clearly contentious, and at its conclusion, Geagea noted, "It was advised that Peter be seen together with his parents in psycho-therapy."

Family therapy. Once again, I didn't know whether to laugh or cry. The absurdity of it. The absolute and utter absurd-ity of it. If *I* felt like tearing my hair out now, I could only imagine what my mother had felt like doing at the time.

According to her, it was after that particular interview, that she'd turned to my uncle, who'd gone with her to the hospital, and said, "We've lost him, Harry, we've lost him."

On Tuesday, September 17, Geagea noted a second inter-view with my parents, detailing my mother's description of my brother, his personality, and his journey from childhood to adolescence. My brother was again called into the interview, and the atmosphere again seemed charged with confrontation and dissension.

It was painfully clear to me that everyone involved was working at cross-purposes. My parents were fighting to keep my brother hospitalized and to get him treatment. The staff was convinced the only treatment he needed was family ther-apy, while my brother himself was trying, simply, to get out of there.

I shook my head when, according to Geagea, my brother explained to them all, that "he was very important in the world of drugs in Montreal, and that he was acting with a group of friends to prevent the misuse of LSD and trafficking in mari-juana, by providing for the young people, who were searching for these drugs, the best environment for using a small amount of these drugs, and then discontinuing the use of them."

On Wednesday, September 18, my brother's case "was again discussed in the ward meeting, with Clinical Director Lehmann as consultant.

"Dr. Lehmann interviewed Mr. Berger to confirm again the general professional opinion that the patient was not psychotic.

"Dr. Lehmann did agree that family therapy would be the choice of treatment in this case. He suggested that Mr. Berger be discharged and family therapy carried on outside the hospital.

"The patient agreed to the suggestion."

Smooth, my brother, smooth. Anything to get out? Or did you, at any time, consider it a viable possibility?

Two days later, on Friday, September 20, he was discharged. Geagea noted, "I contacted Mrs. Berger on the phone. I explained to her that the patient should be discharged and family therapy carried on outside the hospital. Mrs. Berger agreed to this, but would have preferred to have Peter kept in the hospital."

Did anyone detect a change in my brother's mood during his stay?

None was mentioned. There was, however, a single notation by Geagea under the heading, Condition at time of leaving hospital: "Improved."

Who was the last to see him?

This was unclear.

Who signed his discharge papers?

The papers themselves weren't in the file. But there was a DISCHARGE SUMMARY signed by Geagea for Ast.

I turned then, to the DISCHARGE NOTE, written by Ast herself.

"In my interview with Peter Berger," she'd written, "he presented a picture of a highly intelligent, over-idealistic young man, who spoke in terms of lack of communication between parents and children, in terms of human kindness, which is lacking in our 'plastic society.' He accused the older generation of being very materialistically oriented and not paying enough attention to their children.

"This, he thought, was the reason for the young generation to turn to marijuana and drugs. He stated that he knew many facts about drug trafficking, yet being quite vague about this, stating that the kind of information he had, did not pertain to the medical profession.

"He talked at great length about the 'bad trips' of the

young, inexperienced LSD takers. He also stated that, through the LSD experience, he is able to grasp Einsteinian theories. I was left with the impression from the interview that we were dealing with a person subject to the concurrent 'hippie philosophy,' yet having much better insight."

I stared in disbelief at what came next.

"Mr. Berger was discharged on September 20. He planned to go and live with his parents."

How could he have said that? Because he knew it was what they wanted to hear? Allan's words returned, again, to gnaw at me.

"He pulled it off ... he pulled it off ... "

But the words that stung the most and cut the deepest, were those cited in Ast's prognosis: "Good, with psychotherapy."

I wanted to scream. Prognosis good? When six days later, he was found dead with a knife in his chest?

Did the file contain a letter from the Douglas to my parents, asking for their permission to release my brother, because he was a minor? A letter my parents received after *the hospital had already released him.*

Contrary to what Geagea had said, I located a copy of the Application for Discharge. It was dated September 20, but according to my father, he'd received it three days later. It had been returned to the Douglas, unsigned.

What did the Douglas do or not do that caused my father to write to them after my brother's death and threaten them with possible legal action?

There it was. In triplicate, just as Lehmann had said. My father's anguished, two-page letter, written eight days after my brother's death.

My heart broke as I read it. As surely as my father's must have broken when he wrote it. For in that letter was all of his agony. His anger and frustration. His feelings of absolute betrayal by a system designed, supposedly, to protect.

"You discharged my son without my written consent, unconditionally," my father wrote, "and ignoring the fact that in law he was still a minor.

"Not only did I not request Peter's discharge, but both my

wife and I pleaded that you keep him in hospital and attempt to treat him."

I felt the hackles rise as I read, "When he was discharged, your staff failed entirely to understand the implications of his dress and attire when he left the hospital. When I saw him Friday morning, September 20, he was wearing filthy, torn clothes, he was disheveled, and in a state of disarray. Obviously, he was intending to return to the environment and to the group from which we had removed him. He left behind all the brand new clothes he had asked for, and which we had purchased for him a week earlier."

That my father had seen him the morning of his release was a revelation. And a shock. My mother had never mentioned it to me. Was it possible that she'd never even known?

Where had he seen him, I wondered, and when? At the Douglas — that was unlikely — or afterward, at his office, perhaps?

I recalled what Paul had said about there being two bad prognostic signs toward the end of my brother's life. One was his attempt to "razzle dazzle" them at the Douglas. That he'd certainly done. The second was his choice to return, not to his old life, but to his new one. That he'd done, too, despite what he'd told the doctors.

And then, in my father's words, came the confirmation of my brother's own boast.

"You reinforced his sense of mission, whatever that mission may have been, by asking him to participate in a conference on November 29 and again on December 11. He was able to say to me, 'At last I have made a breakthrough. The doctors and hospital need me. I'm going to help them. I'm going to teach them.'"

He continued to outline his grievances against the hospital, then ended with his belief that they had contributed to what he termed "the destruction of my son."

There followed a flurry of correspondence between the Douglas and their attorney, the Hospital Insurance Firm, the Quebec Minister of Health, and my father, all ending in mid-April 1969.

After that, nothing.

Until twenty-six years later. When I entered the picture.

I closed the file and leaned back against the cushions, exhausted. Whatever happened next, whatever price this knowledge exacted from me — and I didn't doubt that it would — I'd accomplished what I'd set out to accomplish. I'd dug up one of the biggest chunks of my brother's missing past. Now, all I had to do was slip it into place.

Twenty-five

I was spent. It was as if the starch had gone from my spine, leaving me weak and limp. There was, about me and everything around me, a sense of unreality now. I was detached from my surroundings, cut adrift from the moorings that had always kept me anchored to the earth.

It seemed as if my head was enshrouded in mist, a gentle, soothing mist, while my body possessed a strange kind of weightlessness.

Without realizing it, I'd begun the process of spinning a cocoon around myself. A cocoon of self-protection and self-preservation. To cushion and comfort me. To act as a buffer, effectively separating me from both the outside world and my innermost self.

Although I didn't know it at the time, I'd set the stage for my withdrawal.

On Saturday morning, I braced myself for the final leg of my long journey. I both welcomed and dreaded it, for I had no idea what I'd find, and how I'd react to what I did find.

With Norah driving, we wound our way through the snow-clogged streets of the city toward our eventual destination: the infamous house on Mt. Royal. But, even with Brawley's diagram, his directions, and his insistence, I was still afraid that it wouldn't really be there.

As Norah parked the car illegally on a narrow, side street,

I started to shake. This was it. I pulled a scarf over my head to protect me from the snow that had started again, and got out of the car.

I rounded the corner and did exactly what Brawley had told me to do. I looked for a hot dog store. And found it.

All right now, I coached myself, continue past the store a few feet. Now, turn your head slightly to the right, and look for a glass door set at an angle to the street.

I did, and then ...

My heart gave a frenzied leap. There it was.

I felt as though I'd stopped breathing as I stared, long and hard, at the three numbers painted on the glass. How could I have missed it before? I wondered. How?

I gazed upward, looking for the answer. Because although the door was still there, I remained convinced that the entire façade of the building had been changed.

With a catch in my throat, I tried the door. Locked. Off to one side, was a battered, black metal intercom with several names and corresponding apartment numbers next to them. I pressed them all.

Seconds later, a buzzer sounded and the door clicked open. I squared my shoulders and pulled it toward me.

It was dim inside the tiny foyer, and as the door swung closed, it grew even dimmer. A narrow staircase rose steeply to the second-floor landing, then continued upward to the third floor at the top. I took a deep breath and started slowly up the stairs.

When I reached the second-floor landing, I looked to the right and saw a single, glass door. Through its dirty pane, I could just make out a large, empty room, its floor heavily littered with trash. I pulled on the door handle, but it was locked.

To the left of me was an identical door, also locked, also looking in on a large, trash-filled room. Both abandoned spaces were for rent.

I looked up then. At the closed door, one flight above me. A tingle went through my body. My scalp began to prickle, and my breathing became rapid and shallow.

That was the one. The door to *his* flat. My brother's flat.

I looked to the left again and felt a stab of instant recognition. Of course. That door had led into the Greek restaurant. I turned slightly, and looked down. And suddenly, I was hurtling backward in time.

It was 1968 all over again. And everything was familiar to me. The feel of the place, the narrowness of the space, the musty dimness.

Even the small, grayish white and black tiles that ran midway up the walls of the staircase. I remembered them. Remembered seeing them each time I came up and went down again.

The past enclosed me then, in its arms, and secure within its grip, I sensed that I'd come home.

I saw myself climbing these same stairs after I'd had a fight with my new husband and needed consolation. I saw myself accepting the occasional pull from my brother's joint as I sought to be part — albeit a small, safely distanced part — of his dark and mysterious life.

I saw myself sitting with him on his bed in his large, black bedroom. I, at the foot of the bed, he at its head, while he spoke to me about having found "the truth." I saw myself seated on the floor in the dark front room, while incense burned and joints were lit, waiting with all the others for the arrival of Bas. I saw myself leaving his strange, new world with a tug at my heart and a growing feeling of trepidation, to return to a world I found equally new, and equally strange.

How many of the people I'd spoken to these last, six months had I met during my visits to this house? I wondered. Apart from Sandy, none of us could recall.

"*Oui?*"

The harsh voice took me by surprise.

The door above me had opened and now, a scruffy young man in T-shirt and jeans, was stomping down the stairs, glaring at me suspiciously. As he drew nearer, I could see that his hair was messy, his eyes were red-rimmed, and his chin was covered in dark stubble. I automatically took a step backward.

"I — "

"Yes?" he snapped. "What is it you want? What are you doing here?"

"I ... Is this number 107?" I stammered.

He slammed the palm of his hand against the wall. "See? What does it say?" he shouted. "Why are you bothering us?"

I glanced up and over his shoulder. At the opened door behind him.

"What is it you want?"

"N-Nothing." I was beginning to shake. Surly and belligerent, he seemed perfectly capable of pushing me down the stairs. "I was just looking for something."

"For what? What do you want here?"

I gulped. "How ... how long have you lived here?"

"What business is that of yours, eh?"

"I-I was just curious."

Frightened and totally unprepared for the man's hostility, I couldn't find the right words. I couldn't tell him that I'd known someone who'd once lived where he now lived. I couldn't bring myself to ask if I could come up and take a look around.

His unwelcome presence on that landing was a violation. A violation, not only of me and of my space, but of the place itself. There he stood, vicious and rude, an ugly obstacle, blocking my way to a lost, precious part of my past. And I lacked both the courage and the password to get by him.

Clearly disgusted, he turned, finally, and stomped back up the stairs, leaving me behind, shaken and speechless.

A young woman appeared in the doorway, with several, small dogs grouped round her ankles. I struggled once again to summon the appropriate words, but when she, too, shouted down, "What do you want?," the words evaporated.

Numbly, stupidly, I repeated the same question I'd asked him. "How long have you lived here?"

Her answer was the same, hostile, "What business is it of yours?"

I cursed myself for my cowardice and for not having taken the time to prepare for just such an encounter. But I really hadn't thought beyond simply finding the place.

My eyes filled with tears as the door to my brother's flat slammed shut in my face. The blaring sound ricocheted off the walls and reverberated inside my head. It was a sound so final, so uncompromisingly final, that it actually made me wince. And as I stood there, staring up at that dark, closed door, I felt a great, leaden sadness settle deep within me.

Robotlike, I turned my head to the left, then to the right. I saw, without really seeing, both locked and dirty, glass doors. Next, I looked at the walls, then at the stairs leading to the ground floor. Again, I saw without really seeing. Angling my body slightly, I glanced up at the third-floor door, then back down at the stairs. And once again, I saw without seeing.

But even worse, I could no longer move. I was rooted to the spot. Stranded in the middle; stuck, literally and physically, on that second-floor landing. Unable to go up, unwilling to go down.

All sense of the present had long since dissolved, leaving me frozen now, in the past. I felt the way one feels when a memory's so vivid, it can actually be smelled and tasted. When the perception of it's so powerful, it becomes real. And for me, trapped there in the dimness of that stairwell, memory had indeed become reality.

I was no longer who I was, but who I used to be. A sister leaving the third-floor flat after one of her nighttime visits to her brother. Perhaps that was what finally restored my mobility, and gave me just enough strength to begin my slow and shaky descent.

As the glass door closed behind me with a muted click, I stepped out into the driving snow, and trudged back toward Norah's car. Then we drove the few blocks to our final destination.

Safe within the thickening cocoon of my withdrawal, I barely reacted when we pulled up before the two-storey house on Coloniale Street, with the "Condo for Sale" sign in front of it.

The building had been divided into four narrow flats. Parts of the façade were covered in cheap, wooden siding, and peeling, white paint barely concealed the original gray stone underneath.

I got out of the car and stood, for a moment, in front of the building. Then I ran the tips of my fingers along the bumpy stone wall, as if feeling for the past beneath the layers of flaking paint. And I tried to imagine my brother living and dying in that house twenty-seven years ago.

Was it my brother's restless spirit, I wondered, that kept driving away the house's tenants? I wouldn't have been at all surprised.

One final look around, and I climbed back in the car.

We had a long and quiet lunch together, then Norah drove me to the station.

I stood on the freezing platform in a semi-trance. Had it only been two days since I'd stepped *off* a train? I gave my head a shake. It seemed like a lifetime ago.

As I boarded the train, I suddenly began to cough. Short, sharp, double coughs. Why, I asked myself, did they always come in pairs? Pairs which, to my discomfort and concern, increased with each passing mile.

Leaning back in my seat, I closed my eyes, and tried to concentrate instead on breathing in and out, slowly and deeply.

My quest was nearly over, and I knew that I should have been savouring my victories. Especially my latest one. But instead, I found myself mentally ticking off the issues that, for me, were as yet unresolved.

I still hadn't received the police report from the Ministry of Public Security.

I still hadn't found Phil.

I still hadn't found anyone who remembered Thomas Garan.

I still hadn't found a satisfactory explanation as to why the drug raid had occurred — coincidentally and conveniently — two days before my brother's scheduled commitment to the Douglas.

I still hadn't found the connection between my brother and Louise's father, or learned how he'd been able to use that gruesome photo, without fear of reprisal, in his book.

I still hadn't erased from my mind the final percentage point of doubt that would allow me to accept my brother's death as a suicide rather than murder.

Despite my best efforts, I coughed all the way back to Toronto. And when the train pulled into Union Station five hours later, I knew that I was sick.

How appropriate, I thought, as I flagged down a taxi. I'd held myself together for the past six months. Six gruelling and exhilarating, excruciating and satisfying months. Six months of brutal blows that my body had borne — for the sake of my mind as well as my quest — stalwartly and well. And now, it seemed, my body was finally preparing to let go.

But before that happened, I had three important telephone calls to make.

The first, on Monday, was to Roberto Iuticone.

"I thought I should tell you," I said, "that I had my hearing before the Commission on Friday."

"Yes, I already know."

"Do you also know that they gave me the file?" I inquired sweetly.

"Yes, I do."

"Well, I thought I'd just tell you myself."

"You're very kind."

I hung up, smiling coldly, and drew a check mark in the air.

The second was to Victor Goldbloom. As usual, he was in a meeting.

"Are you his secretary?" I asked the woman who answered.

In a rather huffy voice, she replied, "I'm his assistant."

"Fine. Then could you write this message down and give it to him when he comes out of his meeting?"

"Of course," she said, and I began, "I thought you'd like to know that I followed the matter I discussed with you in August, through to its conclusion. Thanks to the Access to Information Act, I was able to get everything I wanted from the coroner, as well as the file on my late brother from the Douglas Hospital. I'm sorry you never saw fit to return any of my phone calls or answer any of my FAXes." I paused to let the words sink in, then asked, "Could you read that back to me, please?"

She did, and I hung up, my smile hard and tight, and drew a second check mark in the air.

The third was to Fred Kaufman, who, I learned, was on holiday. I left my name and number, adding, "Tell him, please, that I have some very exciting news."

When Fred returned my call, I said, "I thought you'd like to know that, although it's taken five months, I've gotten every-thing I wanted from the coroner and the Douglas."

He congratulated me, and told me that Victor *had* phoned to discuss the matter with him, but that it hadn't gone any farther.

"He could have at least had the courtesy to call me back," I said, and Fred agreed.

I drew one, final check mark in the air, then took to my bed.

Twenty-six

I was, quite obviously, worn down and worn out. I'd pushed myself to, and then beyond the limits of even my, rather considerable endurance, and now I was paying the penalty for it. Yet, strangely enough, it was less a matter of feeling really sick, than not feeling particularly well.

My doctor diagnosed a touch of bronchitis, and prescribed a course of antibiotics for me. But nothing I took, nothing I did, made much difference. Whatever I had neither got worse nor got better. It simply hung on. And I was glad.

Glad to hibernate. To nestle, like a wounded animal, in the warmth, security, and comfort of my apartment. To barricade myself from any and all intrusions from the outside world.

Glad not to have to talk to anyone or see anyone. Not to have to laugh or smile or be brave or interested or interesting.

Glad to be alone.

But above all, I was glad not to have to start assimilating everything I'd learned. Glad not to have to start putting the pieces of the puzzle into what would be its final form.

Suddenly, I no longer had either the strength or the stomach for it. And it didn't take me long to understand why.

My mind had simply closed down. It had remained behind, frozen on that second-storey landing. Trapped on the staircase midway between the ground floor and my brother's third-floor flat inside that ramshackle building on Mt. Royal.

My mind had stopped where I myself had stopped that

cold, snowbound morning: in the time warp of 1968. And now along with me, it couldn't go up and it couldn't come down.

I was reminded of those children's cartoons, where the character, arms pumping and legs churning, runs off the edge of a cliff. He remains suspended in mid-air, arms still pumping and legs still churning, as long as he doesn't look down. The moment he does, he drops like a stone.

That, in effect, was what had happened to me. For six months, my quest had propelled me forward. Mind pumping and body churning, I'd remained suspended high above the earth. Now, with my quest nearly completed, and with no momentum to propel me forward, I'd dropped like the proverbial stone.

As the days passed, my mind slept on in welcome blankness, while my body burrowed numbly inside the protective layers of its self-made cocoon.

"I guess I'm taking a mental holiday," I explained to everyone who called to check on my progress.

And everyone was sympathetic. Everyone understood. I needed it, they all said. I deserved it, after what I'd been through.

Three weeks later, I was still crawling along the emotional bottom, and I felt no compunction whatsoever about remaining there. For I knew, that as long as I did, I'd be safe. Safe from the images. Safe from thinking. Safe from assimilating. Safe, paradoxically, from ending my journey.

One morning, I looked closely at my face in the bathroom mirror, and I was shocked by what I saw. I'd changed. I'd aged. My skin was looser, duller. There were new lines near my mouth, and fine, tiny lines radiating outward from my eyes and across the top of my nose.

When I told my mother, she said, "Maybe this is what the last six months have done to you. Some people turn gray from such traumatic experiences."

It was time, I realized, to see Paul again.

*   *   *   *

As I sat, slumped, across the desk from him in my chair, it was almost too much of an effort to speak. I felt as if the space around me was stuffed with cotton. As if a pane of heavy glass separated me, not only from Paul, but from the entire world. As if everything I heard was being filtered down to me from somewhere out in the cosmos.

It didn't take Paul long, however, to put into words what I already knew. And feared.

"You're stuck," he said. "Stuck in the mourning process."

I nodded weakly and closed my eyes.

"You'll have to confront it, you know, when you're physically and mentally ready. It doesn't have to be now; it obviously *can't* be now. You need some time away from it first. But it has to be soon."

I opened one eye and looked at him.

"You have to continue the process and see it through," he told me, "and come out the other side."

"Or?" I asked.

"Or you'll *stay* stuck, the way you stayed stuck the first time, twenty-seven years ago."

The days continued to pass with no signs of improvement — either physical or mental. And then, to my dismay, the images returned. More powerful now than ever. How naive of me to have thought that they'd stay hidden indefinitely behind the blessed screen of blankness.

Not only had the old images returned, but they'd been joined by newer ones. The strongest was of myself standing in the middle of that staircase inside the house on Mt. Royal. The second was of the Metro Reference Library, once my favourite resource, now the source of my greatest agony.

Then there were the images from our childhood together, my brother's and mine. The sweet and happy images, the ones that made me smile. And the images from that last, awful year. The dread and frightening ones that made me shudder.

Now, whenever I opened the drawer in the kitchen and saw

the small, old-fashioned can opener lying there, I'd think of
Gerry's grotesque story, and cringe. And each time I took out a
knife, any knife, I'd recoil, as Heather's words, "Peter picked
out a serrated bread knife, that was one of mine," repeated
themselves inside my head.

And then, one morning, I awoke to feel a vague stirring
inside me. As the day progressed, so did the feeling, until I was
seized by an urge I recognized and remembered well: obsession.

Without stopping to question what was happening or why,
I picked up the telephone and dialed the number for the Ministry
of Public Security in Quebec City, to find out why I still hadn't
received a copy of the police report. I left a message for the
advisor who'd written to me at the end of November, then
promptly phoned Montreal and spoke with Dave Schatia.

I discussed my brother's medical file with him, told him
that his signature had appeared on the commitment papers, and
voiced my suspicions about the coincidental timing of that
Saturday night drug raid.

"Do you know what's scary?" he said. "The fact that I don't
even remember signing those papers."

As to whether he'd played a part in my brother's being
arrested, he flatly denied it, stating, "I didn't know he'd been
arrested until after it happened. I would never have had him
arrested. I didn't even know where he lived."

I hung up with a sigh. If he didn't remember signing the
papers, what else might he have forgotten over time? I'd never
know, would I? It seemed this was one more question for which
I'd never have a satisfactory answer. One more piece of the
puzzle that would never fit the way I'd hoped it would.

My next call was to Yale Nerman.

"The incident involving your brother," he told me, "was
one of those things that always bothered me in terms of a system
that really didn't protect him. I'd heard third-hand that what he
did at the Douglas was charm everyone with his personality and
brightness and tremendous knowledge of many things, particularly LSD. He became like a pet, rather than someone who

should have been examined and treated. And I was livid when I learned that he'd been discharged.

"I spoke with Heinz Lehmann afterward and told him that I was very perturbed about Peter's having been released. And he said that, in terms of their examination of him, there was nothing there to hold him."

"In your own, written observations of my brother," I said, "you used the term 'push of speech.' What, exactly, does that mean?"

"It means highly excitable, manic, that there's a lot of activity around the subject when he's talking. My evaluation of Peter was that he was, potentially, highly self-destructive, but I never would have predicted that his death would have been such a horrendous, violent thing. When one does such a brutal act to oneself, when one does such viciousness to oneself, there has to be, somewhere, an enormous amount of rage."

I mentioned the coincidental timing of the RCMP raid, but he could offer no clues other than to say, "Your father was so desperate, so fearful, I wouldn't have been surprised if *he'd* arranged with someone to do something. Back then, if you got a legal document asserting that someone was a danger to himself, the police could pick that person up. You can't do that today, though."

When I expressed my astonishment at the number of people who'd remembered my brother so clearly after so many years, Yale said, "It's not surprising at all. Peter was a very memorable person. A very bright, personable human being. What a horrendous waste."

Our conversation made me think. Long and carefully. About one of the most telling and recurring themes in some people's recollections of my brother: his anger.

From the beginning of his life to the end of it, anger, it seemed, had shaped his personality and foreshadowed his destiny.

The temper tantrums of his childhood. The knife-wielding incident described in my cousin John's letter. His impatience with routine tasks as mentioned by Robin Billick and Howard

Berson. His anger, according to Brian Melzack, with our father over his inheritance from our grandfather. His anger with Joseph St. Denis because his LSD had been seized. His anger, according to Oscar Sanchez, with Bas.

And finally, the ultimate manifestation of that anger. Anger in its most extreme form. When — as much of the evidence supported — he'd turned that anger inward, and directed it against himself.

What, I wondered, was the source of that terrible anger? Could it have been programmed into him genetically? Could it have been some kind of structural, chromosomal defect? Is it possible that he'd been born with it, the way some are born with defective hearts or missing organs or misshapen limbs?

Sadly for me, I'd never know.

That afternoon, Benoit Lauzon, an attorney and political aide to Serge Menard, the Minister of Public Security, returned my call.

"How ironic," he said, "I was just preparing a letter to you. We do these cases in groups of three or four, and we got yours only in the new year. Unfortunately, the law is not clear in your case, and the matter needs further analysis. Your grounds are different from most people's, and our lawyers are trying to see if your request can be granted as a 'moral' right."

He added that it was solely a discretionary matter for the Minister and that mine — and when had I heard this before? — was a test case.

I considered contacting Pierre Trahan again and pressing *him* for a copy of the report, then decided against it. At least for the moment.

But as I sat there, thinking, I was reminded of something an old friend had recently said to me. He himself had been the father of three boys, *two* of whom had, tragically, committed suicide.

He'd marvelled at what I was doing, at how much I'd learned, and how I'd learned it. He told me that he was glad I was putting it all into a book, and how important such a book would be for parents like him. Then, half-jokingly, he'd said, "I should hire you to find out the truth about *my* boys."

A shudder ran through me at the thought. Of so many others just like me ... With the same unanswered questions ... Wondering how to find the answers to those questions ... Asking themselves why? ... Living *their* lives without closure ...

The following morning, I walked into my study and, for the first time in over a month, turned on my computer.

But my leap forward was shortlived. Certain words and phrases sprang out at me from the computer screen, and, like sharpened claws, scratched and ripped and tore at me.

Instinctively, I pulled back. And retreated to the security of my cocoon.

One week passed, then two, while I remained, effectively, in limbo. Still frozen on the stairs. Unable to go up, unable to come down.

Sometimes, as I sat on the sofa in the living-room, a strange feeling would steal over me. I'd sense that I was no longer alone. It wasn't an outer sensation, but an inner one. As if a human vapour had risen inside me, not so much to inhabit me, as to co-exist with me.

And the image attached to the sensation was always the same. It was of me standing, immobile, on those stairs. Not me remembering standing there, but *actually* standing there. For no more than thirty seconds at a time, I'd be aware of myself as two separate entities: the "me" on the sofa and the "me" on the stairs. It was the eeriest feeling I'd ever known, a kind of out-of-body experience in reverse.

My mother suggested that I take off the ring, but I said no. The ring wasn't the problem.

"It makes me feel safer," I explained. "It keeps me connected to him. I need it on me; I feel better with it on."

"You know," she said, "I think there's something you should try to understand about Peter, and about the role the times played in his destruction.

"In a less permissive society, there would have been controls. But every institution, including the universities, had let their guard down. The frontiers had been rolled back, everything was there to be explored, and the sixties sanctioned it.

"Kids could, for the first time, rebel against parental authority. We, as parents, had lost our power, and society gave its approval for the kids' acting out. So Peter went out and tried it all.

"His fatal flaw was his ability to learn quickly, master something, then lose interest in it. For example, when other boys took a year or more to learn their Bar Mitzvah portion, he learned *his* portion in three sessions.

"He didn't have a caution button in him; he didn't have a stop and go light. To him, everything was an adventure, to be greeted with a big grin on his face. If he'd lived at any other time, say, when Christopher Colombus set sail for the New World, Peter would have been on one of those ships."

I smiled at the image of my brother on the prow of a ship, sailing off to explore newer worlds. But wasn't that, in effect, what he'd been trying to do? Except that *his* newer world had been the world of the mind.

A few days later, I went back to see Paul. I told him about being stuck on the staircase, and how afraid I was now to think about, much less talk about, what I'd uncovered in the past seven months.

"The whole purpose of bringing something into therapy," he told me, "*is* to talk about it, over and over again. Because it's in the telling and the retelling that the shock value wears off. The more someone talks about a painful experience, the less frightening it becomes, and the less of a hold it has.

"That's why your mother was able to deal with what happened to Peter and get past it, and you never were. Because you never talked about it. And talking about it is precisely what you're going to *have* to do, in order to heal."

"I don't know if I can."

"Try."

I drew a shaky breath, and gingerly peeled back one of the

thick, protective layers of my psychic cocoon. Out spilled, not only memories, but spasms of pain, and a flood of white hot tears.

Once the emotional storm had subsided, Paul asked me quietly, "Did talking make you feel better or worse?"

"Both," I admitted, tearing at the clump of sodden kleenexes in my hand. "It hurts *and* it feels good. But I know that as soon as I walk out of here, I'm going to cover everything back up and push it all back down again."

"That's okay," he assured me. "At least you know that you have a place where you *can* begin to let it out and look at it. Remember, in the looking and the retelling will come a lessening of the horror, a lessening of its power over you."

"And what about closure?"

"You can't legislate closure," he said, "it's an evolutionary process."

"I suppose I thought I'd just sit down one day, wrap everything inside a nice, neat package, tie it with a ribbon, and declare, 'There, that's it.' And it *would* be it."

Paul smiled. "It doesn't happen that way."

"Then how will I know when I've found it?"

"You'll have a feeling of release, a feeling of peace."

I repeated the words "release" and "peace" as if I'd never heard them before. And my sigh said it all. Then, just as I'd predicted, the layers of my cocoon closed over me once more.

Twenty-seven

*B*ut shortly after that particular session, I had what I considered to be a major breakthrough. I realized that part of my current dilemma stemmed from having tried, and failed, to see my brother as my mother saw him.

Because that just wasn't possible.

My mother and I had always seen, and always would see him from two distinctly different vantage points, two entirely different points of view. She, as the mother; I, as the sister.

My parents' experiences with my brother in the last years of his life weren't my experiences. Their relationship with him was more adversarial and more confrontational than mine had been. Even their fear was a different kind of fear. Their disappointment in him as a son was different from mine in him as a brother.

Whatever my mother had told me over the years about his combativeness, his selfishness, and his hurtfulness, related to *them*, not me. And because our dealings with him were so different, our *feelings* about him and about what happened to him were, therefore, bound to be different.

How many times had my mother lamented, "The drugs changed Peter from a cute, little boy into a monster."

How many times had she said, "It was my anger that saved me. Anger at him for what he did to us, especially to your father, whom he knew was a sick man. Anger at him for destroying his incredible potential, and for throwing his life away, for what, a Bas? Anger at him for ultimately choosing Bas over us."

Unlike my mother, then, I knew that I would never be able to see my brother as a monster. Rightly or wrongly, there was, inside me, a wall of sisterly loyalty and protective love, that could never, ever be torn down. And I understood now, that to try, would be to destroy, not only my brother, but myself as well.

Because all I had to do was remember when he was there for me, and the goodness of him during that terrible time nullified the bad. All I had to do was recall his last, two words to me, and their meaning, obscured forever in ambiguity, mitigated the rest.

It was progress. So sudden and so startling, it left me feeling slightly dazed. Not that this illumination — bright though it was — guaranteed me an unobstructed path ahead from then on. Quite the contrary. For every inch forward, I stumbled back two. But the process, at least, had begun again.

I knew that I was truly advancing when I went in search of one more witness: Tommy Sise.

I called the only Sise in the Montreal directory and found myself speaking with Tommy's stepmother. She immediately gave me his telephone number, and, for the first time in what felt like a very long time, I settled into the slipper chair in my bedroom with my clipboard on my knees.

"I first met Peter through John Shore," Tommy told me. "I knew Peter Brawley and Marshall Hopkins very well. I'd dropped out of school and had just come back from the Caribbean.

"We were all into the spiritual thing at that time in our lives, although I didn't agree with a lot of what they were doing."

"Such as?"

"I didn't agree with Bas. I'd met people like him in the Caribbean. I had no use for magic and all that stuff.

"But Peter did believe, at first, that Bas was very special. He had a power. After a few weeks, everyone thought he was, like, God. A lot of it had it do with his gift of the gab, because what he did, really, was preach. He knew how to manipulate people and how to use fear. I think Peter thought he could use Bas, but in the end, Bas used *him*."

When I asked about the drug dealing, he said, "They were mostly dealing in grass. There's a certain lack of discretion when you're bringing in grass. Then it was big. But compared to now, it was nothing."

We discussed the RCMP raid, and what he said next, took me by complete surprise.

"A lot of people believed that Peter had himself busted to get rid of Bas."

"I'd heard it was just the opposite," I said, and described Jean's recollection of their time together in the holding tank.

But Tommy was adament.

"I was there the night of the raid. I was standing in the doorway of the next room when the bust took place. I was one of the first to see them.

"They came in, one or two of them, and when they showed their badges, Peter said, 'I'm the one you're looking for. I'll give you whatever you want. Don't bother with these other people.'

"He went back to his room and came out with a vial of something and handed it to them. They took him away."

I frowned. His version of events sounded hauntingly familiar. (Upon checking my notes, I discovered that Sandy had told me virtually the same thing, but I hadn't lent much credence to it at the time. Obviously, he'd gotten the story from Tommy.)

"And you all just stayed there?" I asked.

"Yes." Even he sounded surprised. "There were all these people, and they were still sitting around, and smoking dope, and I said, 'What's happening? There's just been a bust.' But they felt they'd gotten Peter, and that they wouldn't be back.

"They returned about a half-hour later with more people. I looked out the window and I could see police cars everywhere. They'd blocked off the whole intersection. The entire neighbourhood was out watching us get busted."

With the Douglas file still so fresh in my mind, I asked him about my brother's demeanour toward the end.

"He wasn't 100% there psychologically," he admitted. "He was warped, and the drugs didn't help. I think he was either manic or schizoid. I think the whole period was basically a breakdown for him, beginning even before the bust. He was certainly not well."

"What do you think was the reason for his strange behaviour?"

"I think he felt responsible for a lot of people, felt the thing was souring. He was in over his head. There was a lot of pressure, both spiritually and materially. I think, also, there was a sense of a change in feeling about Bas, from his being a good person to his being a bad person, an evil person.

"It may have been a few weeks before he died, or in the last week before his death, I can't remember, but he'd started carrying around this stick like a wand. He came to the house, and my mother looked at him and said, 'That boy is crazy.' I didn't fully believe or accept it when she said it, and I said, 'Come on, he's bright, agitated. You don't understand.'"

"If all of this was apparent to his friends," I asked, "how could he have fooled the people at the Douglas?"

Tommy, like the others, was surprised I'd even ask, when, to them, it had seemed so obvious.

"He knew 'psycho speak.' He knew how to talk. He just played with them. He was very, very bright. He could have convinced a psychologist of anything. If he'd set out to fool you, he'd be able to."

Stupidly, I found myself saying, "Why didn't he just go home instead?"

"He couldn't have gone home."

"I know," I acknowledged, and hurriedly changed the subject by asking if he knew about the "can opener" incident. He did.

"Michael Colvey told me that he thought Peter was crazy. It freaked Michael out; he was never the same afterward."

When I asked about my brother's "do not fear death" talk, he said, "I remember something about it. It sounds right."

I asked if it was true that Allan and Sandy had slept at his house the night before my brother died, and he said they had. Along with several others.

"It was weird. Everyone in the house just sat straight up,

wide awake all of a sudden. Then Marshall phoned."

"Did you go with Allan and Sandy to the house on Coloniale?"

"No."

"Did Sandy ever mention finding a note on the table beside the bed in David's bedroom?"

He said no, then added, "Everything I heard, I heard from Marshall. The first thing I asked was, 'Did he leave anything?' I was told on a number of occasions that there was a scrap of paper, and that it was the only thing he left."

When I repeated what Sandy had told me, Tommy said, "It made some reference to *The Tibetan Book of the Dead*, but it was phrased differently, so that it didn't make sense."

"Did you accept his death as a suicide?"

"Yes."

"Did you ever think it might have been murder?"

"No. Except in the psychological sense. I feel Bas killed him in many ways. I always thought Bas was capable of murder. I think part of the reason Peter died was because he'd been mistaken about Bas, and dying was the only way to get rid of him.

"The first time I felt that I might have overestimated Peter was when he committed suicide. He was so very bright, usually in control. Maybe losing that control made him commit suicide."

We discussed the various versions of Bas's death, and agreed that, as ghoulish as it was, we preferred the one in which he'd been killed with a machete.

"At least," Tommy said, "we can draw some comfort from that."

When I mentioned that I intended to turn my writings into a book, he said, "I think it's a great idea. If you can capture some of the feelings, the strength; everything of that age was so strong, so important. Everyone thought they were on the threshold of something new and wonderful." Then he added softly, "To try to understand why Peter did it, alone would fill a book."

Several days later, I returned, one last time, to my research.

There was more I needed to learn about LSD. And for that, I paid a visit to the library at the Addiction Research Foundation.

And what I uncovered, explained, more clearly than anything else, what may have accounted for much of my brother's behaviour, not only in the last weeks of his life, but in that last year as well.

According to the literature, some of the myriad psychological effects of LSD include: changes in the experiencing of time and space; abrupt and frequent mood changes; dual, multiple and fragmented consciousness; heightened suggestibility; depersonalization and ego dissolution; seeming awareness of internal organs and processes of the body; sense of capacity to communicate much better by nonverbal means, sometimes including the telepathic; and concern with philosophical, cosmological, and religious questions.

Many users claim that, under the influence of LSD, all mystic themes, religious concepts, and mysteries become clear to them through what they consider "cosmic revelations."

These so-called illuminations can lead to euphoria, which in turn, can result in a false sense of spiritual pride by those who now see themselves as having found *It*, namely, *the* answer, or *the* truth.

In their apparent yearning for simplicity and wholeness, many users express their disenchantment with Western values by embracing a quasi-Eastern mystique. Unfortunately, drugs like LSD may actually afford them a glimpse of the complexities of Eastern consciousness. But it's only a glimpse, because they lack the stability, maturity, and elasticity needed to assimilate such values.

Studies show that the psychological, perceptual, and behavioural effects of LSD can last between eight and twelve hours, then wear off. If a person takes the same dosage of LSD every day for five days, his tolerance to it will increase, so that, by the fifth day, he'll feel practically nothing. In order to attain the same kind of high, he'll have to increase the dosage accordingly. But if he goes without LSD for a few days, the tolerance he's built up will disappear, and he'll again experience an intense, hallucinogenic episode with only the normal dosage.

The user frequently ignores life-threatening situations because he's convinced his soul will live forever, thereby making his body insignificant. Some, believing they're invincible, stab themselves, shoot themselves, or try to run through walls. Others choose to kill themselves because the LSD has made them so severely depressed, that they simply don't want to live any longer.

One of the most serious, toxic effects of LSD is the psychotic reaction. A single dose of LSD can precipitate a psychosis lasting anywhere from a few hours to a month. During such LSD-induced psychotic states, some users imagine they're famous people or historical figures. Some even believe they're Jesus Christ.

While some researchers consider an LSD-induced psychosis to be separate from schizophrenia, others feel the drug may serve to reveal a user's *latent* schizophrenia.

When seen in a clinical setting, an LSD-intoxicated patient can appear, not only lucid, but can describe his drug usage, even while suffering from illusions, and discussing such abstractions as "universal truth." He can also perform simple mental exercises.

That evening, I settled in front of my computer with this latest data and added it to the information I already had. Then I gathered up the rest of the evidence I'd collected over the last seven months, and spent the next few hours going over it all.

Near midnight, I was ready. Like a projectionist, I set up a reel of film inside my head, and braced myself.

I realized, of course, that what I was about to view could never be more than conjecture. A series of educated guesses, based on a combination of scientific facts and personal recollections. I realized, too, that it would only be *my* version of the truth, not my brother's. He'd taken *his* truth with him when he'd died. But it was the best I could do. I only hoped that it would, ultimately, be enough.

Leaning back in my chair, I let the film begin.

I saw a young man, brilliant and inquisitive, dissatisfied and searching, seeking some newer truths in which to believe, and by which to live.

I saw him embrace the code of the counterculture, steep himself in its myths and ideologies, an acceptance made all the easier by his heavy use of LSD and pure Jamaican weed.

I saw him ride the heady wave of power, exalted in his role, originally as leader, then as first disciple of his own, anointed god. A god who promised both protection from the law and a glimpse of paradise.

I saw that power collapse in a matter of moments, when the RCMP staged a Saturday night raid on the drug haven his god had declared inviolable.

I saw him, stoned, confused, and then defiant, when, in a gesture, part youthful bravado, part misguided loyalty, he sacrificed his own freedom for the sake of his god's, and signed that damning declaration.

I saw him enter the Douglas Hospital on Monday, already emerging from the toxicity of the grass, but especially the LSD. I saw him slip into the role of polite young man, lucid and articulate, easily convincing all who saw him, not only of his saneness, but of his superior knowledge of hallucinogenic drugs.

I saw him leave the hospital on Friday, drug-free for nearly two weeks, and return to the shelter of the counterculture.

I saw him as my mother had seen him that Sunday afternoon — incoherent and high — when, now, even the smallest amount of LSD would have had him flying.

I saw him, either that same evening or Tuesday evening, drugged and delusional, call himself, among other things, the son of God, and claim he could control his own bleeding.

I saw him, on either Tuesday or Wednesday, tell Allan that he planned to kill himself.

I saw him on Wednesday, boast of being the most powerful person in the universe, then prove it by talking the manager of Moishe's restaurant out of six sirloin steaks.

I saw him at RCMP headquarters, demanding his LSD back from Joseph St. Denis.

I saw him on Wednesday evening at dinner with his friends, appearing quiet and introspective.

I saw him on Thursday morning, calmly drinking coffee with Gordie Fulton and Thomas Garan.

I saw him, some time later, lying dead in David's bedroom. I abruptly stopped the film.

Murder? Killed for fear of exposure on orders from Bas or some other drug dealer more powerful than he? Or suicide? A gesture of supreme self-sacrifice to Bas, whether encouraged by him or not? Or, as some had suggested, an act of defiance, born of a sense of betrayal, *directed* at Bas?

And if it *was* suicide, was it a delusional decision either caused by, or aided by, the use of LSD? Or a conscious choice to leave a polluted world and enter a pure and perfect one as described in *The Tibetan Book of the Dead*?

If I were to choose between the two, I would have opted for the latter. It seemed, to me, the most likely. I envisioned him arriving at his decision, then taking LSD to ease what he believed would be his trip through the Bardos toward a good rebirth.

And the reasons for *his* choice? I asked myself.

The world he'd created for himself lay in shambles all around him. He was, in all likelihood, going to be sent to prison. Bas was, in all likelihood, going to be deported.

The dream was over.

He'd crossed the line that separated him from us, his family. A line that he was either too ashamed or too stubborn to re-cross. It was too late. By then, he no longer considered us either a refuge or an alternative.

He saw a path to freedom and he took it. And because he neither feared nor believed in death, he saw his decision as being one of self-deliverance. Whether he'd ever stopped to think about the consequences of his action, I'd never know.

I thought back to the start of my quest and the various hats — lawyer, sleuth, investigative reporter, judge, author, sister — I'd imagined myself wearing. With a shudder, I finally slipped on my judge's hat. Then I closed my eyes and conjured up a pair of old-fashioned scales. In one pan, I placed the word MURDER, in the other, SUICIDE.

I watched as the latter pan quivered a moment, then dropped under the burden of its own weight, leaving the truth, the sad and ugly truth, with no place left to hide.

It was time.

Time to acknowledge that my brother, and not some mysterious figure, was responsible for his death.

Time as well to acknowledge that, after twenty-seven years of believing one thing, I'd now have to accustom myself to believing something else entirely.

I opened my eyes then, and saw only ruins.

It was as if I were standing in the middle of a Dali landscape. Surrounded by ominous, twisted shapes and contorted shadows. And in the midst of that ruined landscape, I understood that to reach a conclusion doesn't guarantee immediate *acceptance* of that conclusion. For me, acceptance would be the most onerous task of all.

Because in accepting that my brother had consciously chosen to die, I would also have to accept that he'd consciously chosen to abandon us. Abandon *me*. And the hurt child in me found it unbearable to believe that, by the end, I'd meant nothing to him. That I'd been easy to leave.

I could, however, draw some, small measure of comfort from the fact that his final decision had been the decision of a deluded mind, a mind so destroyed by drugs, that rational thinking would have been all but impossible.

Staring straight ahead, I envisioned, before me, a series of six, dramatically different doors.

I saw my brother walking out the door of my parents' house.

I saw him walking through the door into the Stygian darkness of that flat on Mt. Royal.

I saw him walking through the door of a prison cell.

I saw him walking out the door of the Douglas Hospital.

I saw him walking through the door into that borrowed bedroom.

I saw him walking through the door of the first Bardo, then onward toward the clear and radiant, white light.

The brother I'd known had ceased to be, when the first of those six doors had closed behind him. His abandonment of me had started then. His death on that September morning in 1968 just made it official.

For me, his only monstrous deed, his one, true crime, was his final act. That was, to me, the ultimate act of cruelty and betrayal.

And I knew, that in order to heal, I would first have to accept that he did indeed take his own life, then come to terms with the truth of *that* cruelty, *that* betrayal.

Twenty-eight

A delighted Paul applauded my tremendous leap forward at our next session. Then I proceeded to spoil it all.

"I'm afraid," I told him in a quavering voice.

"Of what?" he asked.

"Of letting my brother go now."

"If you do let go," he said, "you're not going to lose *him*. What you *will* lose will be the pain and the anger and the grief. He'll still be with you in memory the way your father is."

I hoped to God that he was right.

After what seemed an interminable two weeks, I finally received the letter from the Ministry of Public Security.

A mere two paragraphs, Benoit Lauzon had put into writing what he'd basically told me over the phone. And as I clipped this latest letter to the growing correspondence between myself, the *Centre d'archives*, the Chief Coroner, and the Ministry, I told myself there was nothing more I could do.

For the moment.

A few days later, Bantey sent me a copy of the decision rendered by the *Commission d'acces à l'information*. Although the hearing had been conducted in English, the written decision itself was in French.

I hastily dug out my French/English dictionary.

To my surprise, my name didn't appear anywhere in the

document. I was represented simply by an "X" above the word "*demanderesse*." Nor was there any mention of my brother's name. The two of us appeared, for the record, solely as pairs of squared brackets.

Why? I wondered. To protect *our* privacy?

I smiled at what the Commissioner described as my "eloquent testimony," then went on to read the rest of the four-page document. So, I thought, when I finally set the decision down, there it was. In black and white. It was official.

I began to smile all over again, and this time I rewarded myself with a large, mental pat on the back.

A little while later, I phoned Bantey to ask why neither my name nor my brother's had appeared in the written decision.

"The Commissioner," he explained, "took it upon herself not to use them. We didn't ask her. She did it on her own. They usually don't do this."

"Do you have any idea why she did it?"

"Maybe because you'd said you were from a prominent family, and she felt it wasn't necessary to put your names in the record."

Chock up one more precedent, I thought.

Energized, and happily so, I placed that long, delayed call to Pierre Trahan. My smile broadened at the familiar sound of his low, rasping voice. But after I'd brought him up to date, he told me, "Serge Menard is no longer the Minister of Public Security." And my smile promptly vanished.

"Why not?" I asked.

"We have a new Premier."

"Does that mean Benoit Lauzon is gone as well?"

"I would think so."

I knew what the answer to my next question would be, but I decided to ask it again, anyway. "If the Ministry doesn't release the police report to me, will you?"

Not surprisingly, he said he couldn't. He suggested, however, that I phone the Ministry and give them a push. Which was precisely what I did.

As I'd suspected, Benoit Lauzon was gone, and a man named Artur Pires had been given my file.

When I spoke with him — eager to press my case — he explained that he'd only been on the job nine days, adding, "I'll take a look at the file to see what can be done. I'll try to explore all questions of moral rights versus privacy rights, and I should be able to give you some clearer information soon."

As I jotted down the name of the new Minister, I decided to give Artur Pires time. But only a little. Then, if need be, I'd take more aggressive action.

The following day, I did what I probably should have done long ago. I placed an ad in the Personals section of the Montreal *Gazette*. It read: "Sixties friend from house on Mt. Royal seeks Phil G., 49, born Baie Comeau."

The law, I'd been told, forbids the use of someone's last name in such ads unless the person placing it goes through a social agency or a lawyer. The reason: to protect anyone who may not *want* to be found.

How ironic, I thought. Hadn't that been one of the problems all along: the correct spelling of Phil's last name?

At Norah's suggestion, I put *her* telephone number in the ad. Then we discussed what she should and shouldn't say if, by chance, someone actually contacted her. Which, frankly, I doubted. And yet, as I'd told her from the start, "I have the feeling that one day I'm going to pick up the phone and hear, 'Hi, it's Phil, I understand you've been looking for me.'"

Considering everything else that had happened in the last eight months, it didn't sound that farfetched at all.

I gave Pires two weeks, then called him again.

"I've asked my people to look into the matter," he said, "and I'll keep you informed of their progress. Then, if you can't get the police report through us, we'll try to suggest other avenues for you to try."

"I was told in November that it would only be a matter of weeks," I reminded him. "It's now the second week in March.

That means I've been waiting for four months. I'm tired of waiting, *monsieur* Pires."

"We want to do a thorough and precise job of researching your case before presenting it to the Minister," he explained. Then he pointed again to the "unusualness of my case," and how there didn't seem to be any clear precedents for dealing with such a request.

The weeks continued to pass, and despite Paul's assurances, I found myself in the strange position of not *wanting* to let my brother go. I'd scooped him up from my past and made him a part of my present, and he was bonded to me as securely as a second layer of skin. He now lived with me more powerfully than at any other time since his death. Perhaps because I now *knew* more about him than at any other time since his death.

And oddly enough, I was comforted by his nearness. He was no longer the frightening spectre created by everything I'd learned, but a gentle and soothing presence. The other half of myself who dwelled, not in light, but in shadow.

David Fowler and I had stayed in touch over the months, and during one of our telephone conversations — and in an effort to plug one more leak — I asked him again about Thomas Garan.

To my amazement, he said, "You mean Garam. It was an 'm' not an 'n.' I went to high school with him in North Vancouver."

I held my breath as David went on. "I remember now. He'd been in Europe, and stopped in Montreal on his way back to Vancouver to look me up. He must have been living with us when Peter died.

"The last time I saw him was in Vancouver in '75. God knows what part of the world he lives in now."

I let my breath out slowly and mentally removed Thomas's name from my list of unanswered questions.

My patience with the Ministry ran out at the beginning of May, and I placed another call to Artur Pires.

"My people checked," he told me, "and they found that the law allowing the Minister to use his discretion in releasing the police report to you wasn't in effect in 1968. The matter falls, therefore, under the Access to Information Act, and it's been referred back to the MUC.

"All the documentation has been sent to Lt. Leonard Brochu, and you should be hearing from him soon. *They're* supposed to turn everything over to you."

I shook my head, half-expecting it to rattle. After all this time, the Montreal police would be receiving a copy of the report which they themselves had destroyed long ago. And they — not the Chief Coroner or the Ministry of Public Security — were the ones empowered to release it to me.

Pires had suggested that I give Lt. Brochu two weeks before contacting him. I gave him the weekend.

On Monday, I phoned his office and asked for his FAX number. Then I FAXed him a letter providing him with all the background information he needed, and ended it with a plea for an immediate release of the report. I included, as well, my original letter to the Police Archives and their reply.

I'd told Brochu that I would wait two weeks, then call him. And I was as good as my word.

He promised that because I'd waited so long, he'd do what he could to get me an answer quickly.

I waited another two weeks, then called him again.

"Didn't you get my letter?" he asked.

My heart skipped a beat. "What letter?"

"I sent you a letter and the police report on May 29th."

Above the sudden roaring in my ears, I whispered, "You sent me the report?"

"Yes. But as I explained in my letter, I blacked out the names of everyone interrogated by the police, in compliance with articles 53 and 59 of the 'Act respecting access to documents held by public bodies and the protection of personal information.'"

In other words, the same Act that had protected my brother's file at the Douglas.

"But if you want," he continued, "you can ask the *Commission d'acces à l'information* to reverse this decision."

Never, I thought, as I thanked him — not once, but twice. I had no intention of going through that again.

Then, to my surprise, he said, "We normally take out the names *and* what the people said from these reports, but in your case, I decided to take out the names and leave in as much information as possible."

I could barely speak for the lump of gratitude in my throat. The rules, it seemed, had been bent for me once more. And I was struck once again by the number of people — strangers, all — who'd touched me with their kindness and compassion.

As I put down the phone, I let out a whoop of joy. I'd done it, I'd really and truly done it. It may have taken me a year, but by God, I'd gotten everything I'd set out to get.

The following day, I opened my mail box, and there it was. A large brown envelope with the blue MUC logo in the uppper, lefthand corner.

Back in my apartment, I hungrily devoured each word of the long-awaited police report, then watched as the image of my brother's final morning on earth grew sharper and clearer.

In the opening sentence of the Incident Report, it stated categorically that at 10:45 a.m., the officer in question had "gone to the house on Coloniale for a suicide." The officer described my brother in great detail, from his demeanour and his clothing, to his being "a hippie who didn't work and who lived with other hippies." He noted that both the MUC and RCMP had officers on the scene, that my brother was officially declared dead at 11:24 a.m., and his body removed to the morgue at 1:40 p.m.

The report of Sgt. Det. Lévesque was much the way Trahan had described it to me months before, but it managed, nonetheless, to fill in several, more missing gaps in the total picture.

It noted that photos were taken, but that no valuable prints were found. And that the knife and two letters were sent to the Medico-legal Laboratory.

Allan's poem, it said, had been written on September 25, one day before my brother's death. As a gesture of support? I wondered, if what he'd said about my brother's declared intention to kill himself was true.

And my brother, it seemed, was to have appeared at a preliminary hearing on the morning he died, as a witness for the defence on behalf of Phil.

According to my own notes, my brother's hearing had been scheduled for October 3, and Bas's for October 7.

Had he chosen that day, the first of the three court hearings, to die, because he couldn't — despite his initial boast to "spill the beans" and his signed declaration — bring himself to testify *for* either Phil or Bas?

I'd waited nearly a year for this report. To finally see for myself, in black and white, what I'd only heard about from others. I had in my hands, the final arbiter. It should have been enough for me.

And yet, to my dismay, all the old doubts began resurfacing. It wasn't that I refused to accept my brother's death as a suicide; I still wasn't fully convinced that he hadn't been murdered.

Why, for instance, would he have been fully dressed to go out, complete with David's leather jacket and a kerchief tied around his neck?

Who was to say he hadn't been resting on the bed, thinking about the morning's court proceedings, when someone had sneaked in and killed him?

If he'd been drugged, lying there with his eyes closed, perhaps even sleeping, there would have been no sign of a struggle, because there wouldn't have been a struggle.

From all I could ascertain, a policeman had simply looked at the scene, and "in the absence of proof of a homicide," concluded that my brother had taken his own life.

What made him so certain? No fingerprints had ever been lifted from the handle of the knife.

If the other occupants of the house were back in their own

bedrooms at the time, couldn't a killer have come and gone without their knowing it?

Despite Marlene's and my quip about a killer bringing his own knife, he needn't have bothered. Whether a previous visitor to the house or a stranger, he wouldn't have had any trouble finding just such a knife in the kitchen.

Both Phil and Bas may have been afraid of my brother testifying *against* them, despite his signed declaration. What better way to ensure their escaping prosecution than by ensuring his silence permanently? Then, with only his declaration remaining, the charges against them would be dropped.

Which was precisely what had happened.

In my need to, hopefully, lay the matter to rest, for now and for always, I sought out one final expert. One final (I promised myself) opinion.

I met with Toronto's Chief Coroner, gave him the background of my brother's case, showed him the police report and the deathbed photo, then waited for what he had to say.

Everything I'd considered inconsistent was, to him, perfectly *con*sistent: from my brother's having had coffee with his friends, to his being found fully clothed. Even if he'd been asleep, according to the coroner, his body would have shown some sign of struggle. Despite an apparent window of opportunity, there were too many variables to allow for anyone's undetected entry and successful escape.

There was simply nothing he could see — from all the information at hand — that added up to murder.

His conclusion, therefore: suicide.

But then he said, "You'll never really know, at least not in the way you want to know, because no one was there to tell us the sequence of events. No one was there to tell us what was in your brother's mind.

"You have," he continued, "basically, two choices. You can continue following clues, tracking down leads, ad infinitum. Or you can accept that you'll never know to your complete satisfaction, and learn to live with it."

This was, I realized, the soundest advice of all.

A few days later, I awoke to find myself strangely mired again. It was as if there were molasses in my veins and tar on the souls of my feet, making even the simplest movement an effort.

As I stood in the kitchen, waiting listlessly for the kettle to boil, I could feel it happening again. That strange, other-worldly sensation.

It began in my toes and moved stealthily upward. That sense of being taken over, of being occupied. By that other, vaporous entity. And by the eerie feeling that I was both where I was, and back in that other place at the same time.

The kettle clicked off, but I couldn't move. I was paralyzed again. Frozen in the middle of that steep, narrow staircase. Unable to go up, unable to come down.

Moments passed. Suddenly, a chasm seemed, literally, to open up inside me and around me. I put out both hands in an attempt to steady myself as I started to teeter back and forth on the stairs.

An agonized howl erupted from the deepest part of my soul and I doubled over in pain. A single line from the First Edition's recording, *Just Dropped In*, flared, like a banner, through my consciousness:

"I broke my mind on a jagged sky."

For surely, those eight, telling words, more than any others, told it all.

I imagined my brother then, as a great, dazzling flash of light. A comet streaking through the blackness behind my eyes. I heard a fizzing in my ears and saw, actually saw, a starburst explosion of pure and brilliant white in the air in front of me.

Then a sudden nothingness.

And he was gone.

I landed with a thud at the bottom of the stairs, and when I stood up, I no longer felt the presence of that otherworldy vapour within me.

I was alone.

Epilogue

"*I*f you'd known what lay ahead," people ask me, "would you still have begun your quest?"

My answer, despite the vaguest twinge of pain, is yes.

"Was it worth it?" they want to know.

And my answer, once again, is yes.

In some ways, however, what I saw, perhaps no sister should ever have to see. And what I learned, perhaps no sister should ever have to learn. But I'd gone in search of answers, and, whether I was prepared for them or not, I certainly found them.

Unfortunately, though, I was also left with many questions still *un*answered. Just as I was left with a brief litany of "if only's."

If only the raid hadn't happened when it did ...

If only the Douglas hadn't let my brother go so soon ...

If only he hadn't succeeded in outmanoeuvring them ...

If only he'd returned home as he'd said he would ...

If only he'd called me ...

As I once told Paul, "You know, my brother didn't have to die."

To which he replied, "No, he didn't. But the sad reality is that he did."

It's taken many, painful months for the shockwaves created

by my quest to subside. For the agony to lessen. For the traumatizing images to begin, finally, to fade. And for the darkened filter through which I'd come to view the world to brighten again.

I have, undeniably, begun to heal. But it, too, is a journey. Different from the one I embarked on two years ago, but a journey, nonetheless. And its path has been riddled throughout with unforeseen mental bumps and hidden emotional potholes.

Although I've basically accepted my brother's death as a suicide, that one percentage point of uncertainty still remains, and I suspect it always will.

Although I've yet to hear from him, I'm still waiting for the telephone to ring and for Phil to say, "Hi, I understand you've been looking for me."

Although it's easier to talk about my brother now (To my amazement, I find myself *wanting* to talk about him. And when I do, it's with pride and love, not shame.), I still have trouble saying his name.

And although the rational me acknowledges that I couldn't have saved him, the *ir*rational me still wishes that I'd had the chance to try.

I think wistfully of my brother's many friends, whose lives I've touched, and whose own lives have, briefly, but irrevocably, touched mine. We're linked now, all of us. Part of the same series of concentric, cosmic circles with my brother as its defining centre.

For I remain convinced that it was our very psychic connectedness that led me to initiate my quest for the truth. That, in my need to hold onto him, I'd inadvertently trapped my brother between one life and another. And that because I've agreed now, to let go of my attachment to him, he's free, finally, to make his way through the Bardos until he finds either a good rebirth or his ultimate enlightenment and liberation.

One night, not long ago, I dreamed about my brother again.

He and I were lying on our stomachs, facing each other, with our foreheads touching, on top of a lush, green mountain.

All around us stretched a breathtaking panorama — of other lush, green mountaintops and the clearest of clear blue skies.

We talked for what felt like hours, mainly about my book. Then I said to him, "It's as if we've never been apart. It's as if you've always been here."

He smiled and planted a soft, tender kiss on my left cheek.

I woke up with my left cheek warm and tingling. Alive with my beloved brother's gentle kiss.

Days later, I can still feel its imprint on my skin.

I think back to what Paul said to me so many months ago, and find that time has indeed proven him right. In letting go of my brother, I really haven't lost *him* at all. What I *have* lost is the pain, the anger, and the grief. But *he's* still with me in memory, and always will be.

I lift my hand, touch the phantom imprint he's left behind on my cheek, and smile back at him.